MY DEAR HUGH

My Dear Hugh,

Letters from
Richard Cobb to
Hugh Trevor-Roper
and others

Edited by TIM HEALD

FRANCES LINCOLN LIMITED
PUBLISHERS

Frances Lincoln Limited
4 Torriano Mews
Torriano Avenue
London NW5 2RZ
www.franceslincoln.com

My Dear Hugh,

First Frances Lincoln edition 2011
Reprinted with corrections 2011

A catalogue record for this book is available
from the British Library

ISBN 978-0-7112-3240-2

Printed and bound by CPI Group (UK) Ltd, Croydon, CR0 4YY

9 8 7 6 5 4 3 2

INTRODUCTION

R ichard Cobb was unusual.
His public reputation makes him seem almost conventional.
He was Professor of Modern History at Oxford from 1973 to 1984
before which he was a Fellow of Balliol for ten years. He was amazingly knowledgeable about France and all things French but most of
all about the French Revolution. He wrote several books about this,
the first of which was in French and appeared in two volumes as
Les armées révolutionnaires. He was also a memoirist of brilliance
who wrote several slim autobiographical volumes full of vivid and
evocative scenes described in a style which was lucid, entertaining
and unique.

The entry in *Who's Who* records his marriage to Margaret,
who was a pupil of his at Leeds University, and his five children.
It mentions his education at Shrewsbury and Merton where he
was a Postmaster. His ten years of research in France are listed
together with his early academic career teaching at universities in
Aberystwyth, Manchester and Leeds. There are honorary degrees,
the Légion d'honneur – he was a chevalier – and a CBE. The publications are impressive and include one book which won the
Wolfson History Prize and another which secured him the J.R.
Ackerley. His address is given as Worcester College, Oxford, where
he held a Fellowship from 1973. He died in 1996. It sounds like a
worthy, well-lived but essentially rather dull life.

None of this semi-official stuff provides much of a glimpse of the
real self – 'l'étonnant Cobb' as his many French admirers called him.
He was an extraordinary man in many ways, and although his quali-
ties as a historian underpinned and bolstered his reputation and his
achievements they didn't begin to tell the whole story.

His Frenchness was vital. One of the compliments he most treas-
ured was when a Frenchman described him as 'un titi Parisien',

which meant, essentially, that he was 'one of them'. He spent many years in Paris, lodged as a young man in the rackety dixième district, later had a flat in the Rue de Tournon and eventually, with Margaret, graduated to a house in Normandy which turned out to be one of several essentially disastrous forays into the property market. His ostensibly English writing was conducted in a curious upmarket *franglais* in which his mother tongue was liberally aided by French words and phrases. It was a style that was unique to him and perfectly encapsulated a personality which was as nearly bicultural as it is possible for an Englishman to be. And, in many ways, he was by education and background – his book on childhood in Tunbridge Wells is an uncomfortable classic – the quintessential Englishman.

I remember the first meeting at Oxford between my student history year and the newly arrived history tutor in his narrow room, one end of which overlooked the Balliol front quad and the other Trinity's next door. We all seemed slightly nervous, including our new tutor, until the moment when Bill Trythall asked him a question and used the apparently harmless word 'Sir'.

I knew Bill at preparatory school in Somerset and remembered him being awarded the fourth scholarship to Winchester, which led to one of our friends describing him to his mother as 'fourth cleverest boy in Britain'. Now he was at Balliol as a domus scholar and still fourth cleverest boy in Britain or thereabouts. He subsequently wrote a biography of Franco and spent his professional life teaching history at the University of York. Bill asked Richard a question. I don't remember what Bill wanted to know but I do remember that he inserted the word 'Sir'. This was simple politeness and would have been the custom at Connaught House, Winchester, and possibly at home. Bill's father was an admiral.

The effect on Richard was remarkable. His eyes bulged, he went scarlet, I like to think that the Gauloise which he was still in the habit of smoking trembled from his lower lip. 'Don't EVER let me hear you use that word again,' he said. 'EVER!' He was obviously very angry, and while I suspect that the three other Balliol history tutors would have reacted in a similar way it was not what we were used to. Richard wanted to be Richard and from that moment he was. None of us ever dared address him as 'Sir'.

Roger Highfield, affectionately known to Richard as 'Rodge', had a similar story from much the same time. 'Rodge' was also a historian of the French Revolution and the two had met while working in the Archives Nationales in Paris. Over lunch at the Café de Bretagne, Richard explained the hostility between the Sorbonne and the Collège de France. This was exemplified by a great row then taking place over Fernand Braudel. 'He loved a great row,' wrote Highfield appreciatively.

When Richard was first a Fellow of Balliol, Highfield was Senior History Tutor at Merton and 'I engaged him to take the class for the history freshmen: Tocqueville, L'Ancien Régime et la Révolution Provençale. They didn't know how lucky they were. When it came to paying him for his teaching he said that he could not take a penny from his old college, but then suggested that the sum of money involved should be made available to the members of the class in credit for beer at the JCR bar. In my experience this was a unique suggestion. It wasn't easy to administer, and the bursar hated the idea. But it was carried through – a fine example of his affection for his old college, his generosity and his imagination.'

The Cobb attitude towards money always seemed nonchalant to the point of feckless. It must have been a nightmare for Margaret and his family. Most of the time he seemed on the brink of penury, though to his friends and pupils he was always scrupulous to the point of generosity. From time to time a relation died and instead of spending the money sensibly he would blow it on a party. He loved parties and it was entirely characteristic that he enjoyed mixing up senior and junior members of the university and encouraging them to talk to each other. I remember a formal lunch in the Old Senior Common Room where he alternated undergraduates with Oxford's great and good. I found myself sitting next to Dame Lucy Sutherland, then Principal of Lady Margaret Hall. It was good for me even if it was, as it must have been, boring for her.

In this egalitarianism he was unusual if not unique. Oxford tutors in general and Balliol ones in particular were supposed to make real friends with their pupils, but this was not always the case. With Richard the aspiration to genuine equality and friendship was refreshing and unusual. I remember once leaving Balliol and passing

Richard Scott, an old school friend who held the senior history scholarship at Hertford. He asked where I was going. 'To a party of Felix Markham,' I said, referring to his own senior history tutor, a leading authority on Napoleon and *éminence grise* to the Maltese Prime Minister, Dom Mintoff. Scott was amazed. He had never had more than a formal glass of sherry from Felix. I, on the other hand, was a friend of Richard and because of this we were exalted. On another occasion, in Postmaster's Hall, John Roberts, later Vice-Chancellor of Southampton University and then Warden of Merton, threw me across his drawing room when I questioned his claim to be a karate black belt. It wouldn't have happened had I not been a friend and pupil of Richard's.

He liked a drink. To some of us this was part of his charm, though to others it was an exasperation. Once, years after Oxford, I engineered an invitation for him to speak on a panel at PEN, the writers' organisation. The subject was 'Judging the Booker Prize'. Richard was once chairman and I had lunch with him on the day of the final judgement, at Bertorelli's in London, admonished by what seemed like the entire world of publishing to make sure that he didn't drink too much. I think I more or less succeeded though he made a speech at the Award ceremony in which he said that he had never read Proust. I'm sure this was meant as a joke, however obscure, but if so hardly anyone got it and Richard was roundly abused by a chorus of hacks, most of whom had never read Proust themselves, and almost certainly not l'étonnant Cobb.

On the PEN evening I arrived at their headquarters in the old Sketch Club in Chelsea to find the redoubtable secretary, Josephine Pullein-Thomson (almost as redoubtable in her way as Richard himself), fuming. 'Your friend', she said, icily, 'is in the pub.' I was sent to retrieve our guest speaker and found him deep in not very coherent conversation with a Balliol man he had just happened to pick up in the public bar. Richard was always picking people up in bars, usually when slightly tipsy. I got him back to PEN and on to the platform where a complete nightmare was averted by the shrewd chairmanship of Ion Trewin, who spent much of the evening saying, 'Thank you Professor. That was most illuminating. As I understand it what you really mean is . . .' As none of the rest of us, including Richard, had a clue what he really meant this was pure genius. Richard liked calvados, wine and beer, particularly Guinness. He was once asked to leave a royal banquet when slightly the worse for wear and he had a scary story about being a patient at the Radcliffe Infirmary, festooned with tubes of one sort and another, nipping out for a glass of stout, and then proceeding to the nearest urinal where he was disconcerted to find himself peeing an unusual black liquid. The Guinness had passed straight through him.

Cobb was unimpressed by authority or convention – though intensely proud of his French ribbon and its English counterpart. At his viva at the end of his final undergraduate year in Oxford he found himself confronted by an increasingly irritated Regius Professor, G.N. Clark. After a lengthy exchange of views, Clark, who was chairing the examiners, said in great exasperation, 'Good God, man, you're just a bloody anarchist.' To which Richard, not in the least put out, replied simply and unconcernedly, 'Yes.' He was awarded a second-class degree.

At the regular 'hand-shaking' at the end of term in Balliol, he would sit between the Master, Sir David Lindsay-Keir, and the pupil who was being reported on. His only concern was to make the undergraduate laugh while not being caught out by Sir David. He would therefore sit, po-faced, and scribble on scraps of paper lines such as 'The Master's a Disaster' or 'Sir David's flies are undone' in the hope, often realised, of making his pupils crack up on what was supposed to be a solemn and serious occasion.

One of my favourite memories is of how at the beginning of one term he explained to his two pupils – myself and a seriously aspirant civil servant called Clive Tucker (he went on to head a department) – that there were two alternatives open to us. One was to study all the usual European History questions of the eighteenth and nine-teenth centuries. We could do this easily because he had taught them so many times before. It would be only moderately stimulating but he could guarantee that if we paid reasonable attention and worked satisfactorily we would score marks in the final examinations which would easily guarantee us at least a good second if not a first. On the other hand, we could look at less well-known events which were unfamiliar even to Professor Cobb himself. Such curiosities as the umbrella uprising in Milan in 1815 when a mob beat the finance minister, Giuseppe Prina, to death with their silk umbrellas in the piazza outside the cathedral. Tucker was, naturally and understandably, keen on the conventional path. Richard and I wanted to try something different. He warned us that none of these subjects would appear in the final examination papers. I didn't care. Nor did Richard. We won. Tucker still got a good second; I got a congratulatory third.

I have no regrets about this. It has always seemed sad that a college with such a high opinion of itself as Balliol should be so slavish in its acceptance of the Norrington Table and the excellence of the first-class degree. Whenever someone from another college boasts about their superior qualification, I think to myself (not always, alas, silently) that he or she may have got a first (which I always think of as the academic equivalent of having a personalised number plate) but they didn't enjoy the privilege of a term with Richard Cobb exploring the esoterica of European history. That really was a rare privilege.

Richard was also a consummate writer of letters, prolific master of a dying if not quite dead artform. From the moment I first met him in 1962 until his death in 1996 I was a recipient of his letters. Sometimes the envelope would be handwritten in his instantly familiar spidery writing; sometimes it would be typed with much Victorian style underlining, the typewriter obviously manual and the ribbon worn. I was always dignified with the abbreviation 'Esqre' after my name, which sometimes included his nickname for me: 'Yokello', because I held a Galpin scholarship limited to those born and educated in Dorset. The envelopes were always plain blue Basildon Bond and they arrived at irregular intervals. Once I was away in the United States for a whole year and not a single letter arrived. I feared I had fallen out of favour and, on my return, wrote to find out. 'Far too far to write' was his explanation.

I thought of him as an electrifying tutor, a loyal friend and an eccentric and life-enhancing writer of letters. He was prone to capitals, underlining, codes and to what Americans call 'screamers'. (We British refer to them less colourfully as 'exclamation marks'.) Generally speaking his letters defy mechanical transliteration, so that I spent many hours transcribing only to discover, after tens of thousands of words, that he was a regular correspondent of his old friend Lord Dacre, aka Hugh Trevor-Roper. Despite the kindness and ingenuity of the Christ Church librarian, Judith Curthoys (in both she emulated the librarian of Merton College, Julia Walworth), this meant that I had to write out another tranche. We also changed the title of this collection.

Richard was a creature of his time and place so he may seem parochial and he may seem snobbish. To accuse him of either is the same, it seems to me, as saying that John Buchan was anti-Semitic. Richard was a white, privately educated Oxford don of a certain age. If from time to time he suffers from what a later generation of pupils think of as prejudices which we don't share, then so be it. What you see is what you get and it is not my business to gloss.

The sight of one of Richard's letters on the doormat always raised the spirits. I imagine they did for a quite large number of people for Richard was prolific in his letter-writing. Heaven knows how he found the time for he was also an energetic writer of books and reviews as well as being a conscientious teacher and lecturer. In some quarters he had a reputation for being wayward and late with commissioned work but this was, I always felt, the product of chaos and confusion rather than indolence. He was absolutely not lazy.

I don't know precisely why he was such an avid letter writer. Brian Johnston, about whom I wrote a book, was similarly keen and conscientious about maintaining friendships but he, unlike Richard, was no letter writer. Instead he would take out his phone book once a week and work his way through it, ringing up those listed and making sure that they were still all right, exchanging gossip, telling funny stories, making arrangements, grumbling and doing all the things old friends do when they get in touch.

The telephone was once popularly thought to have destroyed the art of letter writing and this seems from my own serendipitous personal observation to be true. Richard used the telephone but not, in my experience, for fun. He would ring to make or confirm an appointment but not to discuss the weather or the latest episode of *Neighbours* – come to think of it I don't recall Richard once even mentioning television, which might go some way to accounting for the time he found for writing letters.

He came from a generation that preceded the Internet, emails and blogging. Had he been born later I suppose he might have sent emails, though I can't see him as a blogger. I associate him with old-fashioned handwritten or hand-typed letters. He was the only proper letter writer I have ever known and for this alone I am grateful, quite apart from his friendship and for what he taught me, mainly about the importance of the individual and the flaws in popular and majority opinion. He acknowledged me in one book and even dedicated another to me simply and alone. *A Classical Education* was another uncomfortable classic, this one about a school-friend who murdered his mother. Richard used to refer to it as 'our book' which I found flattering if disconcerting. It may, however, help to explain why I always thought of him as a 'friend' as well as a 'former tutor' and why I may sometimes seem to be uncritical.

Originally I worked on letters that Cobb wrote to friends, colleagues and former pupils, some of whom were better known than others. Latterly, however, my attention was drawn (as they say) to a large cache of letters to Hugh Trevor-Roper in Christ Church. Trevor-Roper, later ennobled as Lord Dacre, was very well known and I have therefore relied heavily on the letters Cobb wrote to him. In any case his letters to Trevor-Roper often cover the same ground at least as fluently as those he wrote to others, and latterly at least he regarded Trevor-Roper as his peer and this was reciprocated. Judith Curthoys protests that the correspondence is one-sided. Cobb's letters survive because Trevor-Roper, being a methodical scholar, filed them and kept them. His own letters to Cobb, however, remain largely unavailable because Cobb was chaotic. He never seemed to keep or file anything. Judith says that the correspondence is like listening to someone bellowing down a mobile phone in a quiet carriage on the train. This is true but we still get the essence of Cobb. Besides which I sense what his correspondent would have written back, and in any case some of the most entertaining 'conversations' I have ever heard have been the result of eavesdropping on someone on a mobile telephone. So I'm quite relaxed about this.

Not everyone approves of publishing his letters. I discussed the possibility with him more than once and I remember doing so at some length in the little back bar of the King's Arms in Oxford, which

12

was one of his several homes from home. He affected surprise that anyone should think his letters might be of general interest and I felt he was mildly flattered though, like others, anxious that he might offend friends about whom he had sometimes been less than charitable. He wasn't in the least concerned about enemies, of whom he had several. He hated them and was perfectly happy to have his opinions made public. Above all I sensed, characteristically, that he would have been glad of the cash.

Some of his correspondents, such as his academic friends Professor Bernard Wasserstein and Sir Colin Lucas, seem to have kept all the letters Richard wrote them; others destroyed or lost them (they had better be nameless though some should, having been taught history by him, have known better). I kept mine – at least I kept some though I suppose I may have lost some too. When his old friend and some-time publisher Hugo Brunner, later Lord Lieutenant of Oxfordshire, proposed a collection for the Bodleian Library I gave mine to add to this tranche. This, in my search for his publishable letters, was my first port of call. There were also other nuggets in Bodley lurking, for instance, in the files of old friends such as Sir Isaiah Berlin.

Two other libraries also hold dedicated Cobb collections. Merton College, where he was an undergraduate and where he later became an Honorary Fellow, has a number, mainly from early life. Balliol, where he was both a Teaching and an Honorary Fellow also has a collection, though theirs is, for obvious reasons, from later life. The *Literary Review* and the *Times Literary Supplement*, to which he was an occasional, sometimes unorthodox contributor, published an appeal for letters from myself and John Nicoll, the publisher, who was also a pupil of Richard's. I have also written to as many of Richard's known friends as I could find, although his circle was so wide and so eclectic that I am aware that there will be a number I have simply missed out.

Those who object to publication do so mainly on the grounds that it is an invasion of privacy. Technically I have to admit that they're absolutely right. When Richard wrote a 'Dear Yokello' letter it was clearly intended for me and for me alone. Sometimes there were glancing remarks about third parties which are better excised on the grounds that they might cause undue offence and would have caused Richard grief. On the whole, though, I am more than happy to share his words with anyone who cares to read them. At their best they are marvellous and unique: gems from the pen and keyboard of one of the last of the great letter writers.

This is a personal selection and much is omitted. I have tried to provide explanations and context whenever I could, but it is the letters themselves that count. First and foremost Richard was, I suppose, a great historian; but he was also a wonderful letter writer. I think it is right that this should be recognised and that a selection at least should be published, and I hope that readers who were not privileged to receive them at first hand will derive almost as much pleasure from the pages that follow.

He wrote to a wide range of friends and acquaintances and alluded to an even wider range, often in a manner which will be incomprehensible to outsiders. Where possible I have attempted a translation or gloss, although sometimes I do not know what or whom he is talking about. I have tried to say something about the characters to or about whom he writes but sometimes I have failed. Many of the people crop up in the long 'cast list' at the end and I have done my best to illuminate the script in my links. Some of the people he writes about as if they were household names have faded away so that half a century or so later they have become virtually forgotten. The same is sometimes true of issues which were burning topics of the day but nowadays are tepid or non-existent. Other characters and other issues are as fresh and vibrant as ever. I suppose this is one of history's lesser lessons. Who and what matter enormously at the time but subsequently not at all, and the reverse, perversely, is often true as well. Where readers still don't understand, therefore, it is nearly always – but not absolutely always – my fault. And Richard was something of a fantasist, so it must be stressed that not everything he says, or every story that he tells, is necessarily true or correct.

The Letters

1957

The earliest letters I found from Cobb were written in the 1950s, long before he came back to Oxford, and long before he became famous.

Senior Common Room, University College of Wales, Aberystwyth.
To John Bromley, 7 February.

I have just had a letter from the Warden asking me if I could come and spend a week-end in All Souls. He suggests the week-end of next week (Feb 16–18 or one of the two following weeks). As I am going to be in England anyhow next week, I have written to Mr Stuart Hampshire to offer a choice of Feb 16th or Feb 23rd. I thought it would be more polite to offer a choice of dates à mon tour, as there may be some people who are tied to one date only, and I have no great objections to doing two journeys from here but I rather expect Mr Hampshire will suggest the first week-end, as I've made it clear that I was going to be in the vicinity anyway. As for whether it is best to be seen first, in the middle or last, that is really an imponderable.

This is going to be rather a frightening experience. I shall get a visit in to T. Wells first, to get myself some new clothes and to see whether I can still get into my pre-war dinner jacket. So I don't quite know, till I hear from the Bursar, when I shall be in Oxford. Whenever it is, I very much want to see you. In any case, I think I shall go straight to Tun. Wells. on Tuesday, and await news from the Bursar there. My address is 5a Grove Hill Gds, TW. I shall be there from Tuesday next.

Pray for me.

PS As you said, I am on a short list. I only hope I'm not there the same weekend as Spooner!

Election to a Fellowship at All Souls College, Oxford, always used to be considered, at least by outsiders, to be almost as much of a social as an academic ordeal. This accounts for Cobb's apprehension. Spooner was presumably a rival and familiar to both Bromley and Cobb. Alas, he is elusive as far as I am concerned. Cobb was obviously disenchanted with Aber and eager for Oxford.

12 Rue de Tournon, VIème, Paris. To John Bromley, 12 July.

It was very pleasant to get your letter so soon after my arrival here. I will be checking up at the Hôtel de l'Odéon tomorrow; it is just across the street from here, which is very nice. It was as well you did not come here yet, as the Archives have been shut from the 30th and reopen on the 15th. I quite forgot about this annual holiday. As a result, I have been working at home most of the time on my thesis and last week it was so dreadfully hot that I preferred not to venture out into the streets at all. Next week, I shall start on some visits to village 'mairies' – always the most exciting material comes from there, and it is really amazing how little archives communales have been explored. To me they are far more useful than anything on Department or national level, but of course one does lose a tremendous lot of time in complicated bus and train journeys, not to mention the odd 5 or 6 kms on foot along dusty roads, but the reward is there at the end, and there is also some satisfaction in establishing oneself in the Salle des Mariages on a sort of throne, under the statue of Marianne. What could be more completely French than a rural 'mairie' with its flags and decorations (and photo of Pétain stacked in the attic with the archives). And it is pleasant to look out on a neatly trimmed avenue or on a school courtyard. It is also a relief after the hyper-political atmosphere of Paris. I don't like the smell of things at all just now: France is heading for some form of authoritarian regime, everyone is quite fatalistic about it, no-one is prepared to resist, there is general inertia and this abominable war looks like going on for ever. Lacoste and Lejeune are dreadful people – real Fascists, and there are many such in the SFI. France is still going through a period of acute and petty chauvinism, it is now about the most expensive country in Europe, the State is so bankrupt that everything is held up save military preparations. On Sunday we will have July 14 with paratroops, a sign of the ugly times. I am really very depressed, as I can see no way out, with the extraordinarily mediocre party politicians that at present govern this unhappy country. Algeria may well be the death of French democracy. There is a general atmosphere of intolerance and much talk of 'tired intellectuals', 'defeatists', 'cosmopolitans', etc. Mollet has more to answer for than anyone else.

I haven't put in for Queen's, and the closing date is tomorrow, though I may use the fact that I am here as an excuse for a late application. Your advice is very good. I am desperately anxious to get away from Aber, now that Dick Spilsbury has resigned and Ball is leaving. I shall be completely isolated there and I get so depressed there that I do not make the best use of my leisure. However, one year is no doubt bearable. I feel little enthusiasm about the Revolution Special, as my two students are not at all exciting. The book on the other hand seems to be materialising; Dan [Davin] has just written to say that I should get in touch with Bullock as soon as possible; he would like to see me, it seems, so I have written to him to say that I would come to Oxford during the summer if he felt it was necessary and that, otherwise, I would see him there in September. I think it could be a most interesting project, and the work done by Beau de Loménie, Berthier de Sauvigny, Gossez, etc. on the Restoration and July Monarchy would give some useful pointers on social history. It would be a wonderful opportunity to trace the evolution of French society after the Revolution. I hope Bullock and Deakin don't want a straight political history.

What you tell me about Goodwin and Markham is very flattering indeed. Cobban, of course, will have his Penguin out this autumn. I have seen bits of it; it is well written, but rather unoriginal and marred by his bee in a bonnet about the 'myth' of the Revolution. I think he is particularly helpful on the institutions of XIIIth Century France. I think Goodwin will be about the only modernist at Caen, save for Bury. ALL the French delegates are apparently medievalists. Treharne will be happy indeed and will be able to indulge to the full his favourite relaxation – eating like a pig (without wine!).

My divorce is through. There are still some formalities about the *état-civil*, but I am at least more or less a free man, which is a great weight off my shoulders. I might even get married properly for a change.

You will not need a letter from the Embassy for the OM people. The best way will be to get Outre to write you a letter. I'll introduce you to him as soon as you come.

I hear from Ball that the conference on XVIIth Century Revolutions was rather a flop and revealed the lamentable lack of knowledge of European History of all present.

Personally, if I had a chance, I would very much like to take up Russian History. It has always fascinated me, but I think it is unlikely that I'll ever really switch.

It will be nice having you so near, and I hope that the present cool weather holds. I'll let you know about the hotel. Meuvret will be back tomorrow. Rudé will be off to Saint-Tropez before you get here, I think. Best wishes to Jean.

1958

Aber. To John Bromley, 4 May.

This is not an easy letter to write, as I know how you must be feeling. I read the news in <u>The Observer</u> half an hour ago & since then have been crying like a child. I have written to Mrs Pares – such an inadequate letter. I was such a latecomer among Richard Pares' friends & admirers but even so I felt, when visiting him, that here was the wisest, the kindest and the most courageous man I had ever met. I am very very grateful to you, John, for having introduced me to this great & good man. He is the one person I have ever met in my life I could absolutely respect as a historian & as a man – not only respect but immensely like. So I have some faint idea of your sense of loss – for you have known him for so long & have been such a devoted friend to him. I find myself quite inadequate, John. I keep on thinking of my visits to Holywell – always events in my life – & the tears stop me writing.

I will hardly dare talk of this to you when I see you on Friday. But it will not be for lack of feeling & sympathy, but from embarrassment. You have lost so very much more than anyone of us. My one consolation is that, thanks to you, I met this very great man – everything that a historian should be & so much more as well. He is the sort of person who makes me proud of being an XVIIIth C historian, an Oxonian and an Englishman.

Please don't bother to write & please convey to Jean my sincerest sympathy. Perhaps I shall see you on Friday? It does feel as if something had stopped in our world. Every XVIIIth century historian must be feeling lonely and leaderless – we do such need respect and friendship & Richard Pares was both wise and good. I don't think there are many like him.

Yours ever & in deep sympathy

PS I have written to Mrs Pares at 95 Holywell but I am not sure if this is the right number. I expect it will reach her.

During his post-war exile researching archives, mainly in Paris and Lyon, Cobb struck up a number of friendships with European historians. One of these was Sandro Garrone, also a French Revolution specialist. Garrone died in 2003, leaving his archives to his art-historian daughter Giovanna. Giovanna, born in 1946, was a child in the 1950s when the close friendship between her father and the strange young Englishman first began to develop. 'I also have some funny, nice postcards to me,' she wrote. 'We became great friends. He was terribly funny and I loved him very much.'

Cobb and Sandro Garrone spent a lot of time in Paris together and Cobb often came to visit the Garrones at their home in Turin where Giovanna still lives. They corresponded in French and the translations here are by the publisher and translator Euan Cameron, also an occasional Cobb correspondent. Cobb's earlier life and his French persona both pose problems. The further away the period, the more sparse the correspondence. That is perhaps inevitable. The personality of this younger, fresher faced, conceivably more innocent person also becomes inevitably more elusive. We know him less well than the figure whom we knew at first hand in later, and often real, life.

The Frenchness posed a problem that was solved by Euan Cameron, who first met Cobb when he was an editor at the Bodley Head and who, paradoxically, later translated Jean-Yves Tadié's biography of Proust in 2000. Cobb claimed, famously, never to have read Proust and not to have seen the point. Cameron was educated at the University of Aix-en-Provence and became a professional translator after working in publishing for much of his adult life. It seemed to us that letters in French, even Cobb's idio-syncratic and quasi-English version of the language, would be a step too far. Hence the translation.

On 28 August he wrote from Paris to Sandro Garrone:

I believe Helene will be calling at your place next month, probably around the 5th or 6th. I don't know her itinerary. But I shall write to her at your house. All I ask is one thing. Don't discuss anything with her. I know her. She would be very angry and very upset were she to know that I had spoken to you and others about this business. So it's better not to say anything at all. She probably won't mention it to you, being far too proud.

What a mess! I've really landed myself up the creek and I'm still dancing on a tightrope. I can decide nothing until Helene returns. Much will depend on what she expects of me. I think Laura suspects, and she is worried that Helene's return will be an occasion for reconciliation. I am truly unhappy and, ultimately, I won't be the only one. That's what happens when one involves oneself with two totally exceptional women.

I am pleased to have started work again and to find myself back in my usual role of historian. I am lunching with Cipolla today. Guiral and the friends from Marseille are at the Archives. We're going to try to produce an abbreviated English edition of Soboul's thesis.

Why is life made up of choices? And by what misfortune do these choices depend on me? Ah, Italy, Italy! Laura is so beautiful. Helene too.

Affectionate greetings to Miti and to Giovanna, and a hug for you, you wise old fellow. Have pity on me.

Your poor Richard, weak, indecisive and tormented.

1959

The following year, Cobb was staying near Turin, researching at the city's Institute for European Studies. On 30 July he collected a letter from Garrone and replied, at once, as follows (this too is a Cameron translation):

I am staying on in Italy until Thursday or Friday next week, so we shall have time to see one another. I could come along on Sunday for the day, if you like, or perhaps Monday. I shall telephone you on Saturday at lunch time and we can try to work out something. I'll be in Turin again on Wednesday, to see Marco.

You say some kind things about my work. We're lucky to have that. But history is merely an escape from life, and it seems to me that life is something I cope with very badly. Now there are some extremely philosophical thoughts! It must be the influence of all these Vaudois! You can give me your Romme IN PERSON when I see you, in that way I shall be able to insist on a signed copy! You know, Helene is not in the least angry with you, she is simply an IMPOSSIBLE letter writer. She had written to me from Italy, on her way to Sofia, and I had imagined she had travelled via Turin. She is very fond of you. She has been ill, then she had to spend time looking after an elderly Russian lady, and her life is still just as disorganised. Mine is becoming so. When I write a novel, I shall call it <u>The Waverer</u>, it will be my life story. I am a man who misses trains, and everything else, through indecision. Nor shall I be able to decide when to die! That's what it is to have lived too much for oneself. All right, all right. We can deal with that later (very Vaudois thoughts, these).

See you soon. Must go and buy my <u>crocodiles</u> in Milan next week.

With love, also to Miti and the jolly G.

Euan Cameron was mildly perplexed by the double reference to the Vaudois, which means, literally, inhabitants of the Swiss canton, the Vaud. Cameron isn't entirely happy about this and senses that he has missed something more esoteric which has probably disappeared forever along with Cobb, Garrone and their friends. Cameron also guesses that crocodiles refers to crocodile-skin shoes, a sartorial conceit those who knew Cobb in later life might have found surprising. But there again, maybe not. There was more than one school of thought when it came to Cobb's sense of the sartorial.

1961

The first letter from Richard Cobb to Hugh Trevor-Roper in the Trevor-Roper files at Christ Church, Oxford, was prefixed with the words 'Dear Professor Trevor-Roper' and signed 'Yours sincerely Richard Cobb'. This is uncharacteristic. Later, after the two had become friends, it was 'My dear Hugh' and the signature at the bottom was, simply, 'Richard'. After his return to Oxford as a Fellow of Balliol College, Cobb was – like it or not – to become as characteristic a fixture of the place as Trevor-Roper.

The original letter was from Aberystwyth where Cobb had his first job in a British university after many years researching in various archives in France and eking out an often precarious existence by teaching English. He continued to be ambivalent about Aber, but he was ambivalent about almost everywhere he lived, preferring those places such as Cambridge which he knew only as a visitor.

To Trevor-Roper, 22 January.

Thank you very much for your nice letter & for the magnificent compliment, especially when it comes from a 17th century specialist. It is like being told that one writes like Chesterfield.

Fortunately I am here only half the year, the other half being spent in Paris where I keep a flat. I don't <u>think</u> Mousnier has been here. I saw him in Manchester last year. The man I would really like to get on a visit here is Jean Meuvret, who is a great friend of mine (I am a fairly patient listener!).

I have only just heard of Garrod's death. I cannot imagine Merton without him. I used to live in Fellows when you were there as a Harmsworth. That would be in 37 or 38 I think.

There is not much to be said for Aberystwyth. The students are nice. I am also able to beat my favourite anti-Catholic drum, in lectures & so on, with the approval of most.

I very much hope to see you in Oxford some time. I go to Merton quite often, when Roger Highfield can get me the Guest Room.

Gerald Aylmer has beaten me to it. My own monster is coming out, with Mouton and Co of the Hague, this spring.

1964

By the time of the next letter he had decamped to Oxford.

Balliol College, Oxford. To John Roberts, 12 May.

Those Mertonians were VERY nice. I much enjoyed their visit; I hope I was some use to them.

I see you've been having the Visitor. I well remember Lang's visit in 37. Rather foolishly we were given potatoes in their jackets and they and the bananas were soon flying all over the Hall; it was strange seeing those chiselled features through a haze of flying fruit and vegetables. We all behaved DISGUSTINGLY, three people collapsed and had to be carried out, four were sick. Those were the days.

1967

On 26 April Cobb wrote to his friend John Bromley.

It is a great let-down being back in England and even France doesn't seem very tempting. India was a FANTASTIC, WEIRD, exhilarating, endlessly exciting, totally novel experience – and Calcutta much more so than Delhi. I could write and write about that alarming, violent and incredibly varied city. It has EVERYTHING – every problem of XVIIIth c Paris – and much more visible, I should think. Not that the situation there is potentially revolutionary, it is worse than that, more like Paris after Prairial in one way – for the misery is unmeasurable and indescribable. But the comparison won't do, for it is a modern city – with some fine XVIIIth c buildings and masses of Victorian extravaganza – with a population largely medieval – holy men of every brew, astrologers, quacks, absolutely manic temples (the big Jain temple is a sort of B'pool fun fair gone wrong) – or the facteur Cheval's castle carried a stage further into lunacy. Delhi is a dull place in comparison. Calcutta is a PROBLEM. It has EVERYTHING – cholera, leprosy, the sale of children, abduction of schoolgirls, massive prostitution, extreme nationalism, two CPs, every brand of fanaticism, LOTS of drink, statues of Viceroys and of Bose, a swimming club still all-white and full of Russians and Poles, refugees, etc. etc. I cannot describe it. The University has 190,000 students. I lectured on death and famine last Wednesday, at a temperature of 108 F, in the old University building – like a very broken down and dirty Sorbonne – in the presence of a motley throng like Jesus and his disciples (one is CONSTANTLY amazed by the variety of costume – or the lack of it, for saddus go stark naked, Sikhs go heavily armed, curved swords, sabres, jewelled daggers, bandoliers, the lot – AND they use them, at least they did about ten days ago in Calcutta – variety of transport – rickshaws, cycle rickshaws, motorcycle rickshaws (tongas), cabs, closed carriages, open victorias, donkey carts, mule carts, camel carts, ox carts, a variety of English cars from your undergraduate days, Leyland buses with all their paint burnt off by the heat, B'pool type trams, with clusters of white figures on the outside as well as in, elderly turbaned <u>bearded sages on Vespas</u>, half-naked holy men, saintly looking and absolutely villainous (whorers mostly), charming children who can beg at 3, the halt, the lame, the maimed, the blind, a Cour des Miracles that would make Hugo or Sue look tame – the greatest place for them is on the steps of mosques and temples and, of course, outside fashionable restaurants. The Indian middle class is FAT, horribly so. One can see them being dragged along by Belsen figures, in rickshaws. The Calcutta street is a CONSTANT lesson in social history – for ANY period and for all periods jumbled together. I was surprised too by the amount of Company stuff still about – St John's a pathetic church, half dilapidated, like everything else in that climate, built 1784, with 1800 type monuments on the walls – urns, nymphs, young Company officers, Scots and Devonians, mostly died at Sea, in their 30s, expectancy must have been short, the churchyard is overgrown with lush things, the graves are enormous domed affairs, many of them at an angle, there is a tiny Eurasian congregation (the Presb. Chapel and the Congregationalist one, both built about 1800, are much more prosperous looking and they still have big congregations, there is of course an Anglican cathedral as well, a gothic thing from the 1840s, that is where the buru sahibs go). Of W. Hastings, there remains his house, now the Public Library, in a SPLENDID Park – huge banana

25

and peepul trees – his Residence now that of the Civil Governor of W. Bengal, the military hospital, a school, a couple of streets, the Law Courts, Fort William no – this is William IV – still, quite a bit, and all totally uncared for and yielding to invasive vegetation, animalia, beggary (the steps of the Law Courts offer a fine selection of horror). The degradation is moving and even grandiose. I have written to Lucy Sutherland to say she MUST see the place. AND SO MUST YOU, John. Milner is determined that you come. Delhi is a dull place save for the magnificent mosques and forts, all Moghul stuff. The rest is George V AT ITS WORST – SUPER-LUTYENS, like Cardiff Civic Centre. Two of the most fashionable schools in Calcutta are called La Martiniere, I talked to the girls at one and told them about the sister school at Lyon. (Certainly I NEVER thought I'd see General Martin's other foundations when I was in Lyon!) They still celebrate in both places Founder's Day, 13 September. Chandernagore is a PATHETIC dump, in a very seedy suburb, ONE boulevard that might be out of Châteauroux or some such dull place, NO French, a poor little museum with nothing much in it other than the iron bedstead of a Governor. Gandhi must have been an awful, miserable, pleasure-hating backtotheland, puritanical little shit, an Indian Robespierre. Nehru seems mushy, messy, squashy-squishy, full of Great Sayings, a hypocritical charmer, the Congress Party are a nasty lot, TRULY hated, completely chucked out in Bengal. India, like XVIIIth c France has too many lawyers – 'a point of order sir' – and Bengal is full of Balliol-type debating smarties. No wonder the Raj liked the Punjabis, etc. I found the Sikhs much the nicest collectively, but the Bengalis ARE intelligent, they are very WELSH, I was constantly reminded of Gwyn Alfred Williams! And the Indian papers ARE VERY Welsh too, in their endless chiselling malice, their slightly obscene harping on seedy scandal – there were eight references to a necklace given to Indira Gandhi 8 years ago (I was unaware of this one in Delhi and was surprised when I produced such a titter when talking of l'affaire du collier!) – being a VC is a dangerous job, being an invigilator is a suicidal one. (I must say I do LIKE the idea of VCs – AND REGISTRARS – getting beaten up by their students, we could do with a bit of that in Redbrick.) I discovered that Philips, of the SOAS, was UNIVERSALLY loathed in India – a true London Professor-

bureaucrat – Keith and I thought he was quite odious. So is Max Beloff, the fool had been telling the Indians how to organise their Universities, I am glad they gave him the cold shoulder, for he is one of the biggest frauds in Oxford, and one of the noisiest too.

I could go for ever, John, but mustn't. I want to get back to Calcutta, as soon as possible, and for much longer. England seems so appallingly pointless. Even France seems oddly ORDINARY. I have told the Indians I'd like to come to one of their universities – Calcutta or Aligarh, for a term or two. This IS possible. I am so excited about it all I've decided to write up my Delhi-Calcutta lectures, in view of the discussions we had with the Indians – some of it VERY good and suggestive. This is the most important thing that has happened to me since I went to Paris at 17.

By 24 July the friendship with Professor Trevor-Roper had blossomed to the extent that he had become 'Dear Hugh'. This was how Cobb addressed him in this letter from Nyon, a small town in the Vaud.

Here is my piece on van Severen; it is also in the TLS along with a short piece of mine on Follain's little dictionary of ecclesiastical argot. I wanted to put it in a collection of TLS and other stuff (including a couple of jabs at Caute) that the OUP are doing, but Bert Goodwin seemed to think it would not fit in with the rest which are about Belgian history; still, I rather hope to persuade John Bell to take it, along with Marie Besnard. One can surely have fun sometimes? Old Bert is so serious! I don't think I have ever laughed so much as when reading your splendid piece on Toynbee. I was invigilating an exam at the time & got furious looks from eager candidates. The Joris piece produced a couple of furious letters from Flemings, one of whom lived ... in Dublin. I must admit to some prejudice as, when I was in the army & my unit went to Malines in September 1944, the young bloods of the UNV & former SS from Flandria or Langetmarke used to shoot at us at night – fortunately they missed but one of my pals was shot in the arm. I saw one thrown off a rooftop by a crowd of Belgian railwaymen; certainly a very large section of the Malines bourgeoisie was involved in the UNV &c. I am generally in trouble in that quarter, as the Belgian <u>Ambassador</u> (my!) wrote to the editor of <u>The Times</u> to protest at some remarks I made about Ghent &ca. in an article on translations.

I had a piece on 20 April on a peculiar chap called Georges Darien – a French linguist & author of <u>Le Valeur</u> – & in March a piece on the <u>Enrages</u>. Otherwise nothing much. I am doing a long piece on Simenon (a <u>nice</u> Belgian!) whom I am going to see next week. At the moment I am writing up my Delhi-Calcutta lectures into a small book for Dan Davin.

I haven't seen <u>The Times</u> for a month. What is C. Hill on about? I think I am becoming politically more & more inactive; I seem only to react <u>against</u> people – e.g. the revolting Brown.

<u>Some</u> of Balliol I like very much – e.g. Maurice, Jack Gallagher, the Dean (who taught me at Shrewsbury), our good Etonians, our equally good Barry Tech people, our flippant Sherborne fellows, &ca. But the PPE Fellows I find I do not <u>enjoy</u>; that I think is where the power lies under the new regime. There is far too much talk of 'Balliol leading the way' & all that, these Balliol people take themselves so <u>seriously</u> & most of them <u>revere</u> ambition, which I find distasteful. Apparently, in the last two terms, there has been a move on the part of the <u>Do-Gooders</u> to give the College over, in the Long Vac, to Boys of Deprived Backgrounds. I would put myself in that category, as a son of a Sudan Civil man, having, at my prep school, been deprived of everything save lentils, & at Shrewsbury, of everything save cat bones; but I don't think Christopher and Montefiore mean <u>that</u> sort of Background. Christopher, for all his Left-Wing views – or maybe on account of them – is really a Milner <u>elitist</u>, he thinks Balliol important & that Balliol men have a <u>duty</u> to lead. I suppose he's been there much too long. The worst thing about the place is that they HATE PLEASURE. Still, there HAS been a difference lately. Our Thursday guest nights are quite gay affairs. Jack and Maurice do NOT hate pleasure. I do wish you would come to one of our Thursday dos. Another displeasing thing about the College is the love of money: we accepted money from <u>Maxwell</u>, I think the college would take it – would have taken it – from Rachman. The place is quite shameless. But there are always some <u>very</u> nice undergraduates, Griffin & Lonsdale & the librarian are pleasant, decent people. The place is too

complacent & too arrogant; if a pupil of mine from Wadham, BNC, Magdalen, New College &ca. gets a first I am JUST as pleased as if it is a Balliol man – Christopher CANNOT see this. Personally, I very much welcome a bit more centralisation & far more exchanges – one should have the feeling of teaching in a <u>University</u> (this is one of the things I liked about Redbrick, but then, of course, one gets Power Groups, VCs and Registrars & bureaucrats and senates & <u>that</u> is sinister). I have always imagined that the nicest college to be in is Magdalen – Merton is <u>pleasant</u> but sometimes a bit fey. I quite like some of the young bloods I meet at the <u>Gridiron</u> but I don't think I'd like to live with them! (By the way, I am <u>delighted</u> the House has given a research thing to Geoff Ellis, a <u>very</u> good Magdalen S. African.)

I did like Christopher's piece on Laslett! Splendid.

Certainly he <u>loves</u> being Master & he is really very good. But what an ambition! <u>A life for Balliol</u>. Is it <u>worth</u> it? I think I would feel different about Balliol if I had to live in Oxford in the vac.

I wonder who Cobban's successor will be? I should think Douglas Johnson is a likely candidate.

Please send me U.S. back sometime. I'll be here till the end of September. Nyon is very <u>dull</u> – Macmillan came here for a quiet time in October last but I find it conducive to work.

PS In Balliol I am one of the leading Reactionaries, on pretty well <u>every</u> issue.

PPS It seems the <u>verdinaso</u> did NOT carry arms outside.

The 'verdinaso' were Belgian fascist paramilitaries but evidently not as military as previously supposed. Joris Van Severen, about whom he was writing for the Times Literary Supplement, was the Belgian nationalist who founded the organisation. He was shot by the Germans in 1940, after which the organisation effectively collapsed. The Balliol analysis is partisan, of course. Nyon is about 25 miles north of Geneva and is best known as the HQ of UEFA, the European soccer body. Its rugby team is twinned with that of Ealing in West London. Enough, probably, said.

1968

On 19 May he wrote to Hugh Gough in Dublin complaining about an ethnic minority and extolling a new acquaintance.

'The Flemings are my favourite hate nationality,' he wrote in what was to be a familiar refrain, 'they used to shoot at me from rooftops ... had another go at that rotten language in a TLS piece I did on Why Translate? Ghent reacted. Still, I am now learning Afrikaans, prior to going to the Witwatersrand for the long vac.'

In a handwritten postscript he added, 'I met Davidge for the first time, chez Felix: VERY good value! He doesn't like 1) PPE, 2) the late Lord Lindsay, 3) Nuffield, 4) economists. This shows taste. He was splendidly rude to Chester.'

This last passage is so arcane it is practically in code. Translated it means that Cobb had met Christopher Davidge, the notoriously philistine oarsman-loving Bursar of Keble College at a party given by Felix Markham. Cobb sympathised with Davidge's prejudices; PPE was Politics, Philosophy and Economics – a degree course of which Cobb disapproved; Lord Lindsay was a left-wing Master of Balliol who went on to found the University College at Keele in Staffordshire; Nuffield College is and was a graduate college popular with sociologists to whom the boss, Norman Chester, was sympathetic. Cobb didn't like economists either. His prejudices, usually profound, fluctuated violently.

On 20 April he wrote to a former pupil, David Long:

I'll put you down then for 8th June and will tell the bursary.

Things are much the same. The bump supper resulted in a stained glass window in Trinity hall being smashed – a bad business.

Maurice is getting married in August. A lovely redhead from Somerville reading Greats. I shall miss him at breakfast, but am v. happy for him.

I am lecturing at the university of B'ham next October. I am even quite tempted by the chair vacant there; it is a VERY nice university. But I expect I'll stay put.

That year Cobb went as a Visiting Fellow to the University of Witwatersrand in South Africa. From there he wrote to his former pupil Tim Heald on 15 August.

Just recovering from an IMMENSE lunch for the Br. Minister in Pretoria & some do-good character called Lord Walston. I am gasping. Food after moral uplift (the lord's lecture was laid on by the students and was all about JUSTICE & that sort of thing). An enormous amount of my time here goes on food (happily free mostly). The sociologists are after me now, & so is The Star. It makes me feel very important.

NEVER travel Union Castle, a floating Lyons. One lectures to lots of lovelies. The students here are all pretty affluent & beautifully dressed.

I soldier on (going about doing good). It is bloody hot, although late winter, and Jo'burg is about the most unattractive, crudest town I've ever seen. Yesterday, in a bar, an old man (white, of course) died (his address c/o the Salvation Army). They laid him out on the floor, put a tablecloth over him, but someone took the cloth away. The ambulance people took him away after 2½ hours of uninterrupted drinking (& eating). It is, somehow, quite a good description of Jo'burg.

The minister was fat, avuncular, fruity with a skinny wife in an outrageous hat. I liked them both. M thought the minister quite sexy. He looked, in fact, rather like Reggie Maudling.

People eat too much in this country.

After the usual expression of love he added a PS: 'I cannot help feeling I am not doing enough GOOD.'

1969

On 30 January he wrote to Trevor-Roper.

I am glad you liked Simenon. It was rather a rush job, as the TLS were being harried by Hamish Hamilton. What is the Coffin

Memorial Lecture? It does sound rather sinister. I have since moved to <u>Vespasiennes</u> & to Gwyn Williams (but am NOT responsible for the heading NO TROUSERS).

<u>Mercurius</u> does seem rather to have gone to earth (upset no doubt about the Merton <u>gazebo</u>) but expect we'll be hearing of him again soon. He must surely rejoice (as I do) at the thought of the <u>Agitprop</u> Robin Blackburn (Eton, Balliol (?), Nuffield, LSE, NLR) being 'investigated'. Don't you wish someone would 'investigate' (à la française preferably) Gareth Stedman-Jones, the People's Friend. But there! I am being un-Balliol. Master Hill, who has studied Machiavelli, is schooling Don Pennington (who I believe wrote a demi-book) to be the next Tutor for Admissions, which will mean, I suppose, that we will get no more Etonian peers or even <u>any</u> Public schoolboys at all. However, there does exist a corrupt, unaustere, non-chapel minority, including Big Jack (the Bonze), Maurice and my corruptible self. And Jack can <u>write</u>.

I will write to James. He should <u>never</u> have gone to America. I was <u>frightened</u> all the time I was there. On my first visit to N.Y. I saw 3 corpses in four weeks.

George Morpeth is difficult to stop. He is financed by the Army though he must be the <u>clumsiest</u> officer they have ever had. He moves in jerks like one of old Garrod's clockwork toys.

If it weren't for the <u>Grid</u> I <u>would</u> feel v. lonely. It is a pity Merton will not give me dining rights.

Michael Prestwich is too melancholy to be <u>Mercurius</u>. Would he not be that fey gadfly Gerald Aylmer?

PS I hope the Ranter man got his B. Litt.

'Mercurius Oxoniensis' was the by-line attached to a series of gossipy articles in the weekly Spectator, written in a cod-seventeenth-century style and widely assumed to be the work of Hugh Trevor-Roper. Cobb, described as 'a ranter', featured regularly in them. The Grid was the club which is sometimes unfairly linked with the Bullingdon. At the time it had cramped premises above Woolworths in the Cornmarket and offered cheap meals and drinks as well as the papers. Members tended to divide into two groups – on the one hand Eton-educated Christ Church men such

as the Earl of Ancram and Lord Irwin, who were indeed natural Bullingdon bloodies, and on the other Balliol men who were lower class, had less money but thought they were cleverer. Cobb belonged to the Balliol group though he had leanings towards the other.

On 14 February Cobb wrote to Bernard Wasserstein. This time he identified himself only as 'Richard (moral tutor)'. 'Dear Bernard,' he wrote, 'The Dean has told me all. I am <u>very</u> sorry. If it is any consolation, may I remind you that <u>many</u> fine works have been written in prison: <u>Pilgrim's Progress</u>, Russell's treatise on mathematical logic &c and prison inspired Silvio Pellico. I can keep you supplied with paper.'

Later that month Wasserstein received a communication along the lines of a Private Eye piece. It purported to be from a firm of solicitors in Cambridge called Ranter, Ranter, Ranter and Rant. Their senior partner, Emanuel Scribnet, said that Mr Richard Cobb had placed his affairs in their hands and that a writ would follow shortly. On All Fools' Day that year Wasserstein received a letter signed in Cobb's inimitable scrawl 'Bridget Page, College Secretary'. It told him that the Wigmore Hall had been booked for his performance the following Friday and that the Master and Lord Michael Pratt hoped to attend. Needless to say Wasserstein did not play the piano or any other musical instrument. On 13 November Wasserstein got a slightly more conventional letter from Cobb. It was headed St John's College, Cambridge, and was an attempt to change a date at Nuffield College where Wasserstein was studying and which Cobb christened 'The Penitentiary' because it was opposite Oxford prison. The letter began 'Dear Rotter' and concluded with a PS which told him, 'You'd better be grovelling to me, as I am doing a piece about you for the Friends of the Hebrew University of Jerusalem, am in fact perjuring myself by saying you are a DEDICATED SCHOLAR HA HA.'

Several of Cobb's correspondents were as chaotic about filing systems as he himself. One such was Tim Hilton, son of a Balliol-educated history professor who himself read English at the college and went on to become a distinguished art historian, a biographer, for instance, of Ruskin in more than one volume. At Oxford Hilton cut a louche figure and was, to Cobb's pleasure, an enemy

of his contemporary Anthony Cheetham. On one memorable occa-
sion Hilton set fire to Cheetham by dropping a lighted match into
his pocket at a riotous party hosted by Cobb and Maurice Keen.
Hilton was dubious about sharing his Cobb correspondence dis-
persed over a variety of attics and between the leaves of a number
of books. He was bothered because in his letters Cobb revealed a
private side which accentuated the less respectable side of his life.

Just four days after one such (suppressed) letter from the Angel
Hotel in Cardiff, Cobb wrote to his former pupil Martyn Lyons,
who had moved into Toulouse to read for his doctorate and was
staying at '5, rue des Quatre Billards', an address which caused
Cobb much amusement. He was not impressed by French history
in France and thought it was 'going down the drain'. The letter is
dated 28 July.

'Godechot,' he wrote, referring to Professor Jacques Godechot of
Toulouse University with whom Lyons was in contact ...

... is a dull dog and also something of a <u>bonze</u>. He is a great power
figure in Toulouse, of course. Soon, the only people who write
HUMAN history will be the English – Colin Lucas, the Revd Jack,
Olwen, etc., and also, of course, the marvellous Richard Andrews.
Goodwin and I examined Colin's thesis on the 16th. It was first-rate.
I think the Clarendon will publish it. He really KNOWS his area.

I shall be interested to hear what you can find especially about
the Thermidorian committee. The best thing I ever got on Toulouse
in the year II was the registers of the orders of the day of the <u>com-</u>
<u>mandant de la place</u>, in Vincennes. You are quite right about the
priority of military matters in the Toulouse context.

Balliol, bloody Balliol, has got SIX Firsts. Disgusting.

In a letter dated 28 August Trevor-Roper has finally and irrevoca-
bly become 'My dear Hugh'.

I have just returned from Co-Durham; my wife and I reached Darlington
on Monday two hours before her mother died and since then we have
had all the dreadful business with undertakers, the church service
and so on. The one redeeming feature was that we met an extremely

sympathetic and sensible curate, new to the North and very nice indeed. So it was very pleasant to receive your friendly letter on returning here. The death itself was not the worst part of it, as it was very peaceful; but what has to be done afterwards is really fearful. I was abroad when my father died in the 30's and my mother died in hospital, at 85, so I have never been through this sort of thing before.

I am going to Trinity, Cambridge, tomorrow, for a couple of nights, to remind myself what a college CAN be like. What you write about Oriel could well be applied to Balliol, though, fortunately there is quite a strong opposition there to those who would sell us out to the PPE Etonian New Leftists. But it is also true that the most zealous and indefatigible reformers are exploded academics who have become burnt-out (if there was ever any fire there in the first place, which is doubtful). Could you imagine any fire in PENNINGTON, one of our most relentless levelling men? Christopher is devious. But our worst demagogue rather oddly, is a Law tutor – one would expect THEM to be sensible – and a Scot – and one would expect THEM to be – Neil McCormick, a former President of the Union, a good piper, but a tireless People's Friend, who after only two years in the College has acquired all the positions of power. There are one or two silly scientists, but most of that lot are remarkably sensible and do not want their time wasted with a lot of disordered <u>palabres</u> with anti-democratic representatives of the JCR. Our greatest danger, I think, is Christopher, who is secretive and has a CABAL. I have always disliked ALL the Seton-Watsons; it is just not humane for historians to write so badly and to be so dull as those two. What is so particularly awful about Balliol – apart from the discomfort and the loneliness – is that no item of business ever gets completely disposed of. No sooner have we rejected, after agonising soul-searching, some impudent and ridiculous demand than it turns up once more on the agenda under some other head. I am DREADING next term, as it is all to start again. There is a proposal that senior men should be disciplined in the same way as junior ones. This would mean that Jack G. or I, while having a noisy party, could be told to shut up by some little PPE twit. The Penningtons, who never set foot in college after 6pm, would be quite prepared to agree this. Now you can see why Jack looks so nostalgically eastwards.

I don't think <u>Mercurius Dublinensis</u> is ever in a condition to put pen to paper. He is seldom out of Hartigan's tavern, a low place, frequented by jockeys and hucksters. And it is not known where he lives; or rather it is supposed that he sleeps where he falls, which is never far from the Green.

I hope to get to Paris later next month. But even there I suppose I'll be confronted with revolting students, though the Archives are happily free of that type. Laslett is apparently under the impression that I wrote my <u>Armées</u> in English and had it translated. I am DEEPLY hurt! He wears sandals or funny cloth shoes. He came to a talk I gave in Cambridge and kept on interrupting: FIGURES, FIGURES. I did not have any, that is why he says I cannot count. I can't.

Well, let us not be TOO Gloomy. There is the Grid; and even our Thursdays have remained unsullied by moderation. We have Marder with us this coming year, and a naval historian must SURELY be a good drinking man? He is an American, of course, so might not be.

I am tickled at the thought of Robert Ogilvie in Johannesburg.

Remember me to Xandra, I will write to James.

I am to become external examiner some time to the National University of Ireland. This may well shorten my life. Perhaps I had better not. I have acquired a great taste for a Cork whiskey called Paddy, introduced to me by Maurice.

On 2 September a relieved Cobb wrote to Martyn Lyons congratulating him on settling in to Toulouse and giving further information about Professor Godechot. He was, according to Cobb, 'chatelaine of le Bousquet-d'Orb, a towered and moated place with a lavatory in la Tour de l'Est. I gather he goes around wearing puttees, in a countryfied kit.'

Cobb had recently returned from Ireland where he 'had the pleasure' of seeing the Union Jack burned in Merrion Square, had a letter supporting Jack Lynch published in the Irish Times, drank too much whiskey with a much-decorated former Master of Foxhounds and his Anglophile friends. On a more serious note he had some professional historian's points to make. 'Mallarmé', he wrote . . .

...is a very interesting chap. He was a very active dechristianiser and ultra in the East in the winter of 93. I agree. I think there was often a revival of dechrist. etc. AFTER Thermidor. What surprises me about Toulouse is that the Thermidorian Reaction was so comparatively mild – take a look, for instance, at Saverdun, Pamiers, and other places in the Ariège, where Protestants were massacred in the year III and the year IV. Colin Lucas has been having a look at the Loire in the years III–VI. I think one has to take the whole range, up to Fructidor, to understand what is happening in terms of local personnel.

And then, suddenly and seamlessly, one is back in the twentieth century drinking too much whiskey with the Anglo-Irish in an ancestral home in County Wicklow.

On 7 November he wrote a brief letter to another, younger, historian of Revolutionary France, Sandy Murray. Murray, lecturing at the University of Newcastle, had recently at his brother's wedding introduced Cobb to a Mrs Isadora Caplan. This was, in Murray's words, 'a mistake'. Cobb's brief letter on Balliol writing paper begins and ends with a block-capitalled imprecation against Mrs Kaplan [sic]. At the wedding, Murray conceded, 'there had been a coolness'. Instead, Cobb wrote imploring details of the whereabouts of 'the lovely Jacky Turner'. In the rest of the brief letter Cobb referred again to the 'SUPER' time he had enjoyed in Dublin 'lecturing to nuns and J's' and giving a glimpse of the revolutionary 1960s, which, especially in Balliol, made life so uncomfortable for tutors, particularly for those, like Cobb, of an essentially traditional disposition. 'Life is BEASTLY', he told Murray, 'as we have a mannerless, humourless revolutionary JCR committee. Thank GOD for the Grid and for Etonians – they preserve what little sanity I have left.' In fact Cobb was not naturally well disposed to like toffs but he liked good manners and good humour while disliking many agents of change.

On 3 December Bernard Wasserstein received what sounds like his first normal Cobb letter. It thanked him for a party the previous night and was stapled to another, genuine-looking one from Bob Edwards, then editor of The People, alleging rather pompously that Cobb had obtained copies of his headed writing paper

37

which he was using for 'certain humorous purposes'. Edwards said that he had consulted solicitors and that Cobb would be hearing from them shortly. In his letter to Wasserstein, Cobb says that he, Wasserstein, would have to come and testify on his behalf in court if the matter ever came to trial.

1970

On 25 July he wrote to John Bromley from 'Ward 7, the Royal Free Hospital, NW Branch, NW3'. The letter was handwritten, covers six sides of paper and has 'love from Richard' on the first page, above 'Dear John', presumably because he had run out of space. Alongside there is a note saying that his hospitalisation was due to the demon drink and 'a punishment for my intemperate ways!'

I've been on this Health Farm for about 10 days, & by the time you get this, I think I should be back home. I broke some ribs & punctured a lung, in a bad fall – a combination of <u>wine and gin</u>. The ribs hardly hurt at all now, the lung is still a bit deflated. But my breathing is normal and I feel indeed much better from this compulsory rest. Time goes v fast. I potter about, explore the hospital & the surrounding streets. (I have however, resisted the temptation of having a drink in the Railway Tavern in my pyjamas! Unfortunately, I have no clothes with me!) Writing & receiving letters are the main satisfactions; I have also read a great deal of Arthur Marder – a <u>stupendous</u> book though I do feel he is much too nice to Beatty, who has always seemed to me the nastiest type of social climber. How discerning to make 'Ms' so much more important than 'Dr'. It reminds me of Trevor-Roper's use of 'Dr' Hill. I don't think he sufficiently emphasises the Navy as a social unit; but this is hardly his brief anyway.

Hospital life is intensely <u>interesting</u>: it is much more hierarchical than the Army. I doubt if Nicolas I radiated quite the POWER that one feels in a series of shock waves, 2 or 3 hours ahead, before the bi-weekly visits of Mr Quist and Mr Hopewell, the 2 consultants, who are also <u>Professors</u>. (This is a teaching hospital. I am a

Hopewell problem. They arrive, 3ish, Wednesday & Friday, preceded by a flutter of nurses & ward sisters, straightening beds – we all sit up on piled pillows, hands on the outside of the turned-down sheets – les mains étendues reglementairement a deadly hush, then a loud voice; Mr Quist is tiny, crisp & incisive; Mr Hopewell is a big blonde man, rather nice. They both wear roses (provided daily by a student). The procession moves from bed to bed in V formation: Mr Hopwell at the apex, the Registrar, the Deputy Registrar, 15 or so students (lots of girls in the Royal Free), the Ward Sister, the 2nd Ward Sister, the nurses in order of precedence (you can tell their ranks by the colour of their blouses, their belts & the number of rings on their bonnets), the physiotherapists, & various technicians. I have been inspected, in July 44, by Monty, in Barbeville, but this is far more impressive: sheer, utter POWER. No wonder, in Bichat & Lariboisière, they talk about le Grand Patron. Incidentally, they are met at the doctors' entrance, when they arrive in their Mercedes, by the housemen. I cannot see much sign of Student Power here! This is, in itself, a welcome change from the anarchy & appeasement of Balliol. The Royal Free is, in fact, unlike Balliol, an institution; & the ward, too, is a collective. Some of my fellow patients are marvellously funny – especially a cockney guard on the Tube who has a talent for the obscene metaphor equalled only by a Mancunian WWII Colleague of mine in Brussels in 45. He has been very bad for me, as once he gets on his favourite themes of knickers, panties &c he has me in fits, and laughing hurts my ribs. He is a completely natural humourist with an amazing verbal inventiveness. It's nice, too, to see people, even in the short time of 10 days, visibly getting better, sitting up, walking about, eventually leaving. And it is quite wonderful the trouble they all take – doctors, housemen, nurses – when one is really in pain or in danger. I am a natural optimist, but never more so than having seen National Health in action. (I suppose our present unspeakable govt will destroy it, as it does so much good & is entirely free.) Certainly a spell in hospital is the most powerful argument I know in favour of Labour.

People are v. kind to one another. There has been one death – poor old thing, I saw him being taken away and they did everything for him, they were all there, Quist &c&c at 1am. Goodness! Hospital doctors do work hard and they are so <u>interested</u> in what they are doing. With my 'floating' ribs I am a 'problem' & have been exhibited breathing, viewed from behind, by students & nurse-trainees; I suppose I am an <u>easy</u> problem like 'account for the dissolution of the Polish State in the XVIIIth century'. It would be more flattering to be really difficult. 'Discuss the significance of the career of Georges Clemenceau' but this, I think, would be in the kidney or liver or rare cardiac groups, whereas my lung is straight de Tocqueville. Still they have to learn that too!

I feel almost indecently well – all this rest, sleep, regular meals (I even down the prunes and custard), the total irresponsibility of being a patient – a similar attraction to that of the Army – just NOT being one's own master; one is not <u>entirely</u> safe even here. 2 days ago I was run to earth, on the balcony of Ward 7 – where I sun myself – by one of my most neurotic researchers, come up specially from Oxford – fortunately the end of visiting hours came quite soon (there are far too many visitors).

You <u>are</u> nice about my book. I cannot judge it; it is like an un-trimmed garden, some parts have grown & grown (e.g. the White Terror) as I've collected more & more stuff. I think Johnson's has been the only review; I don't know. I can get the dailies but not, for some obscure reason, weeklies; it is impossible to buy either stamps or weeklies in the hospital &, like a schoolboy (it is awfully like Shrewsbury – matron & all that), I am too afraid of the Ward Sister to go as far as the newspaper shop, 5 yards down the road. (Lucy and little Richard's school is less than 100; but I don't want the children to come into the ward, it can be frightening).

When I couldn't get up I spent a lot of time looking at a small garden, the leaves moving from sun to shade, a Victorian one-storey workshop with steam coming out of the chimney. Now, between showers, I can sit on the elaborate Victorian iron balcony & watch the comings and goings of ambulances, doctors, garbage, haemo-philiacs. I have not yet been <u>bored</u>. But I do long to go back to reviews and writing. I should have been in Paris as from Thursday morning! But I am <u>so</u> glad to be better. I am going to take more care of myself when I get out. Think! I have not had a drink for 10 days! Well, there is no problem, as I <u>can't</u> anyway! But I gobble a lot of chocolate & even eat <u>fruit</u> – something I haven't touched for years.

The hospital chaplain is rather a hearty Keble man of my age – very <u>red</u>, played hockey for the university &c. I seem to be his <u>only</u> communicant in this ward – all CLASS, I suspect! He talks rather too much about Keble …! Still I might have had a <u>Balliol</u> man! As one of my fellow patients keeps on saying: 'Never mind, my friend; there is always someone worse off!' Anyhow, the Royal Free can always be used as autobiographical material. Actually I feel like writing to <u>The Guardian</u> to say how <u>jolly</u> good our hospitals are.

PS If you are ever <u>ILL</u>, go to hospital, to a public ward.

Most of Richard Cobb's letters are typed erratically on his own manual typewriter, but in September he borrowed a Hermes from Bernard Wasserstein and in a letter typed on it at Balliol he pronounced it 'a super dream' and added that it was assisting his latest projects as it was 'giving wings to my most mellifluous prose'. Four days later he wrote Wasserstein a cod-letter purporting to be from his secretary, Anthea Knatchbull-Hugessen, re-emphasising his delight with the Hermes and asking if he could keep it a little longer as he still had no news of his own, which was presumably undergoing repairs. Needless to say he never had a secretary and Anthea was a creature of his imagination. On 5 October he wrote a third time, this time in his own writing, to say that he would return Wasserstein's 'lovely toy' before leaving for France the following Thursday. He clearly did return it but was missing it, for on 14 October he wrote to Wasserstein again saying that he would have to re-borrow it to finish his latest book. Two days later he wrote thanking Wasserstein for offering to 'give' him the typewriter and suggesting a formal ceremony complete with speeches and sherry. Wasserstein says the offer was a complete fantasy although, as he was going abroad, he did agree on a sale. Cobb agreed to give him thirty pounds though as his overdraft was over £900 and the bank was 'persecuting me' he was afraid the cheque might bounce.

1972

On 7 December Cobb wrote to John Bromley from Balliol:

I finished marking Prelims on Christmas Eve. What HAS happened to Upper Basset? I am glad you found THE POLICE useful; it is, I fear, very destructive. I hope you enjoy REACTION; it does at least have some good stories. Now at last I'll be able to get on with the next book.

I have been examining an Eng. Lit. thesis on Carlyle. Gosh, what a TERRIFIC historian he is! Imagination, compassion, a sense of place, a sense of colour and of sound, even of night and day, a master of words. I think I had never quite realised how much I admired him. I have been re-reading him – he is sensational, though often wickedly inaccurate. Now THAT is GREAT history. The furniture of the former Fellow of Belial (as from 1st January) is being pushed on trolleys down Beaumont St. On the 9th I am myself being CARRIED, accompanied by Devoted Pupils & a Band. I thought it should be done in style. Drinks <u>au depart</u>, more, far more <u>à l'arrivée</u>. I thought it best to break the Provost in early on, in case he should think that, coming from Belial, I am a pleasure-hater.

As Hervey once said of George II: 'never a kind word'. This applies at least to C. Hill, who has never expressed, at least to me, a word of recognition of the quite hard work I have put into this place. But Belial is famed above all for its GRACELESSNESS. It simply does not know how decently to send someone on his way. No, but I have been warned that I must get out of my house and clear my battels.

Well, as I am going I prefer to go in this way. One does expect Belial to live up to its own high standards of callousness. I feel EXTREMELY bitter.

PS I am exaggerating, as usual. A number of Fellows have written and said very nice things.

The references to 'Police' and 'Reaction' were to two of Cobb's best-known historical works – 'Police and the People: French Popular Protest 1789–1820' and 'Reactions to the French Revolution'. The 'Fellow of Belial' is, presumably, Cobb himself and Belial, meaning devil, is a word-play on Balliol College, which he affected, sometimes unconvincingly, to dislike.

1973

On 9 June he wrote to Oliver (Gilmour?) thanking him for taking him home the previous night. 'I would never possibly have made it on my own.' David Gilmour commented laconically, 'It was not Oliver but I who took him home.'

Cobb moved to 165 Godstow Road, Wolvercote, on the outskirts of Oxford in August and on the 23rd of that month he wrote to David Gilmour saying, 'This is my new home. And very nice too. FIVE pubs within 3 minutes on foot and the Paper Mill opposite chugging out paper for MY books.'

He suggested dinner in 'rather a drunken restaurant frequented by surgeons, always joyous people. They tend to go there after long sessions with the hacksaw.' He had also noticed a picture of Gilmour's father, who was very tall, with 'the TINIEST Arab officer I have ever seen. He was about 4ft.' And in The Guardian ('Floreat Salopia') he had 'a reference to my school friend who did in his mother'.

His elevation to the university Professorship of Modern History meant a translation to Worcester College, where he had rooms and enjoyed the status of Fellow. He referred to his new college, affectionately, as 'Wuggins'. He was glad to be out of Balliol, as he wrote to Gilmour, gloating over the 'weeping and wailing in Balliol JCR' over the assassination of Allende in Chile. 'I really AM glad to be out of the place. You and John must go on visiting me in Worcester.'

On 27 September he wrote to Sarah and David Gilmour apologising for not having managed to get to their wedding even though he had bought them a present 'neither practical nor useful, but merely designed to entertain'. He had hoped to get a lift from the Warden of All Souls, who was not after all going, or Maurice Keen, who was in Ireland. 'Perhaps it was just as well, from my point of view, that I did not come as I have been having tests in the Radcliffe and it seems that I may have something wrong with my kidneys, in which case I'll have to watch the demon drink.' He was heading off for a few months *in Los Angeles and commented, 'If England gets too awful, we'll have to consider emigrating, though I really rather like it here. Worcester, of course, is utterly dull, and I find myself missing Balliol!'*

1974

By now Cobb and Trevor-Roper had clearly become close friends – a relationship marked by the mode of address which was always 'My dear Hugh'.

To Trevor-Roper, 17 June.

There are so many silly and wicked people about. I expect now we will be faced with a gush of protests about this wretched student who got himself killed in London. Why do Left Fascists so much hate Right Fascists, when they have so much in common? And then there is Chile, about which I seem to have such unfashionable views.

I have just completed revising my lecture. It is still a bit of a chronicle of names.

PS We have started on soundings over the Provostship. It is a pity that our mutual friend from what used to be Herefordshire has apparently ceased his correspondence, because I think that before long there might be occasion for his pithiness.

The student who was killed in a demonstration in London was a New Zealander called Blair Peach and there were allegations that he had been murdered by police. The Provostship refers to the head of Worcester College, Oxford. The mutual friend in Herefordshire is the fictitious 'Mercurius Oxoniensis' who enlivened The Spectator for several years and which numbered among its cast list of Oxford characters one Cobb, 'a ranter'.

On 4 September he wrote to Trevor-Roper:

The only news I have of you are your excellent pieces in <u>The Sunday Times</u>. I particularly enjoyed the last one on all those mendacious mediaeval historians and I hope <u>you</u> will approve of <u>my</u> piece in Friday's <u>TLS</u>. It was a great pleasure to write. Don't you think Balliol should change its name to <u>Woolstonecraft College</u>?

We've spent the summer in Wolvercote but will be going to Lyon at the end of this month to attend some Anglo-French historians' do & will then work in Paris till the first week of term.

George [Morpeth] invited Michael [Pratt] to lunch at the Turf Club. Michael managed to break a chair but there was no damage to <u>persons</u>. George is umpiring between Turk & Greek. <u>What</u> a job!

There are lots of things I want to talk to you about when you are back in Oxford.

My best wishes to Xandra.

PS One of the pleasures of the vac here is that we take our meals first in Trinity, then in St John's & the former I find particularly pleasant.

I wonder what you think of the book on Robespierre.

The only book on Robespierre to come out at about this time was J.M. Eagan's 'Maximilien Robespierre: Nationalist Dictator', which was first published in 1938.

On 17 September Cobb wrote to Trevor-Roper again.

Oh dear me, yes, the Heavenly Band are after me alright including one of the <u>Feet</u> (the Minister), Arblaster <u>et al</u>.

I am <u>astonished</u> that there should have been any difficulty about Dmitri's election. I fear some sections are very remiss; & the philosophers very silly (why should <u>Kenny</u> be an FBA?). Would there be any hope of having a drink together on <u>Monday 23rd</u>? I <u>would</u> like to see you if it is possible – 6-ish or on <u>Friday 20th</u> at much the same time. Monday would be better for me, but Friday is alright. I could meet you at the <u>K.A.</u> [King's Arms] or wherever you like. I, too, will be away for the beginning of term.

Drop me a note here if you can manage either time.

Michael has probably left a trail of wreckage in various houses. He seems to have it in for <u>chairs</u> as well as <u>Fuman Beens</u> (as my youngest calls them.)

Best wishes to Xandra. I've just had a nice note from Constantine.

PS One of the Balliol Firsts was a <u>very</u> trying, pretentious man I had for a pupil who kept on dropping names of French XVIIth C historians. I was <u>very</u> sorry to hear he'd got one.

The Foot concerned can only have been Michael; Arblaster was the equally left-inclined Balliol man of that ilk, and the Heavenly Band was a blanket dismissal of those to the left who were baying for Cobb's blood.

To Trevor-Roper, 12 December.

I am so sorry I missed your lecture on Clarendon. I went to Zaehner's funeral in the morning, a v. long, elaborate affair, already full of 'flu & felt so rotten that I went straight home to bed where I remained for another day – in the past I have been immune, but having given up spirits, my immunity has been lessened. There is little to entertain me in this dull place. This term I have retired more & more to Wolvercote.

I had an agreeable visit from Michael Pratt. Otherwise, little to report. I <u>am</u> reading Ch Dickens on the Americans & find him very up-to-date.

I expect you are off to Melrose.

1975

To Trevor-Roper, 15 April.

I entirely agree with you about the Donnery <u>en masse</u>:'see how I bleed, my heart bleeds for Allende', and so on. Balliol is full of bleed-ers of this type, there are one or two in Worcester, though on the whole, the Fellows of Worcester do not bleed, most of them do not seem to have any blood. It IS curious, though, why the Congress Crooks should have been so successful in selling themselves to our Hampsteadians <u>et al</u>.

I hope Mrs Tomalin sent you my Bowra piece. I was reluctant to write for the N.S. but she is very persuasive, and their Book Page is not so revolting as their politics at the beginning.

I must report one thing about Asa Briggs that you may not know. I had a long session the other day with J.C., who opened up for my benefit, part of his dossier on your appointment to the Regius Chair. My goodness, to think we might have had A.J.P.T.! Or Lucy [Sutherland]! There was a Divine Providence at work, clearly. But J.C.

wrote to Asa, who wrote a very clear and pleasant appreciation of you. Did you know that? What a wretch old Galbraith seems to have been! And, what very nice things did Neale write about you and your justifiably severe article on Stone. So there ARE good and wise men about; I came away from Beaumont St. quite encouraged. J.C. has such a tremendous regard for you.

I have a book coming out, most unsuitably, on May 1st (for it is counter-revolutionary). Anyhow, I shall be delivering it at No. 8.

I shall be spending the second week of term working in Paris.

I shall look forward to seeing you at the BA dinner. Now that I have – alas – renounced whisky, I manage to get through such occasions more or less coherent.

J.C. is a reference to Masterman, the former Provost of Worcester, author of a fine Oxford novel and sometime spymaster. The clear inference is that but for the intervention of Lord Briggs the Regius Professorship might have gone to a rival historian such as A.J.P. Taylor or Lucy Sutherland.

To Trevor-Roper, 21 April.

It is good to have such pleasant news of your father. It was my misfortune hardly to have known mine; he died when I was 17, very shortly after his retirement, and for most of my childhood he was away, in Port Sudan, Wad Medni and Khartoum. My sister went several times to the latter, but I never got nearer than Cairo, where he was in the habit of taking his holidays. I think if he had not been so insistent on retiring to England, he would have lived longer, and I would have had the opportunity to have known him better. He was only allowed one leave from the Sudan Civil throughout the War; and I had the usual childhood of the sons and daughters of servants of our former Empire – boarding schools, grandparents, uncles and aunts, and so on. My father had a passion for the great churches of north Essex and Suffolk, and I owe at least to him my own glimmering awareness of our national past. He ended up in the Sudan, almost by accident, and not at all through the usual channels of examination. He volunteered for the Boer War, serving as a lieutenant in the REs, then he stayed out there after the Peace, meeting my mother in Bloemfontein, transferring to Somaliland, and then to Port Sudan, as port engineer. When I was in South Africa as a Hofmeyr [scholar], in 68, I went over most of the places my parents had been to. Later, as Deputy Director of Public Works, he was mixed up with early plans for the Aswan High Dam. Some years back, I found all his papers in Peterborough and gave them to the University of Durham, where there is some sort of Sudan Institute. It is curious to think that what my father started was eventually completed, I suppose, by the Russians. I have never been to the Sudan, Maurice Keen went there, and was bitten in the bottom by a scorpion while swimming in the Nile. I have a remarkable photograph of General Sir Bindon Blood and Staff, all wearing high collars. My father's brief military career served me well, as I got a Kitchener scholarship, along with my Postmastership.

A long digression. Now I must tell you about myself, about a Fate, literally, Worse than Death, that nearly overtook me. For some time George Cawkwell has been harrying me about a Certain Matter – and, like the great Kaunitz, it is a word I prefer not to mention in respect to myself – he is apparently the Obit man for THE TIMES as far as the donnery (what WOULD be the right agglomerat for the collectivity of Tender Consciences and Bleeding Hearts?) – anyhow, it ended up with my receiving a letter from Dan Davin telling me that he had been asked to write my obit. I was HORRIFIED – well, you can imagine the sort of thing, can you not? It would have been another rumbustious Myth, my late self merely being the pretext for Dan to write yet another duobiographical Dan-and-Winnie piece, with myself as a shadowy figure, vaguely seen, and described in Dan's own unique style. (I KNOW, for I have for review, a series of his Death Evocations, about to be published by the OUP.) Whatever should happen to me, nothing could be worse than that I should add to his already well-furnished Gallery of Death Masks. Dan has always regarded me as in some way his property, and it is true that I have known him ever since the 30s – but, in fact, I have never at all belonged in that galère. So I wrote him a polite letter, more or less on the lines that I'd like a fellow French Rev man to write about me, so I escaped at least that fate. Anyhow, I am doing my best, in each successive book, to get in first.

I always thought Eden was a DISASTER, and now you fully confirm my views! Poor V/C Smith, but it serves him right. What a HIDEOUS fate!

I am sad to hear of my succession as Ralegh Lecturer. But I console myself with the thought that, in November, I will be appearing under a new alias, as Zaharoff Lecturer. This I owe to the present V/C.

I hope all goes well on Thursday. I will have to come back on that awful last train. The Warden is going to tell me about Zaehner. I am glad of one thing: that is that I do not have to do an <u>éloge</u> of his predecessor in the Spalding Chair, if possible an even bigger fraud than Gandhi!

I would very much like to visit Pakistan universities some time, and would be very grateful if you would let it be known in the right places.

No, I don't know Raine, I DO know rather a nice chap with the suitable name of Wordsworth. I must make my peace with the SUNDAY TIMES, having had a book on the Bordeaux parlement for ages; the trouble is that it is in horribly small print.

Lukes is not a Bleeder, he is much worse. I had a brush with him last year IN THE TIMES over the Indian Institute violence.

I am happy that Xandra and you liked my Bowra piece. I really was rather sickened by Annan's.

The Dan Davin 'Death Evocations' were 'Closing Times'.

To Trevor-Roper, 21 April.

Just a postscript. The Philosophy tutor you mention must surely be that self-righteous Michael Hinton? I had a terrible row with him in Worcester, by coming into lunch rejoicing at the overthrow of the frightful Allende. He is certainly the College Resident Bleeder. He bleeds all the time and has a Maoist wife though a bit younger than the Chairman.

PS Alas, Michael Pratt's book on the Illyrian Is. has in the end been rejected by the OUP. Perhaps he should try an autobiography: <u>PEOPLE I HAVE SHOT</u>?

Just over a week later, on 29 April, he wrote again to Trevor-Roper.

Gosh, <u>quelle purge</u>! I left the Fishmongers' dead sober and in an appalling temper. At least I got driven the whole way back to Oxford, by a rather nice archaeologist from Belfast. But Wilson on Innocence was too much.

I am glad – and proud – to be in such good company in the TLS.

My book has reached me, so I will be leaving you a copy at No. 8 tomorrow, when I come in. I have to go to Cowley Police Station as the silver that was stolen from my room in Balliol, my last week in that college, and which includes my christening mug, my mother's travelling clock, etc., has been discovered in the course of a raid on a house in Cowley.

I will not see you on the 1st, as I am going to London for my publication lunch. But I hope to see you soon.

On 25 May he wrote once more to Trevor-Roper.

You will have read the appalling news in yesterday's <u>THE TIMES</u>. It came to me earlier in the week as a complete shock, as I had completely withdrawn from the whole sorry process. The only tiny speck of satisfaction is in the fact that he is unlikely to remain with us for long. Meanwhile, I only wish we had the Cambridge system, for I would so dearly love to take my chair away to some other College. WHAT am I to do? WHERE am I to go?

You were entirely right about Bhutto, and I reproach myself for having not turned out a second time. The left is always so assiduous. How fortunate Cambridge is! No fuss at all about General Gowon (a good man too, I feel). I suspect there is a powerful Bangladesh lobby here. And it is always a bad sign when Peter Levi adopts a cause. I suppose he has to find a new one, now that he is out of Greece.

I managed to get a reference to our old Herefordshire friend in my piece on Bowra.

PS I hear very horrid rumours that there is a Keith Thomas lobby in All Souls.

The 'appalling' news was the election of a new Provost of Worcester College.

To Trevor-Roper, 27 September.

I hope you have had a good vacation. For myself, apart from a brief visit to Paris, another to the Suffolk coast, I have hardly moved; and much of this month has been taken up with tests in the Radcliffe (I was in there for a week); I will be hearing the results next week. I suspect I have some kidney trouble, my evil past having caught up with me. At the moment, I am drinking enormous quantities of <u>Evian</u>, and feel quite fit on it, though I would much prefer Fleury. Today I should have gone to Gilmour's wedding, but was unable to obtain transport to Newbury. Anyhow, I am now feeling fit, <u>despite</u> Evian, and thanks to daily walks in Wytham Woods.

I hope you managed to hear my talk on Robespierre at the end of August. It was really about many more people as well.

Tell me about Natalie Zemon Davis. I have a book of hers for review for <u>The Spectator</u>, a book of essays, that I find humourless and uninteresting. She drops all the 'right' names, ranging from Keith Thomas to Eric Hobsbawm, and she seems to be very much part of <u>la Secte</u>. She is undoubtedly very <u>learned</u>, but I find her learning overpowering and pedantic & totally uncritical. I don't think I have ever met her. Anyhow, I intend to write a fairly scathing review.

George has invited me to the Beefsteak but I have not really been in condition for such occasions. Today week I am going to the Merton Gaudy, and they have put me next to Reggie Maudling.

I am depressed by all these dreadful Marxists. Late in life I have reached the conviction that there is nothing more entirely evil, hopeless and wearisome, than Communism in <u>any</u> of its forms. I don't know why I took so long to hit on this very evident truth. Portugal was the final light.

Worcester is SUCH a dull place. I hardly ever go in there these days.

Warmest greetings to Xandra.

PS I am eager to get a first-hand account of Constantine's experience of the 'Alexander Pushkin'.

I called in at Worcester Monday last, on my way to the Radcliffe, and found your very nice letter, which in fact could not have come at a better time and one when I needed a bit of encouragement, as I was to have an operation on Tuesday. The operation, as it turned out, was a fairly minor affair, and not the one the surgeon had warned me I might have to have; what is more, having turned my testicle inside out, in the course of it, they found nothing wrong with it, and I came out much as I went in, with two not one, and, generally, with a clean bill of health. But the night of Monday–Tuesday (I was to have my pre-med at 7.15 on Tuesday morning) I did a good deal of pretty hard thinking – the great Doctor had something to say about how the Steps & the String could 'concentrate a man's mind', and so on – and it seemed the only thing that really mattered was to have a happy home and family though, of course, I do enjoy writing. The trouble is I am not at all a 'belonger' and all those others, including the vain, self-persecuted and rather unpleasant, are. I do not at all like their history, it is arrogant and ill-tempered, and blows on the dead ashes of XVIIIth century resentment, in a vain effort to get the fire of a civil war that never was going. I think all of them, middle-class intellectuals and arrogant historians, are absolutely determined to recruit into class attitudes simple people who did not think in those terms. But I am no judge, as I do not read their books. I am quite happy to go my own wayward and unplanned way, though I do like having readers, especially when they are people like you who think history is a form of literature. Last week I reviewed a book by N.Z. Davis, an American woman who has written, among other things, a piece on popular forms of entertainment; it is a very boring, very intellectual piece, seeing all sorts of symbolism in various aspects of Carnival, and never for a moment does it seem to occur to her that these people were trying to have a bit of FUN. She quotes everybody under the sun, from Keith Thomas to Christopher, so I suppose she is one of the <u>secte</u>.

This month or next, you will be getting more of my autobiography, when one of my Duckworth books comes out; and I hope you like it. I'll give it you as soon as I get the advance copies.

So, you see, your note came at a very good time for me, and gave me a great deal of pleasure and encouragement. There are so many NICE people around, especially in hospital wards, both nurses and patients.

I have transferred to Guinness. Hope to see you soon in the Prince of Wales. I might go there Wednesday evening, as I give my first lecture that day. I went there last week in dressing gown and pyjamas, via the back entrance of the Radcliffe, and neither Charlie nor Edith, nor the old Welshman, showed the least surprise. Now I have got my clothes back, and can go ANYWHERE. The back prospect of St Paul's is interesting as a study in ivy, pigeons and decrepitude, but I am glad of a change, and now I can see the autumn trees.

Thank you, dear Tim, for your letter.

The letter is signed 'Love from Richard' and accompanied by two spheres or balls, one bigger than the other with the hand-written legend under the second, bigger one saying 'enlarged'. This was presumably a testicular reference. He appends a post-script: 'I shall be back in Bodley, as I have discovered, much to my surprise, that it has quite a range of <u>livres bleues</u> on Cartouche & Mandrin and similar bright sparks and there is much material in these, especially on coining and, generally, on frontier areas.'

To Trevor-Roper, 17 November.

I was so glad Xandra and you were amused by my piece on Malraux. It really wrote itself, the poor author was so visibly embar-rassed by his subject's peculiar attitude to evidence. Originally I had intended to have a few references to the various charlatans who had been awarded honorary degrees by Oxford, then I thought better of it, and after all, I was able to include the Heights of Bangla-Desh anyhow!

Yes, Pitt, Campbell &ca are <u>ninnies</u> and ninnies are now reveal-ing themselves all over the place, including Cambridge. It will keep <u>The Times</u> going for weeks (just as Hexter – who IS he – will keep the TLS going for weeks – I so disliked the tone & substance of his inquisition that I could not resist in putting in a word for Dr Hill, as historian, not as my ex-Master).

Oliver Franks is still in the Lodgings. I am much better and am greatly enjoying myself with the admirable Hickey, which I have for review. We must meet for a drink soon; I have taken to Guinness and have abandoned beer.

I don't think I really like the sound of St Jerome!

Pitt and Campbell were Fellows of Worcester and 'ninnies' because they disagreed with Cobb. Hexter and St Jerome also had the misfortune to express different views.

1976

To Trevor-Roper, 10 February.

Margaret & I listened to you last night on Radio 3. All those terrible people from Central Europe! I had no idea. What an awful crowd they must have been – and what an odd way of preparing for the Second Coming! We really did enjoy the talk, and I enormously enjoyed your piece on the Calvin book the other Sunday. Calvin seems quite as unpleasant as Robespierre, and far more effective and dangerous, because Robespierre fortunately did not last, and Calvin did. What a ghastly religion! How did someone as nice as James Douglas-Hamilton subscribe to it? Or does he? He used to when he was in Balliol.

How odd it feels to be the Zaharoff Lecturer! It makes me feel quite sulfurous; and it certainly is the strangest of my aliases, stranger even than being the Deputy to the Regius Professor of Greek, as I once was at a Degree Ceremony. Anyhow, my lecture is now ready, and of manageable length at last.

Do please give more talks. My publisher will be pleased with that one. I am still basking in the rays emitted by Anthony Powell on my Duckworth books.

On 25 June Cobb sent Blair Worden a letter on one of 'about a thousand' sheets of 'prestigious and vaguely unsuitable' paper with a printed legend saying that the letter was 'From the Professor of Modern History' at Worcester College, Oxford. Worden had been a boy at St Edward's School, Oxford. Cobb was particularly pleased to learn that Worden came from a village he knew quite well.

How extraordinary that you should be from Hemingford Greys. In 1940, my sister and her husband moved into the Old Cross Keys, a former pub, just in Hemingford Abbots, but really a bit nearer the Greys; and they were there, more or less, till their ground floor got flooded in 1947, when they moved to Bedford. I was actually billeted by the Army on my sister part of 1942–3 when I was attached to the Czechoslovak Independent Brigade Group No. 24 Liaison, with headquarters at Kettering, but with units scattered all over Hunts and the Soke of Peterborough. I did the rounds of my parishioners on a bike, and acquired in the process an intimate knowledge of pubs in St Ives, St Neots, Godmanchester etc. etc. as well as all those on the road to Cambridge where I spent most week-ends, to visit a refugee Belgian historian. But my local was the pub in the Abbots, near the church. My sister's main friends were the Gaselees, the husband at one time librarian of the Foreign Office. She still keeps up with Lady Gaselee. My brother-in-law was industrial manager at Papworth St Agnes. So, you see I know – and much appreciate – the area. I used often to wake up to the sound of bombers returning from night raids and, occasionally, exploding on landing. Of course, it is MUCH the best part of England, surpassed only by North Essex and Suffolk. Two of my nephews were christened in the church at the Abbots. I once bought a fine little table in an antique shop and wheeled it home. My sister still has it. And there was a VERY nice pub in St Neots.

Stephen Gaselee was Pepys Librarian at Magdalene College, Cambridge, before moving to the Foreign Office. When he died in 1943, The Times described him as being keen on 'travelling, shooting and bridge' but he sounds much more interesting than that suggests, writing a book about the Foreign Office, and being a noted bibliophile and classicist.

On 6 July David Gilmour had a letter on one of the official 'From the Professor of Modern History' pieces of paper about which Cobb still appeared to be quite excited. 'Pretty impressive paper, wot!' he scribbled in a postscript to the fading typescript. He aplogised for missing the Gilmours in Paris and typed with a shaky left hand induced by too many end-of-term parties. He was particularly pleased with the peerage awarded to his friend Hugh Trevor-Roper and had enthusiastic words for the Upper House.

The House of Lords is the right place for a historian who, unlike Marxists and AJP <u>fantaisistes</u>, is a friend of truth. I have always thought that foreign affairs were far more important than domestic ones – though I suppose they cannot really be disentangled – and <u>I</u> should know, having gone down in 1938. So I feel that one of the best things about the present Government is that these important matters are in good hands and that there is now much greater awareness of the Soviet threat all over the world. I shall never agree with you, however, on the subject of the PLO, the allies of the IRA, ETA and similar murder gangs. I know you don't like Egyptians, but you must admit that Sadat has a great deal of courage.

To Trevor-Roper, 6 July.

I think and indeed pray that you have both abandoned the miasmic swamps of the Isis – or what is left of it, and, up here, it looks a mere clutter of dried mud, unmentionable debris and empty cans – for what I imagine to be freshness of Melrose. Never have I experienced such an awful summer and I have always had a deep loathing for the heat – one of the reasons why I seldom move south of Lyons. I pretend it is NOT hot, and, during the Giscard visit, moved around London in morning dress, so utterly unsuitable and yet just so good for morale, and I soldier on with my count of the drowned, the <u>suicides</u> and the murdered, for my next book. It CANNOT go on like this, we are not a TROPICAL country. At least I attempt to console myself thus.

I was glad to see you at the BA dinner though sorry to have had so little occasion to talk to you (I was seated between Ireland in the Troubles & Military History, quite an agreeable position in fact). I would have asked you – for you would know – by what extraordinary quirk of circumstances Margaret and I should have been invited to the State banquet for Giscard; you did in fact mention the magic name of Beaumarchais. I think we both conducted ourselves correctly, though the appearance of our last most recent PM trussed up in a Garter, as though he had a hernia, in tights, pumps with mauve pompoms and looking just like the White Rabbit, did cause me some amazement. It seemed well established from the start, when the Lord Steward introduced us to some of the other guests, that I was a Professor of Modern Languages at Cambridge, and it seemed tactful to let this ride to the end. The Dowager Duchess of Gloucester even asked me if I had known her boys at Magdalene, and I said I had not been at that College, leaving the matter of University open. But she then gave me the benefit of a very good knowledge of the Cambridge-Hunts-Northants countryside. Anyhow, it was a stupendous occasion. Margaret was next to a very very nice Major-General who started the conversation going with the remark: 'Well, now, Mrs Cobb, what have YOU done to save France?' which really made her evening. I had next me rather a horrid MP called Cronin, who actually got the wine waiter to take back a perfectly gorgeous claret 45, remarking with a smirk: 'I bet no-one has ever done that before at the Palace' and with this I did indeed agree. My other neighbour, Mrs Jocelyn Stevens, looked quite put out. Who IS Cronin, apart from being an MP for Loughborough? Apart from Cronin, it was an absolutely marvellous evening, especially thanks to the Army people.

It is good to see that Corpus has given James a permanent base. I went to the farewell dinner for the Franks in Worcester last week – a melancholy occasion, enlivened however a little by the presence opposite me of the Lord Vaizey who spent the evening holding forth, in a very loud voice. I did enjoy that, but some of the others did not. It was at least pleasant to meet once more my predecessor, Wernham, a nice, gentle, pleasant person I thought.

Tomorrow I am having lunch with Anthony Powell. I have never met him, but hope he lives up both to Widmerpool and Venusburg.

And on Friday I go to a dinner at Westminster School, of which I know NOTHING, save that Bowle once taught there and the young Ribbentrop was briefly a boy there. Will we have to eat pancakes in this awful heat? For isn't that the pancake place?

I am glad – and relieved – about Denis Mack Smith, not glad about Hobsbawm – at least I had NO hand in that! I wish I could move from Worcester, but whither and how?

While in Paris in the last week of term I had lunch with Le Roy Ladurie and found him both charming and modest. I shall have to think again about the <u>Annales</u> school. Anyhow he is a complete individualist.

I will look for you at THE SPECTATOR party on Thursday, but without much hope. Xandra and you are bound to have taken refuge north of the border, where presumably it is COOL.

Jeremy tells me you are writing a book about an academic fraud. Did you ever know a man called Peters, who once rang me up about something, and who married rather a lot of people?

PS Nothing could have been nicer than the way in which EVERYONE put us at our ease, from the Duchess of Grafton onwards, at the Palace. One of the Equerries said: 'You will have a super time, enjoy yourselves,' and we did, both. I suppose what pleased us most was the fact that the Queen Mother was there. Also I was pleased to meet, once again, a splendid Breton admiral called Le Floch, or something like that, who used to be in high Gaulliste circles and who I think now must be Naval Attaché.

Cobb wrote a similar account of the Buckingham Palace banquet to several of his friends. They varied, but not a lot. On 15 September he wrote to Trevor-Roper again.

You are very much in my mind at the moment as I am reading Bethell's <u>harrowing</u> book on those poor wretched Russians. What a cold-blooded creature Eden was! It makes me wish I were going to Gunnersbury cemetery on Saturday.

Now that it is cool again I begin to revive & find I can <u>think</u>. I too have almost finished a small book on <u>Death</u>, & now I have to start thinking about lectures having been imprudent enough to put myself down with the Mod. Lang people as well as History. Meanwhile The Telegraph has asked me to review the 1st volume of Anthony Powell's autobiography & this I think I'll enjoy doing.

Yes, tell Xandra please, Margaret's quite delightful neighbour at the banquet was Major-General Patrick Ward. And he obtained for her from a black-&-silver wine waiter an extra round of the superb Chat. Latour 45 (the same that my neighbour, the unspeakable Cronin, had sent back).'Your husband works on the French Revolution, I believe. What does he think of that fellow Robespierre?' 'Oh, he doesn't like him at all!' 'Good show! Must be a good chap.' Her other neighbour was a Regent of the Bank of France whose eyes nearly popped out when he saw the Sèvres hand-painted Louis XV dessert plates: a gift to George III.

I am slightly embarrassed by the enthusiasm displayed on my behalf by Bron Waugh, a dangerous advocate, I should reckon.

That really is most of my news, having not moved at all from Wolvercote, save for the Banquet & the Election Dinner at Westminster School, an original occasion as the dinner never arrived, it got held up somewhere in a caterer's van between Eastbourne & Westminster though the Head Boy gave us news of its progress, from an external pulpit facing into the quad, every half-an-hour or so, as we drank more and more sherry: 'the food is now reported at Guildford', but I had to leave, to get the 10.15, when it was still in the neighbourhood of Penge. The result was I fell asleep in the train, overshot Didcot, woke up at Chippenham, got back to Didcot at 4.20 am, & to Oxford at 7.30.

I do hope Constantine will not be leaving Oxford.

Best wishes to Xandra, to whom I'll be writing.

PS Princess Margaret has an extraordinary resemblance to Queen Victoria; I was quite fascinated by it. Wilson looked quite grotesque, a gnome with the large head of an ageing & wicked child, wearing, so one of the Ladies-in-waiting said, his garter on the wrong thigh. Mrs Thatcher appeared to be entirely constructed of some vaporous cardboard substance in electric blue. Mountbatten looked absolutely splendid.

Gollancz have sent me a very vulgar unseemly book about the fate of the Russian Imperial Family.

Do you know Anthony Pagden? I'd like to meet him. I believe he knows Anna Somers-Cox, who was at one time married to the <u>awful</u> Martin Walker.

This letter was, unusually, handwritten. The book by Nicholas Bethell is 'The Last Secret: Forcible Repatriation to Russia 1944–47'. 'Who Was Who' has no record of a Major-General Patrick Ward but does have a reference to Major-General Sir Philip Ward (1924–2003), who would have been General Officer Commanding London District and the Household Division at the time of the banquet. It seems reasonable to suppose that Cobb got in a muddle over the General's Christian name.

On 12 October he wrote to David Gilmour after an interview in the London Evening Standard by Maureen Cleave:

I owe you at least 3 letters having heard from you in suffering Beyrouth, scruffy Cairo (a town my father adored and that I <u>must</u> visit) & now from the rue de Foin, near the Archives. I will be calling on you both in December, when I am giving some lectures in Paris & Sceaux & when I'll be staying, <u>aux frais de la Ville de Paris</u>, rue Geoffrey-Larnier in the IVme, not very far from you – an arrangement I now have permanently & that saves me the hell of a lot, apart from being very handy for the Archives de la Seine.

Yes, the lovely Maureen Cleave (Cleavage, as Auberon Waugh calls her) did me proud for <u>The Standard</u>. What's more I got a free trip to her home in my beloved Manningtree, on the Stour Estuary, in lovely flat country. She lives in Lawford Hall, a v. handsome 17th C in pink brick. Quite a change from beastly Oxfordshire! Anyhow the Royals all believe I am a Professor at <u>Cambridge</u>.

He then repeated the story of the Buckingham Palace banquet and his cross-purpose conversation with the Dowager Duchess of Gloucester. Cronin came in for further flak and Mrs Jocelyn Stevens received a further endorsement. The Irish Guards, however, came in for mild criticism because they played too fast but he was most impressed by the Lord Steward and another 'Court High-up' who walked backwards in front of the Queen.

To Trevor-Roper, 9 December.

I was so glad that several critics have picked out Backhouse as their favourite book for 1976. The book has a fervent admirer in the present Director of the Maison Française; he was talking to me about it yesterday, when we were on our way to what turned out to be a very dull party at the French Embassy. He was in Peking as a child & is very keen on Segalen, who, he reckons, must have known Backhouse, if not personally, at least by repute. He very much wants to talk to you about Segalen.

The party was a very dull one grouping all of London's professional Francophiles, wearing their appropriate rosettes; there was a great deal of kissing & embracing, though I could not see our Provost par eclipses (1) anywhere present; & one of the translators of what must be a very dull book, as it is about Lenin & is presumably favourable to that horrid man, made a long and catastrophic speech in 2 languages, equally unfunny in each, which kept the buffet + champagne & ourselves at bay for over 20 minutes (the scramble that ensued reminded me of my most desperate sponging days in Paris at receptions in obscure East European embassies where people of rugby build would pocket the sandwiches & those of my build wld be marooned against pillars).

I believe we may be meeting at the Savile; M.R.D. Foot, on the strength of my review of his book, has invited me to some discussion there on S.O.E. & such matters though in fact I have nothing to contribute. Still, it sounds a pleasant occasion, though I always find Foot rather elusive, even mysterious, as if he were engaging one on some slightly disreputable secret mission. He reminds me in some ways of my old pal, Goronwy Rees.

I was glad you gave that Helvetian such a trouncing in the TLS.

Please excuse the envelope. I have none to hand; & it is early closing.

Should I read the Merton History of the World?

If there is any suggestion at the BA of putting up the name of E.P. Thompson (2), next month, I shall oppose it. As I recall, there was no support for the idea last year.

Warmest greetings to Xandra.

PS (1) I gather he has not been seen very much in Worcester this term.

(2) I have just discovered that E.P.T. has completely misquoted me, though perhaps not deliberately, in his book <u>Whigs and Hunters</u>; but I think it prudent not to take it up with him as I find the less one has to do with him, the better.

Merton could <u>still</u> make Backhouse an Honorary Fellow; or perhaps they could name a building after him.

To Trevor-Roper, 16 December.

I am sure you'll find Segalen in the library at the <u>Maison Française</u>.

It was <u>you</u> who told <u>me</u> about Lady B's comments on conversations with the Queen. You told me you had heard it from that great French royalist, John Rogister.

Ellmann: now I have looked him up, <u>&</u> his letter, in which he uses the word 'memoirist' & makes the astounding statement that a <u>typescript</u> is a <u>manuscript</u>.

Roland de la Margerie ... I was introduced to him in 1939 when, as I recall, he was <u>chef du cabinet</u> to Paul Reynaud, & he was exceedingly helpful. He must be pretty old now, though, of course, he might have been quite young then, though not to one just down from Backhouse College.

A friend caught me yesterday on Bodley stairs gazing at the Marble Tablets. I was having Doubts about the Knightly or Baronial COBB!

Oh yes, I have to go to some wretched thing in B'ham on 4 January, so I'll miss the BA.

The Segalen whom Cobb had been discussing with the Director of the Maison Française must have been Victor Segalen who was born in 1878 and died mysteriously in the French woods with an open copy of Hamlet by his side. He was in China from 1909 to 1914 and again two years before his death. He wrote poetry and must surely have been known to Backhouse although not apparently to Trevor-Roper.

1977

To Trevor-Roper, 31 January.

No, she has not been eaten by the Pope; but she has been taken over & _entretenue_ by a rich Englishman who works for FAP or some such set of initials & I fear that the Legate's papers in the Vatican are not getting her attention. In fact I think she is quite lost to research. She is a poor lost Californian girl who fell for a married man, lived with him & was abandoned by him when, like a good repentant Welshman, he dutifully returned to his wife. In some ways, FAP was a mercy, as she wept so much over us all here in Wolvercote we thought the meadow and our house really would be flooded. As I have heard _nothing_ for the last 6 months I can only presume she is in good hands.

I was hugely pleased by your remarks on those awful Bloomsbury people; but I have been a boob over Tawney & have made a sort of apology. Malraux got a tremendous bashing, & I was glad you had a word for the fraud Teilhard de Chardin.

I have just been nationalised by the French, via the Embassy, a blue ribbon, in the rather Russian-sounding _Ordre Nationale de Merite_. Well, it _is_ rather nice – even if it makes me sound like a _Monument Historique_ (open to visitors) – & I really am _most_ gratified.

I think M. de Beaumarchais – or his predecessor – may have had something to do with it. And all this despite my crime of _lese-Malraux_.

I am being pursued by an elderly lady with a French name (but _not_ a French accent – sounds _Greek_ to me) on behalf of Felix Markham, who is desperate for a _red_ ribbon (my blue one mercifully has no Napoleonic connotations); he feels he should get one, as Enid Starkie and Warden Chester; & he is brandishing a letter he has had from the Prince Napoleon. But I am not Grevy's son-in-law & do not see what I can do. Poor Felix, he is apparently very wretched and disheartened. Is there anything that could be done?

A visit _en coup de vent_ from Michael Pratt. He talked so loud the house _shook_! I don't think he's been _shooting_ lately, but he's writing a book on Sicily.

The awful Ellmann has at last shut up. What's the matter with him? Everyone I know has adored your book. My OUP editress gave it to her father, a judge, for Christmas.

It looks as if I am going to have to look after Mousnier. Harry Pitt has not come out with any very helpful suggestions. It was all Matthias' idea: why can't All Souls look after him.

Section XIV: Robert Blake sends me very bad news. Anyhow I'll not vote either for Lord Briggs or for Matthias. And Hobsbawm has put Labrousse up. Oh dear!

Does this make me an Homme de Merite? Or an Homme meritant? (& of what?)'

Best wishes to Xandra.

(notre Richard national as they would say in Brussels).

PS Good heavens! Prince Charles of Belgium the Regent! A prospective husband for our Queen. He looks just like one of the Fish Footmen in Alice.

1978

To Trevor-Roper, 8 January.

The C.B.E. is very mysterious. Who can be my Protector? Qui veille sur moi? Not Marcia certainly. I have not had a 2nd lavender letter, there does not seem to be any trace of feminine influence. But what have I done for the Empire? It is much more a matter of what the Empire has done for me: (i) my parents first met in Bloemfontein; (ii) I, I presume, originated in Khartoum; (iii) I got a Kitchener scholarship as the son of an officer who served in the Boer War; (iv) I went to Johannesburg on Hofmeyr money; (v) I went down a gold mine, with 2 intense young executives of the Dresdner Bank, at a place called Doris (about as unattractive as any girl thus named); & (vi) I gave a paper on French Protestantism to a Pretoria aeropage of Afrikaans Professors of Protestant Theology. And now I am to be Il Commendatore.

I do wish you could unmask another Backhouse, several others. More? I don't envy you that! I am surprised Evelyn Waugh never wrote a novel on him (Waugh on More). I am at present reading a biography of him & find him pretty <u>awful</u>. Catholicism does not seem a very <u>happy</u> religion, judging from their converts.

I too read through the list, at least to the end of the CBEs, & was indeed gratified to see the name of Jean Rhys, whose quiet melancholy I rather admire. But, best of all, my Bank Manager was impressed!

George Morpeth has told me of your father's death. I lost my mother when she was 86. I think the loss is correspondingly greater with such an accumulation of years.

Now I suppose I'll have Levin buzzing at my ears.

All best wishes to Xandra & you.

This letter was signed 'Bokassa II Imperator (nothing less will do)', which was, presumably a facetious nod in the direction of the notorious cannibalistic diamond-loving African dictator of the day. The reference to 'Marcia' and the 'lavender letter' is to Marcia Falkender, an important figure in Harold Wilson's 'kitchen cabinet' at Downing Street. He never did establish precisely why he was awarded the Commander of the British Empire but he was glad to have what Harold Macmillan, as Prime Minister, always referred to as 'a little something to hang around the neck'. Ms and Os are worn on the chest; Cs and above elsewhere.

To Trevor-Roper, 9 February.

Margaret tells me that Xandra & you were literally cornered by one of the 2 ex-Tunbridge Wells Jumbos. I seem to have been rather luckier, & I tend to be quite ruthless when confronted with the masculine vision. They are both, I fear, somewhat lacking in self-awareness (just as well, perhaps, for <u>them</u>, but hard on those they encounter for the first time, though they are both perfectly good-hearted & kind but kindness is not an excuse for lack of social graces). The wife I have known since we were both 13, & her brothers were in my house at school. The husband is an Anglo-American, with the bellowing pomposity that sometimes accompanies that combination; he is also a Fishmonger or a Skinner, or something of the kind. He came round this afternoon to say how much he enjoyed himself. I do so hope he did not prevent Xandra & you from enjoying yourselves.

Poor Prince Fred, Geoff Ellis, Father James & others were likewise cornered.

They have just moved here, &, imprudently, I suggested to Maurice & Robbie that they ask them. I had rather forgotten how amazingly obtuse they can be.

So my apologies; & may I please be forgiven?

The B[ritish] I[nstitute in] P[aris] has gone to an <u>awful</u> man called Campos, who is French, I think and who once savaged me in the <u>TLS</u> on the subject of the destruction of Paris, calling me 'an occasional tourist'. I'll be seeing John Rogister tomorrow.

My excuses to Xandra.

To Trevor-Roper, 12 July.

I have hardly seen you this term. Perhaps you have been away. You missed a very cantankerous Faculty Board!

Your brother has been awfully kind in lending us his house near Bridport in September. It will mean a real holiday for us, & we don't know the West at all. Richard Brain will be coming too.

My book has been delayed – Union trouble at the printers! (Clay.) It is terribly frustrating, as I'd kept rigorously to my timetable.

Perhaps you are now in Melrose. I was outside No. 8 the other day & someone had put up notices suggesting it was the Citizens Advice Bureau.

So Oriel is to have a new Provost – a <u>male</u> one I hope!

The sociologists are hounding me in <u>New Society</u>. Well, it's a sort of honour.

Warmest greetings to Xandra.

To Trevor-Roper, 19 September.

We are having an extremely pleasant stay in your brother's house here. I did not know Dorset at all before; it is full of beautiful village churches & strange earthworks: & this is a very attractive house. At times I feel I am invading your childhood as I keep on finding books that belonged to you. I was delighted to rediscover <u>Ruthless Rhymes</u>, a humour very much to my taste, & a book first read at my grandfather's in Colchester. One way & another, we have been extraordinarily happy here, & I read no papers & gave no thought to

Oxford. Anyhow, I've finished a book & various reviews & have not read a word of history since coming here.

Oh yes, I am to write a biography of Simenon. I hope I do not come to dislike him! He's pretty crude but then he is a Liègois. It might be quite interesting, & he is prepared to co-operate. It will also mean a change of publishers. I think really that only a Backhouse is worth a biography but then he's hors concours.

When we first came here, three of your brother's Westminster students were here. We found them very pleasant & direct – I have always had a penchant for medical students, having lived as a child for a time in Charing X Hospital (one of my aunts was matron) & all my mother's family being GPs or nurses (one of them marrying a naval surgeon). The three young people absolutely revered your brother.

Sometimes I quite look forward to retirement, though I do enjoy teaching & lecturing. What I cannot abide is College business. How can anyone enjoy committees? Yet many academics do!

My most awful Balliol pupil, S.K. Holland, has been adopted as a Labour candidate. It is the best argument for voting for Mr Patten, which we will do.

I have no other news. Still, I am sure I'll soon be getting gossip from George, Michael (the proto-Home-icide) &ca. One of my Army pupils has been playing practical jokes on members of the garrison of Windsor Castle.

Best wishes to Xandra. C. Hill is now a Professor (of a sort) as well as a doctor.

PS In Askerswell Church there are 2 tablets to Gerald Aylmer's parents. On each it is stated that their son is Professor Gerald Aylmer almost as if they'd produced a prodigy. But I am being uncharitable, am fond of Gerald A (despite his Winchester education) & hoped he'd get Balliol.

To Trevor-Roper, 9 October.

Richard Brain has just received, belatedly, a letter from your brother. It was addressed: 'c/o OUP, Walton Street, Cambridge' was sent on 'Address unknown try Oxford'. I think this shows the right attitude to the Morgue and its occupants; & it reminds me of Emma Howard's telegram to George: 'Darling George, so sorry, thought

Balliol in Cambridge.' So let this greet your return to the miasmic valley of Thames & Isis. I am reading with a sort of sombre fascination – a <u>huge</u> book on Germany by Gordon Craig. What appalling people they were! Or most of them! Craig I can remember as a very solemn, rather pompous Rhodes scholar, in the late 1930s.

I attended a veritable <u>orgy</u> of Balliology on Saturday. Of this, more later.

Perhaps if I wrote more in <u>English</u> Princess Margaret might read <u>me</u>. I'll take your tip when I write up Simenon – no great French stylist himself.

The 'huge' book was Craig's magnum opus and concerned Germany between 1866 and 1945. It was a bestseller in Germany and the USA. On 12 October, just three days later, Cobb followed up with another letter to Trevor-Roper:

First of all your queries. For the Observatoire, I can recommend the re-editions of Germain Brice X, <u>Description de la Ville de Paris</u> published by Droz, 1971, p. 348 (ie in the pagination of the 1752 edition, tome 3me, starting p. 151) to p. 351. The foundations were laid in August 1667 & despite the difficult terrain, the building was completed in 3 years. The architect was Claude Perrault. The astronomers who first used it were Jean-Dominique Cassini & Philippe de la Hyre, then by Jacques Cassini aon of J-D. At the end of the XVIIth century, it also housed le chevalier de Louville & Claude Couplet. Brice is much impressed by the solidity of its construction & describes it as the finest building put up during Colbert's ministry. There is an early XVIIIth c print of it on p. 349. On p. 36 (1971 edition) it appears that the initiative for its foundation came from Jean du Clos 'Medecin renommé' & Amable de Bourseis 'Abbé', who in Dec 1666 prevailed on Colbert to have it built for the members of <u>l'Académie Royale des Sciences</u> 'le Roi y fit pour plus de 6 millions de depeuses . . .' and this is all I can find in Brice. I can let you have my copy, if you want to have a look at it.

I fear that all the records of the old Sorbonne disappeared during the Revolution. The more recent ones were burnt in May 1968! It is easy to get lists of <u>professeurs</u> in the XVIIIth century, in the annual Almanach Royal. But these only started circ. 1720, & I don't know

<u>what</u> one can use before that. If <u>anyone</u> knows it would be my friend <u>Michel Fleury</u>, 8, rue de l' Université, VIIme & President de la 4me Section. He is a charming man, 6 foot 3, with a daughter, Pauline 6 foot 2, married to the current Headmaster (6 foot 4) of Haileybury. Write to him <u>de ma part</u>. I mean to Fleury.

I think I have met your brother but it was <u>not</u> an auspicious occasion & I am glad he does not recall it. It was after a BA dinner; I had fallen down the steps of the Fishmonger's, you had kindly carried me off in a taxi, & all I can remember of your brother's house was the pattern of a very fine rug! I was <u>exceedingly</u> drunk, it was in my worst whisky days (now happily a mere memory). I would very much like to meet him in more favourable conditions. I have sent him one of my OUP books, am sending him another concerning <u>le Boigne du Mais</u> & similar one-eyed bandits, & will eventually send him my 2 Duckworths when I can extract them from the publisher.

Jeremy tells me Michael Howard is a strong contender for Turps' succession. But <u>why</u> don't they ask <u>you</u>? And <u>what</u> is to happen in your old college?

I could do without <u>The Times</u> but I <u>cannot</u> do without the Obits. Could there not be an Obituary Supplement?

I am still reading about Hitler. It <u>does</u> seem entirely appropriate that his (half-) brother should have been a <u>waiter</u> (in perhaps rather a <u>seedy</u> commercial hotel?) in Liverpool.

Back to College tomorrow.

PS <u>Poor, poor</u> Foch! At least Xandra's father did not have a Chair named after him, he was spared <u>that</u>.

I send separately my Foucault piece, for your information. Please let me have it back. & thank you for the letters.

To Trevor-Roper, 23 November.

I quite agree one should not underestimate Hitler. But what <u>was</u> it about him? I have just been reading Craig. & am <u>appalled</u> by his utter callousness (v. Paulus, Berlin &c). Even <u>Napoleon</u> was not <u>quite</u> so awful (though he was quite as <u>vulgar</u>.) I have reviewed Beryl Bainbridge's <u>Young Adolf</u>. I think it shows some insight. It is hard to realise that even Stalin was once a child.

How is Xandra?

1979

To Trevor-Roper, 5 March.

I went to a party in New College on Saturday & met, for the first time in <u>years</u>, James, <u>also</u> with a crutch, but also on the way to recovery.

Re <u>Chaumont</u>, it occurs to me that the chap to ask is a former Oriel pupil of mine, <u>Justin Wigoder</u> (his father is a judge), who is doing his thesis on the The Marve & who has spent years there.

I have been rather low lately. I went to York, to give a lecture there, on 15 February, & spent 13 hours in the train, getting there a bit before midnight. The train gave up the ghost altogether at Northallerton. I have had a bronchial cough, though a bit better now.

On 14 May he wrote to Michael Hodges concerning a complicated-sounding meeting: 'Where <u>is</u> Porlock?' he enquired plaintively. Whatever was happening in Porlock it conflicted with a Degree lunch so he would be 'in Wuggins before taking the lads off to the Sheldonian'. Much of the rest of the letter was taken up with the possibility of inserting Hodges into a future Degree lunch but his heart was not in it – nor the letter. 'Very shaky! Dined last night in All Souls with John Sparrow & Frank W-B & put away an awful lot of claret, & a heavy evening ahead today, first of all talking to the Ruined Boys of your old school, then drinks with some of the masters.'

A week later a meeting with Hodges still seemed problematic. 'Alright then, Balliol Buttery at 6.30 & then a meal somewhere.' He qualifies this with a note saying, 'I suppose we <u>could</u> eat at the <u>Grid</u> if it is not too awful.' He had just come back from a '<u>most</u> agreeable' visit to Eton where his talk was chaired by a handsome, dark boy in a 'gorgeous' waistcoat of Lyon silk. The boys were polite even if the masters, presumably after years in service 'looked a bit <u>worn</u> and dusty'. Everyone seemed to approve his welcoming of the Tory election victory and there was 'plenty to drink'. Perhaps best of all he caught sight of a copy of his book 'A Sense of Place' in the library. It had been presented by Anthony Powell.

To Trevor-Roper, 6 July.

Here is a proper letter, to add to the brief note of congratulations that I sent you as soon as I had heard the good news of your Peerage. I am sure there is still plenty of room for the voice of sense and justice in the Upper House, particularly when the boring gnarled subject of Scottish devolution turns up again, as no doubt it will (how surprising, though, that the Welsh should have displayed so much more sense than those north of the other border!). I think it will be of great value to have a historian, who is a friend of the truth – as any historian should be, but which some are not, either because they are Marxists or because, like A.J.P., they are <u>fantaisistes</u> – in an assembly that sometimes has time to devote to the recent past and to getting the record straight (for instance, during the Occupation years, the Breton autonomists collaborated with the Germans etc. etc.). For myself, I shall have the satisfaction of feeling that I have a friend in high places. It must greatly delight Xandra. Let us hope that you are going to be in Oxford for a bit, before moving north, so that we can celebrate this happy event in some suitable place & not, I feel, the K.A. any more, because it has become rather horrid; but I find that the Eastgate still has quiet corners.

This typewriter is dreadful, but my handwriting at the moment, following various end of Term rejoicings, is even more so. The BA dinner this year was monumentally dull: a long, dreary speech from, I think, a Lord Flowers – anyhow not a man to enliven your House – but I did enjoy sitting between Tony Quinton and old Michael François (old Frenchmen are so much nicer than young ones). I made quite a fuss about Hampson's name not having been accepted by Council; as far as I recall, Section XIII has always been allocated two names. It seems to me that the mediaevalists and all the other archaeologists are over-represented, and that we are under-represented. I hope that Hampson will make it next year.

I wish I had time to write. I seem to spend my time reading typescripts for the OUP AND the CUP and ploughing through ill-written theses. But perhaps next month there will be a respite. I went to Paris in June and have come back with some excellent material for my next counter-revolutionary allegory. I feel at the moment quite pro-Swedish – not a sentiment normal to me, because I always associate that country with the awful Bergman, with the equally awful Borg (who, on appearances, MUST be left-wing) and with an accent that goes endlessly up and down – my little book having been given a tremendous boost in <u>Svenska Dagbladet</u>, by a reviewer not over-partial to the Left in his country. I managed to get it translated by the Danish wife of one of my Worcester colleagues (there is some sort of Station Road Law by which Cambridge undergraduates who read English ALWAYS marry Scandinavians – though they don't always stay married to them) and it really is very nice indeed.

I went, on the 30th, to a Balliol Gaudy, and enjoyed myself greatly, meeting some of my first pupils and a very tough Anglican missionary in Guyana, who came up in 1927, and who was extremely amusing on Guyanian Marxist-Leninists. <u>Le père</u> Kenny, unlike his predecessor, Dr Hill, is not an enemy of pleasure, and we all had a very good time. Jeremy was there – it was his year – also my old friend Tyacke.

Tomorrow I go to Brighton to talk to the Sussex Branch of the Oxford Society – a dull occasion, I fear, also a reminder of time passing, as nearly all who are coming are apparently, like myself, in their 60s. On Monday, we are hoping to meet your brother, who is coming up for a conference and whom Richard Brain is going to try and bring round to see us.

Now I must get back to multiple chores. I wonder what style you will adopt, in respect of place.

Warmest regards to Xandra, and, once more, many congratulations.

PS I ordered this notepaper in an endeavour to keep up with the Revd Jack McManners; but never fear, it does not mean that I intend to follow him into D. Littery. I shall remain an (increasingly lonely) MA.

Trevor-Roper was now Lord Dacre in public but still 'My dear Hugh' to Cobb in epistolary mode. On 16 July Cobb began another of his letters in just such a fashion.

In <u>your</u> case the Fountain of Honour was well directed, firm & as decided as <u>les Grandes Eaux</u> at Versailles. Yes, John Vaizey went on and on to me, at a Worcester do, about all the <u>perks</u> of the Peerage as though describing the <u>jetons de présence</u> used by members of the French Academy. He insists on his children being addressed as Hon'ble. He's like a happy child with a new toy.

We had a visit from your brother last week – a very happy occasion. It was the first time we'd met. It turns out that he knows my cousin John Cobb who is a consultant at St George's.

I approve <u>more & more</u> of our P.M. (the <u>real</u> Mrs T.).

Once when abroad for a longish period Heald received no letters from Cobb and assumed that he had committed some dreadful faux-pas and been ostracised. When approached about this Cobb seemed incredulous and merely protested that North America was 'far too far to write'. By 13 July 1979, however, Heald was back in England and had a letter from Cobb on his official paper with the word 'Famous' inserted between 'the' and 'Professor', plus in brackets the words 'Englands finaster forfattere' with a footnote explaining that the description was from the Svenska Dagbladet on 15 March 1979 and was, therefore, as Cobb put it, 'official'. He, characteristically, ruined the effect by typing in the words 'a fraud' after his name at the bottom of the page.

He would be returning to 'Yokelloland' for the first half of September ...

. . . Patrick Trevor-Roper having once more lent us his house at Burton Bradstock. Perhaps you will be in those parts then? I have just been acting as guide to 60 members of the Sherborne Historical Association, one of whom – I think a former chaplain – knew both Yokello and Matthew. I took them round Worcester. I also thought I would find you at the <u>Spectator</u> party, where I missed Edward, but met Enoch Powell, Michael Foot and wife (who upbraided me on the subject of Mary W), an elderly queer called Crisp, a topless lady journalist etc. I do quite a lot for <u>The Spectator</u> these days – very much my style. (I also voted for Cricketer's homonym – well how COULD one vote for a party that chose Horrible Holland for a safe London seat?) In fact things seem to be on the up: and I was delighted about Hugh's peerage. (I suggested that he take the title of Lord Melrose.) Of course, I have been offered various things by Marcia and Mrs Thatcher, both letters recognisably written by Edward (the <u>fausse Falkender</u> was shown to the Queen Mum among others). I have also been talking to quite a lot of Ruined Boys: Sherborne, Shrewsbury (Visibly Ruined), Eton (terribly good-looking with lovely coloured waistcoats), Haileybury etc. Edward is in Burford so I'll probably see him soon. I am writing a new book – my little Death thing has had a super boost from the Cruiser (Conor Cruise O'B) as well as in Swedish. Then I must get down to the biography of Simenon, I am seeing the Maitre in Lausanne in November.

Cobb's footnote to this letter was almost as long as the main letter. It mentions an old school friend, John Heath, who was Consul-General in Chicago, where he employed a former pupil named Caroline Cracraft (née Pinder). Heath was due to get an Embassy in South America and had worked in Mexico under the Ambassadorship of Sir Edmund Cheetham, father of Cobb's former pupil and bête noire, Anthony.

At one point he takes to what seems like free verse, so:

> Maurice has been on leave.
> My hair is falling out.
> Margaret is on a diet.
> Nicky is a teen-ager.
> The Russians are very nasty.
> Carter is a disaster.
> Thank God Trudeau is out of the way.

I rather liked Canada, could even live there, were it not for the ghastly climate; but Canadians are rather DULL, and French Canadians are utter bores and almost as nasty as the Irish, the Basques, the Bretons, the Turds (Edward's friends), the PLO, etc. I am quite pro-Israel, but am told I would hate the place if I went there, which I am not likely to do. David Gilmour is TERRIBLY pro-Arab, I suppose he caught it from his father, an excellent man in other ways.

He concludes:*'L'appétit vient en mangeant (French). I want some MORE Honours. At the last BA dinner I went absolutely covered in medals making an appearance first at a pub called the Edgar Wallace (his son was at prep school, no, dame school, with me, in Tunbridge Wells). It was full of journalists and loud-talking barristers. My pupil Justin Wigoder has a wig. What are you writing and where? What about that character, Burwash, or whatever?'*

A week or so later he wrote to Heald again, this time inserting the word 'stunning' between 'the' and 'professor' and signing himself 'Menilmontant', which was one of the titles he had decided on in the event that Mrs Thatcher were to offer him a peerage.

'What a corvée to have to write a life of the Prince,' he remarked, in response to Heald's news that his latest contract was to write a biography of Prince Charles. 'Worse even than to have to write one of Simenon; at least I do not have to be discreet about his sex life.

'Did you hear Warden Sparrow's marvellous talk last night on Growing Old? A very ACTUAL subject, I find, though I do not remove the white hairs from my eyebrows, as then I would not have any eyebrows at all, and the ones I have have been white ever since I was 12 or so.'

On 27 July he wrote to Trevor-Roper after a champagne-fuelled meeting which was presumably an opportunity to congratulate the newly ennobled peer in person.

I greatly enjoyed our meeting last week and the two bottles of champagne we shared filled me with optimism, to the extent that I actually forgot – for a moment – this perfectly horrible weather. I hope you had a satisfactory meeting with Garter. I must say I find the Dacre title extremely attractive, it has a Norman sound about it, and Dacre of the North is even better. Why does the North carry with it so much more power and prestige than any other point of the compass? I have always thought that Le Nord was much the most romantic-sounding of any of the French Departments: it is simple and a tiny bit threatening. Lord North too is a great title, though I am not so sure about its holder, a man much abused, however. Anyway, Dacre, with or without North or South, sounds tremendous. I will much look forward to hear what you decide.

A call from Hartmut from Riga. I didn't think they let anyone in at those places, much less a descendant of a Baltic Baron.

A pleasant visit from Bert Goodwin, a simple soul and a good, honest historian. In his last book he has placed several small bombs beneath the dreadful E.P. Thompson, the very <u>worst</u> sort of left-wing millionaire.

I am sending this to Melrose, in the hope that you have now reached a cooler place, well away from the miasmic swamps of the Isis and from the squatters on your doorstep in St Aldgate's. I shall see August out here, but will be rewarded, in September, by a stay at your brother's house in Burton Bradstock. Warmest greetings to Xandra.

He wrote twice to Bernard Wasserstein that August, still debating with himself the question of what title to take if he were offered a peerage. Ménilmontant was mentioned but he seemed to prefer Lord Tour-de-France or Lord Barbes-Rochechouart. He voted for Mrs Thatcher, a switch in allegiance for which Wasserstein chided him for he replied, 'You may well remind me of my voting position in 1970; but things have changed since then, and the PLO, the IRA, ETA, Baader-Meinhof, the Red Brigades, NUPE, the strikes, Jean Genet, Horrible Holland, etc. etc. have caused me to become more sensible and I shall continue to vote for Mrs T, for the time being at least.'

Towards the end of August he wrote to Sandy Murray advising him to send a manuscript to Oxford University Press on the grounds that 'they are about the only academic publishers these days'. He was also dropping the name of Auberon Waugh. 'Bron Waugh fawns upon me. He says I'm <u>WITTY!</u>'

On 14 September Cobb wrote to Trevor-Roper aka Dacre from the Regius' brother's house in Burton Bradstock:

How I wonder are your proceedings? Has the new Garter proved amenable? It seems to me that you must have had a terribly busy holiday whereas here am I, at the end of a fortnight in your brother's house, who have done absolutely nothing at all save visit Dorset churches, walk on the cliffs, go & see Goodwin

(French Revolution, ex-Jesus) in Sherborne, & spend half-a-day at Anthony Powell's in Frome (this is becoming an annual fixture), read <u>Villette</u> & a Turgenev, & get stuck in a boring trendy, Lefty novel by Heinrich Böll, for whom I have now conceived a strong dislike.

I expect everything here is familiar to you: a picture of the Clifton Suspension Bridge, a Victorian print entitled <u>The Sabbath Morn</u>, a collection of sticks, one bamboo with Chinese decorations & inscriptions on it. But things have changed since last year, a local man - ex-Navy - is attacking the garden, planting grass seed, clearing the kitchen garden, &ca &ca, all of which seems to indicate that your brother intends to spend more time in this potentially delightful house.

I have done <u>no</u> work, have written <u>nothing</u> for a fortnight. And I have no news of Oxford during the vacation, save that James Forbes seems really very ill though I do not know the outcome of his last operation. I have discovered no more Aylmer Tablets, though local churches abound in ones that mark the places in church of admirals, widows, numerous in these parts, in monuments to captains who perished in Antigua & the Windward Isles, &, in Charmouth churchyard, a vast sarcophagus of an ex-Capt. R.N. who was killed in a duel in August 1793, a bit of a waste at a time when he should have been fighting the French. I have to bring to London various objects - gold cuff-links, a Senior Citizen's* Railcard left behind by one of your brother's friends.

The sea has revived me - as it always does (no doubt the result of having survived my first four years on the East coast). Our Government seems to be doing well, but <u>what</u> can anyone do about the hideous IRA?

My nearest approach to history is to learn, from the book page of the D.T., that Hexter regards Lawrence Stone as a great historian! Tell me about Hexter. Hasn't he written about my former Master? Or is it the same Hexter?

I do hope you now have your title settled to your satisfaction & to that of Xandra. Perhaps you will end up with something Northumbrian. All this I will learn next term, it will be something for me to look forward to. At least Northumberland has retained the name; recently I wrote to <u>The Spectator</u> asking that Cambridgeshire should be forced to disgorge poor little Hunts & that Salop should get back its Montgomery twin.

Poor Maurice Keen is being made to teach <u>Marx</u>, an author of whom I have never read a word.

I gather Lucy Sutherland is not at all well.

Stay up north as long as possible. Oxford is too near Cowley, shop stewards and TUC bullies.

Best wishes to Xandra.

* I don't want to <u>be</u> a Senior Citizen, having never been a Junior one, nor a Middle one. Anyhow I thought citizens were Quakers, Unitarians, Baptists, members of the Labour Party &ca.

Three days later he wrote to Trevor-Roper from Worcester:

My return to beige-coloured envelopes, entreaties for yet more testimonials, & other grim signs of the on-coming Term has at least been enlivened by a hilarious letter from George, now keeping the peace between Johnny Greek and Cruel Turk in Cyprus. The news is that <u>Michael Pratt is in love!</u> As George says, it places the Russian Revolution in its true insignificance. The lady is the daughter of a Kenya judge; George does not seem to know whether she is black, white or brown. But the father was an energetic hanger of Mau-Maus.

I await with eagerness further news of your title. George has a word about a female Dacre married to William Douglas-Home, who writes plays.

Now I must write to thank your kind brother for our excellent holiday. In the fortnight we were there we were able to follow the progress of the grass seed; soon it will be a very fine border.

For <u>unctuous</u> reading, I strongly recommend the current number of the Oxford Diocesan Magazine, which includes 3 valedictory pieces on Henry Chadwick, the first by the Chairman of the History Faculty Board & which is so sycophantic as to arouse in me unsuspected depths of anticlericalism (also aroused by the appearance & statements of Bishop Runcie, even more by those of Mrs Runcie, <u>Madame L'Évêque</u>). Do you ever read this forward-looking publication?

I note en passant from the latest literature of the BA, that I have been quietly dropped from the British National Committee for the World Conference of Historical Sciences or whatever, & that I have been replaced by Hobsbawm – no doubt a step in the right (Left) direction. There are many mysteries about the workings of these BA committees.

I wonder how you'll find Runcie as a colleague.

Now that John Heath has been appointed to Chile I shall endeavour to get myself invited there. Miss Santa Cruz was a pupil of mine & I think my version of the French Revolution would not be taken amiss on that side of the Andes. Every time I turn on the wireless I hear earnest Scottish voices talking about Devolution, so then I turn it off again.

1980

The 1980s, which were to be the years of his penultimate decade, seem to have been his most prolific in epistolary terms, though it may just be that more of his correspondents from this time were still alive in the first years of the twenty-first century and they were better at hanging on to their letters. He was now in his sixties and sounding grumpy.

To Trevor-Roper, 22 January.

I think I'll be doing a piece for <u>Encounter</u> called 'Goronwy Rees in Aberystwyth', as I lived through that sad and rather seedy affair and indeed appeared before Willink, a very NASTY, narrow man, as a witness for the Principal. But WHY he let the <u>Sunday People</u> have those awful articles is a mystery to me; I feel he needed the money. But WHY, even more did he agree to see this Boyle – 'investigative historian' is a horrid invention – on his death bed. I cannot make it out. And why did he bring in Liddell? Goronwy was a charmer; but I would never have attached much importance to what he said. He was quite unreliable (as I discovered). Do tell me what you think.

I hope you had a good holiday. I have been busy writing, so am in a pretty good mood. Oh dear, the press do come out with dreadful things: Hugh Thomas as your successor . . . I cannot believe it will happen.

I am giving a talk in Cambridge at the end of this month.

Warmest greetings to Xandra. Is not this Runcie a bit 'tinkle-tinkle'?

To Trevor-Roper, 2 February.

Just back from Cambridge, full of nostalgia for that beautiful place and that perfect part of England. Yesterday I walked among sluices and locks, bridges and ducks, a pause at King's Chapel, an undeserved adornment to a perfectly ruined College. I had a long talk to Maurice Cowling, who is writing a book about Christian historians, a circle into which he tells me he has introduced me. If only I were a little younger, I would put in for that Cambridge chair; but with a bit over 4 years to go, I am just not a worthwhile proposition. A pity, because it would be exciting to have 4 years there, finding out how it all worked, before retiring further east. I found Trinity Hall quite appealing, rather like a Dutch Town Hall. It is down a long alleyway, with bicycles coming and going. Cambridge seems somehow closer to the 30s. I looked at your beautiful Lodgings and felt very envious. You will both love it there.

After all this death-bed business I feel I no longer WANT to write about Goronwy Rees. Really I don't know <u>what</u> to think.

PS Maurice thinks Elliott could have the chair if he wants it. Apparently he has a house in Cambridge. Then there is Norman Stone. I am still almost tempted to express a positive interest, though from what Maurice tells me, I am almost certainly too old for their purpose. If I were to move, I could probably get myself taken by St John's, where I have some friends and which is opposite my favourite pub, the Baron of Beef.

Our friend Jack Gallagher is in hospital again, not at all well by all accounts.

I am making my first trip to the House of Commons at the end of the month. Chris Patten is a former pupil, Ian Gilmour is the father of one.

The Baron of Beef was a favourite meeting place of Cobb's particular Cambridge chums but seems to have slipped into a relatively faceless anonymity, rating absolutely no superlatives from any guide. This may, of course, have been why Cobb and his friends liked it.

To Trevor-Roper, 11 May.

Belated thanks for a delightful evening in my old College. I was particularly happy to discover that Hugh Lloyd-Jones is as passionately pro-feline as I am; and Anne Whiteman and I were able to have a really long talk about Jack Gallagher. I cannot tell you how <u>envious</u> I am of the D[octor of] D[ivinity]. I hope they do the thing properly, black gloves with long sleeves, a red robe. And I shall expect Hugh to be wearing it at the <u>Maison Française</u> Garden Party, so as to put to shame the Marshal Foch Professor in his canary robes. I think, after all the nice things I have said about the place, it is more than time that the University College of Wales gave me some colourful hood and gown!

I have referred to Backhouse, in a review I have just done for <u>The Spectator</u> of <u>Madoc</u>, the myth of the Welsh Indians.

I do think I should be a DD. I have preached in at least six College chapels, in the University church in Leicester, and in the school chapel at Shrewsbury. Surely that is enough? What is more, Maurice Cowling has included me in his book on Christian historians!

To Trevor-Roper, 18 February.

As I said, alas, I cannot make your Valedictory Lecture, <u>History and Imagination</u> (a necessary combination in which some of our colleagues are sadly lacking). I am guest speaker at the St John's annual history dinner in Cambridge. This was fixed up last February, and I cannot get out of it at this stage. It is all the sadder, as I would have been coming on for drinks at Jeremy's. Please forgive me, it really cannot be helped. I heard about your succession from one of the monks when I was in Ampleforth last week. I had been talking to the boys there, and a very nice lot they are too. I am not sure I entirely envy Michael moving from All Souls to Oriel. I am glad above all that you HAVE a successor.

I think Merton should have a Backhouse Room. They have a Beerbohm one. The Backhouse Room could be a chapel of retreat for meditation on Truth. I shall put the suggestion forward.

To Trevor-Roper, 31 August.

Of course I shall withdraw my resignation, your arguments are irresistible. Indeed both Regiuses (Regii) have written to me in the same friendly way, and oddly the Marxist Hilton. And Haskell has passed me on what appears to be a message from Blunt. So I will be writing today to poor Dover. AJP will not be pleased, but then I did not resign to please <u>him</u>, and was indeed most distressed by the whole business. It would never have happened had I been in Oxford among my friends; and it would not have happened in Shrewsbury, as I never read the papers when on holiday – well I did get the <u>Shrewsbury Chronicle</u> to find out about the Flower Show. Unfortunately, a former Classics master put cuttings from the Guardian through my door, and this is what impelled me into unwise action. I WAS jolly fed up with the rearguard action of the Minority. And, unfortunately, the Guardian journalist was a former pupil of mine. I shall own up to my foolishness and ask to be readmitted to the Fold. Perhaps the whole thing may be regarded as an August Folly, and dismissed as such. I was surprised to read in the Telegraph that I was on holiday in the Lake District. Shrewsbury near Windermere!

So I hope they will have me back. Apart from that, I had a nice holiday, even read a splendid book by Norman Stone on the Eastern Front, all the more appealing because he shares my own dislike of the Magyars. I also read a v. charming book by v. Rintelen. We were living in the Georgian town house of one of the History Masters*. Shrewsbury is a nice town, but the churches are dreadfully HIGH, indeed Popish; and the school chapel, which is LOW, was closed.

I shall avoid St Aldate's. What will happen to No. 8? And I shall send you my piece in the <u>Cambridge Review</u> about Jack Gallagher. I must also get myself invited to Cambridge each term.

Thank you for telling me not to be silly. I AM, but it can be remedied.

*Le Quesne, coming to the House this term as schoolmaster student.

This 'resignation' appears to be from the British Academy, the association of the supposedly eminent, which was set up in 1902. The year before, the eminent art historian Anthony Blunt had been exposed as a Russian spy along with Burgess, Maclean and Philby. Blunt had become a leading member of the British Establishment and this included Fellowship of the Academy. The President, Sir Kenneth Dover, came under pressure to expel Blunt but he refused. This caused some dissent and provoked some resignations including, it would appear, that of Cobb. The matter was later resolved when Blunt himself resigned.

To Trevor-Roper, 10 September.

Many thanks for your letter of the 3rd, which I got yesterday while on my way to the funeral of my old History master at Shrewsbury, a Christ Church man called Murray Senior and an absolutely marvellous teacher, though given to 'Georgism'. I travelled down to Sandwich with his clerical brother and family and a mass of punters with a most inventive Cockney vocabulary who were attending Folkestone Races. They must be awfully boring; but I don't know. I have never been to one.

I have just learned that those people in the Walton Street Morgue have made Richard Brain, my editor and fellow Salopian, redundant. It looks very much as if I too will be moving east, as the CUP is gradually building up a corner in French history. The OUP are foolish for they have now sacrificed the General Division, which was their one really good section. There is some dictator who is sacking all the former Ely House people, just like a purge in an E. European CP.

Of course I'd LOVE to preach in Peterhouse, I have the greatest admiration for the Dean, one of the few really sane people in the C of E, or indeed in any other church, at the present time. He is not the sort of person to go on and on about P Pinochet.

I feel sorry for Dover. Terrible damage has been done to the BA as an institution. I do not share AJP's sense of 'fun' and I have tried to avoid publicity, refusing to make any comments on TV when they got onto me in Shrewsbury. I hope that the BA is no longer news.

I am sure you will be getting the <u>Cambridge Review</u>, from now on, as Head of College. But I'll send you a copy in any case. I am sure you'll miss St Aldate's, just as we are all going to miss you & Xandra. But I do think Cambridge has SOME advantages; for one thing, it is in a MUCH nicer part of England, within easy reach of Suffolk and Norfolk, the Stour and the Orwell, of Hunts and of North Essex. When I retire – as I'll have to quite soon – I am hoping to persuade Margaret that we should move in that direction, though preferably off the Felixstowe container routes which have so much ruined charming little places like Stowmarket. Still, Felixstowe brings in <u>huge</u> amounts of money to Trinity. I think you'll find Peterhouse interesting; Maurice C is; King's is, of course, utterly RUINED. I wonder if old Mercurius can be enticed out of retirement from the Welsh Border. I think there might be work for him in the Fens.

Having, foolishly, agreed to give a lecture in Sussex on Belgium and the North of France under German Occupation 1914–18, I am reading up on the First World War, indeed with considerable fascination. A welcome change, for a bit, from the Directory. I have just been reviewing a book on the British Germanophils of the 30s, for the Sunday Times.

I hardly dare say best of luck for the move, it is a dreadful, surgical operation that one hopes to get over as soon as possible. I am pretty used to Pickfords et al. from childhood, as pretty well every time my father came back from the Sudan on leave, we would move; and every time he went back to Khartoum, we'd move again. All very obscure to my sister and myself, and related no doubt to low salaries. But when my mother died, I had to dispose of her place in Tunbridge Wells. I still dream about the disposition of each room. Perhaps, after all, we will NOT move away from Wolvercote, even to the skies of Old Crome, when I retire!

My typewriter is having ribbon trouble, so I am having to use Margaret's which has no accents.

Anyhow you are moving into the most lovely house and I do like Trumpington Street. And there are lovely walks around Cambridge, and Hunts is quite close. At one time, during the War, when I was with the Czechs, I actually got myself billeted on my sister, in Hemingford Abbotts, a beautiful place 12 miles north of Cambridge, on the Ouse. You must persuade the Lords to re-establish Hunts, which has been <u>devoured</u> by Cambridgeshire (so has the Isle of Ely, so that the

84

Cambridge War Memorial is now out of date, it is to the men of Cam. And the I of E).

Oh yes, the BEER is very good, Abbotts Special; and the landlord of the Baron of Beef, opposite St John's, is an ex-CRS paratrooper, and a great pal of Robbie's, it was Jack's pub. I recommend it most warmly. MUCH better than the KA. Robbie is to be found there at week-ends. Best wishes to Xandra.

In a letter dated 28 September, he wrote to Michael Hodges from Wolvercote telling him that he was to give the address at the Memorial Service to his old friend the former Dean of Balliol College, Frank McArthy Willis-Bund.

'No easy task. I seem to be very much engaged in funereal activities just now. I suppose it is the penalty of being 63'. He seemed mildly put out by the news that Edward Mortimer had grown a beard ('I suppose that goes with his fashionable pro-Arab sentiments') though less than by his infuriating new typewriter whose carriage kept slipping. 'I hate all machines especially those that don't work properly, though I suppose there is nothing worse than a car. I have never had one of the brutes.'

He was, however, keen on bicycles and, at one point, owned a state-of-the-art Moulton which folded up. On balance, though, his tendencies vis-à-vis machinery were predictably Luddite.

On 15 October he wrote a congratulatory letter to Hugh Trevor-Roper:

I am so <u>delighted</u> to read in today's Times that Merton has elected you to an Honorary Fellowship. <u>Please</u> use it to come there with Xandra. I have started <u>lunching</u> there this term & it is most agreeable. I am transferring from the OUP to the CUP (after a lunch with Patricia Williams) & am coming over to give a talk to the Trinity History Society towards the end of next month so I shall call on you both in Trumpington Street.

There are rumours suggesting that old <u>Mercurius</u> is coming out of his Leintwardine retirement & may be taking up his pen again about Recent Events in Port Meadow &ca. I've heard this from an impeccable source.

I am reading up on German history. Of course, I am only an <u>Has-been</u> (à la française, As-bin) in any case! There is a Tutors' meeting in the next room. I suppose you'll have to go to Governing Body meetings too. Perhaps in Peterhouse they don't go on for 5 hours.

Xandra and you are sadly missed here. How is the East wind down Trumpington Street? I saw ex-Master Dr Hill in Bodley yesterday. He dyes his hair.

To Trevor-Roper, 21 October.

I would love to call on Xandra and you some time on the 27th, and get all your news. At Matriculation on Saturday I noticed with satisfaction that most of the young men had short hair and there were very few beards, a sure barometer of decency. Favier's letter has made me feel quite Francophobe, rather as Xandra's father must have felt every time he had a meeting with Pétain. Still, I must not give way to such silly sentiments.

I shall miss the Faculty Board on Thursday; tomorrow Robbie and I are having lunch with the Foreign Minister of Mali, plus acolytes; and THAT will get me out of College Meeting!

To Trevor-Roper, 16 November.

Alas, the Pembroke lunch was so splendid, I never managed to make Lucy's Memorial Service, being enticed away by the Bursar, a Salopian. I had really meant to go to it, but was tempted away by the offer of Pleasure (claret).

On Thursday the 27th I am having lunch with Bill Davies, of the CUP, who I rather hope will be my future publisher. Are you driving to Oxford that afternoon? If not, I'll come back on the 6.15 bus, I expect I'll be getting a return anyway.

Alas, your successor is giving himself airs. He does not seem quite to understand that we are a sort of democrat body. I fear worse will follow.

Would it be in order for me to propose, for the n-th time, Piers Mackesy, who was originally Lucy's candidate? I shall of course oppose Thompson if he is dragged in again. I have been circulating your story about Xandra being asked if her father were an academic. It greatly pleased Maurice and Jeremy.

I am feeling rather ill as a result of yesterday's overindulgence.

PS Lovatt is silent and sombre but Maurice says he's <u>learned</u>. He did once speak to me at breakfast in your College: 'Please pass the salt.'

To Trevor-Roper, 1 December.

Thank you for making the journey from Cambridge to Oxford fly by in such an agreeable manner, much of it to the tune of Peters, a minor Backhouse in his way, though presumably not of Quaker background. I do feel, though, that he merits further study, perhaps even a short biography, as he is fairly outstanding both as an academic fraud and as a bigamist. I presume he is a very HIGH Anglican. He rang me up once and his very fruity voice certainly suggested a great deal of bowing & scraping and what Xandra calls 'tinkle tinkle'. Do you think he is related to the Bishop of Medway? No, I think not, for Medway was after ruined boys, or he ruined them afterwards, and Peters seems quite straightforward.

I did so enjoy seeing Xandra and you, I hope you have at last some heat and that Hinton has been dealt with. Also I was delighted by the thought of a tavern-frquenting Milton. How does Dr Hill <u>know</u>?

Less than a week later on 7 December he wrote once more to Trevor-Roper:

I am adding to my piece on Jack Gallagher, if I can persuade the <u>Cambridge Review</u> to take a supplement. Last week I dined in Ch.Ch. with a group of worthy but rather dull graduates. We had drinks in the MCR, which I was told had once been Keith Feiling's rooms, at the end of Hugh LJ's corridor. It was as if they were playing at being dons. I felt hopelessly frivolous. There was much weighty talk about research on the diocese of Périgueux in the XVIIIth C all very worthy no doubt. And they all seemed to think I had been very unfair on M. Favier (well, of course, I had not tried to be fair). A solemn lot. They will all become strict adherents of SCR Rules. Still, they got thoroughly bullied by a butler in Hall. From where I was sitting I had a distant (just as well) view of Kreielsheimer, & rows & rows of clerics, from behind whom a portrait of Henry Chadwick looked out, rather startled, but quite benign. The food was a curry of a disagreeable hue and uncertain content. Later I had to drink Madeira. I was driven home by a solemn Canadian in a Japanese car with a dashboard of flashing lights like a cockpit.

I shall make a point of going to Peters's next nuptial mass. Perhaps I could call out: there IS an impediment?

To Trevor-Roper, 13 December.

You are wise, I am not. I need your advice. I've just had a letter from Bernard Levin. John Gross has shown him a copy of M. Favier's original letter to me, & Bernard Levin is anxious to use it in his column in <u>The Times</u>. The letter <u>is</u> a masterpiece of its kind, & it has already done the rounds on both sides of the Channel. On the other hand, I might well need to return to the <u>Archives Nationales</u> one day. I have written to Levin asking for time to think about his suggestion, telling him that I'd like to consult my French friends. My instinct is to say NO, eventually, & to let the whole thing drop (I am not replying to the Favier letter in the <u>TLS</u>). As it is, I have given myself more time. I am not <u>mad</u> keen on Levin, though he is very funny when he writes about Robespierre Benn, & he is quite often right about things; but he does go on & on about poor old Pretoria & I don't think Pretoria is all that bad (an unfashionable view) & he wants to let out that horrible woman Myra Hindley (whom Lord Longford has canonised).

What do <u>you</u> suggest? I shall be back from Paris on the 21st.

Myra Hindley (1942-2002) was found guilty of the notorious Moors Murders with her friend Ian Brady. Despite her apparent reform it was made clear that she was to remain in prison all her life. This indeed happened but Lord Longford (1905-2001), former Labour cabinet minister, head of the famous literary family dynasty and prison reformer, was well known as her friend and champion.

On 27 December he wrote Trevor-Roper a final letter of the year:

I sent you a meandering letter this morning, with some Oxford news; but then realised I had not sent you my <u>A.N.</u> piece that had provoked the Favier letter. I have now found the (rather smudged) proofs of the offending piece. You will be able to judge whether it quite deserved the <u>Has-been</u> reply. It is, of course, somewhat exaggerated in places, though the general impression given is accurate enough.

Also I did not thank you for your Jack Gallagher gem. Of course, he waded ashore, with the only other survivor, after his Tank Landing Craft had struck a mine off the Greek Island, so he was used to taking to the water, though not walking <u>on</u> it (like Namier, according to Lady Julia). I am asking the <u>Cambridge Review</u> to let me do a Supplement as I have come by much more material all of it unsuited to a BA memorial piece.

My letter of this morning went – or will go, when life is resumed in this country, & in Scotland – to Melrose. So this I am sending to Peterhouse.

I have no news of George, last heard of in Singapore. Michael Pratt, 'Camden's Boy', is madly in love, may even be <u>married</u>.

PS I am told that your successor has taken over <u>most</u> of Oriel, well a quad or two. I believe he lives in great splendour, in a style appropriate to velvet cap & scarlet gown (the everyday garb of Rae, headmaster of Westminster, who also wears Geneva bands).

The same day, 27 December, he sent Trevor-Roper another missive.

On returning from Paris where I managed to do a lot of work in the APP (where I am still received) & where I tripped over a step and fell headlong in the <u>Collège de France</u>, to be picked up by a solicitous <u>appariteur</u>, who turned out to be the <u>introducteur</u> & acolyte of my <u>Leçons</u> of 1971 – how marvellously <u>formal</u> the French are! – I found your two excellent & heartening letters. <u>The conversation through Cambridgeshire, possibly a bit of Beds (?), Herts, & my native Essex was pure honey as far as I am concerned. To have brought consolation to the sick, to the prostrate!</u> What a compliment! & one I received originally from Lord Vaizey (not then so styled), who, in one of his numerous spells in a London hospital, had read my <u>2nd Identity</u> (one was pretty well lost). I am glad too to hear of ONE sane

King's man. One of the advantages of Cambridge is that it leads you to Liverpool Street, my favourite terminus, & the only one containing a memorial to a British general murdered by the IRA.

Harry Hinsley is a good <u>home-spun</u> man, who wears home-spun suits that actually seem to have a life of their own, the wool on the tweed is so abundant & flourishing. Sitting next to him recently at lunch in St John's I actually felt that his suit might take me over and <u>devour</u> me. Alas, since your departure, Robbie & I are now the only non-D-Litt professors, Jack McManners having gone for the scarlet so as to show up in his cathedral. Fieldhouse (in Gallagherese FIELDMOUSE) is the latest D. Litt. But as Maurice Cowling has officialised me as a 'Christian historian' (C of E, I hope) I have my eye on that longed-for DD (Durham would do).

Your second letter has decided me that I must write to Bernard Levin & tell him to make whatever use he can of the Favier Letter (not, I hope, a <u>Faux Favier</u>, no it is well done, too good even for Etonian inventiveness). Anyhow I do not see why Favier should be left with <u>le beau rôle</u> in the <u>TLS</u> with toadying American female professors writing in: <u>come back Cobb</u> (which was hardly the message Favier delivered to <u>me</u>!)

Oxford is closed & shuttered, though I did meet John Sparrow on the High between 2 affluent fur-coated ladies, one of them Mrs Ian Fleming, a Farringdon millionairess (they seem to congregate in that place), all 3 looking <u>most</u> festive (3pm). On the 12th I went to quite a grand lunch at the <u>Maison Fr.</u> attended by the V.C., who looks more & more like a monk (of the Port-Royal rather than the Tuck Connexion). The <u>M.F.</u> has a <u>superb</u> chef, a vegetarian, who <u>hates</u> his job, never eats the food he cooks, lives off nut omelettes & rhubarb steaks & who is returning to France as a <u>commis</u> (a typewriter-basher). What a sad story! But chefs are quite abundant in France. Alas, Bouillier is going too & rumour has it that he is to be replaced by a deeply pious Catholic pederast called Bruno Something. Perhaps we will all be served by scantily-robed Senegalese boys. And then <u>la Fin des Ambassades</u>, but the <u>beginning</u>. I think the new style might bring old <u>Mercurius</u> out of Powys or Clwyd.

I <u>should</u> be marking exam papers for Max Beloff's Buckingham. But it is still <u>almost</u> Christmas.

Warmest greetings to Xandra. I am feeling frivolous, perhaps it is just what I am.

This is the 'meandering' letter that Cobb posted earlier on the 27 December and which was posted to Trevor-Roper's home in Scotland rather than Peterhouse. It would have been written and sent before the one printed earlier but received later. Hence the order of publication.

1981

To Trevor-Roper, 15 January.

I am enormously gratified for I have now received an invitation from your Dean, a very sensible & good man whom I admire, to preach in your chapel on 22nd November. What shall I wear? Alas, no hope of a DD even from Ian Paisley or Billy Graham. No hope of Geneva bands. Anyhow, it will be a sermon that Jane Austen would not have taken amiss, but it will have to have Fenland connotations. Will Cowling be there to test my Christianity? Will Wormald be there to denounce my Anglicanism? Will Lovatt be there to stare angrily? I am already looking forward to the occasion. Is Cambridge in the diocese of Ely? I hope it is, as Ely could be a useful cue.

The Death colloquium was a bizarre occasion, illuminated by your address. The room in which we were somehow squeezed looked like a giant coffin. Professor Niklaus, of the enormous strangler's hands, seemed to have been one of the better impersonations of the late Peter Sellers. My own talk was frivolous & irreverent. But I am glad you met Hampson. Jeremy & I sped back to Oxford, our journey illuminated just outside Oxford by a car burning like a torch (no one inside, fortunately).

Next week I hear Owen Chadwick lecture on Pius XII, & attend a dinner given for him by your successor. Perhaps they will all be in velvet caps.

I have just finished some writing which I hope you'll be reading before too long. I fear it is v. impious.

The friend of the tavern-crawling Milton is now in Canberra, very hot I reckon, under his brocaded D. Litt. gown.

Warmest regards to Xandra. I am writing to Levin to go ahead.

PS I see that you are on the board of the Cambridge Review. I am very anxious to do a supplement on my Gallagher piece, but fear that the Master of Emmanuel – a grim, gloomy College presumably founded by Barebones – will be against after reading my November piece. Some of Jack's pupils have passed me on some rather splendid quotes.

I hope you managed to find Tour de France. Duckworths are quite agreeable publishers, but they never give their authors any books.

All the gossip now here is about the successor to the Chair of War, Margaret Gowing is the Grand Electress (among others). I am hoping to win her over to a John Keegan candidature. Keegan is very good on wounds that should interest her. 'Copper' Le May (of Le May's Pilsen Lager, Lourenço Marques) is also an Elector. So is Raymond Carr.

To Trevor-Roper, 27 January.

I shall get Geneva bands from somewhere & I shall have Ely very much in mind.

I went to the first Ford Lecture. It was, in a way, about English history, as the principal hero of the discourse was the British Minister to the Holy See – Osborne (?) or a name like that – who had a monocle & a very large dog who shared the Legation with him, & who, on retirement, went to live in Leeds Castle, in Kent; the lecture was most entertaining, none the less so from three quartos of the typescript having cascaded from the lectern to the floor half-way through. The lecturer was dressed very soberly, like a Bishop in mufti. Pius XII will be making his entrée this week. Most diplomats accredited to the Vatican seem to have spent most of their time somewhere else – in Monte Carlo &ca, but there was a German aristo who seems to have been most assiduous.

Your successor, weighed down by an immense & heavily embroidered black gown with various fittings such as Brandenburgs & tassels, but all in black, broke with tradition by introducing the Ford Lecturer in his quadruple character (Regius, Master, ex-VC, Ford Lecturer) & this took a little time.

In the evening there were drinks in an extraordinary room off a staircase of washable bricks, in a distant part of Oriel. I was told it had been Powicke's. Later we had dinner in the room you had decorated. All ended sharp at 9.45 (there were bottles of whisky & brandy laid out on a table: but we were rushed away). As Robbie & I left (we had 2 pints in the KA) we heard your successor ask Henry Mayr-Harting: 'tell me, who <u>pays</u> for all this?' During dessert I was placed next to the son of a Petty Officer in the Navy, & now the son is at All Souls. There was a big, very <u>red</u> man from Oriel – also there was the Squire of Cassington, looking very rural. And young Beddard was there. But, alas, no Jeremy. The Squire retires a year before myself. He was complaining about sand-pits.

It looks as if we have won the first round against the OUP, as the Planning Department has not approved their plan to ruin Wolvercote. I have written to John Patten & hope to enlist the only Salopian in the present Government (Heseltine) if the scheme comes up again.

Of course, Cambridge is <u>bound</u> to have trouble as it possesses an utterly ruined college, King's, a nest of vipers and Marxists. I am <u>delighted</u> to hear Balliol Ricks described in a Sunday as reactionary. Soon I will be having an <u>utterly</u> reactionary piece in <u>The Spectator</u>. Here all is quiet, even dormant.

I am coming to a wedding at St Catherine's (Christopher Bayly, a pupil of Jack's) on 22nd March.

Your old house appears to be <u>in ruins</u>, or not far off. Ch.Ch. do not seem to know what to do with it. I <u>believe</u> the Catholics opposite have designs on it. But you must not tell Xandra this. She would be too upset. It may be a rumour put out by the Benedictines, who don't like the Campion Hall people.

I am to go to Brandeis at the end of March. Perhaps they'll make me an honorary Rabbi. Do Rabbis wear robes, I wonder?

I saw a notice in a window of a house – alas the property of Merton – in Holywell today announcing a Christian–Marxist dialogue. I shall preach against it. But not at Peterhouse.

I wonder if George went to Sir Oswald's funeral.

The Direct Descendant of the Lord Chancellor of Ireland (of Askerswell Tablets fame) was present at the Ford Lecture, looking learned & very serious.

I have an offprint from a Cambridge man called Blanning, it is mostly about rather nasty Marxist historians. Blanning seems a sound fellow.

The Kingsley Club recently had a 12 course dinner, with 25 different wines, in our XVIIIth century Hall. It went on till 1 am. I believe young Soames was in evidence. Very little was broken, but half a grouse got stuck to the ceiling. Of course, Worcester IS a bit old-fashioned, though your Magdalene is even _more_ so.

I must stop, as it's time for my local pub.

I hope Xandra is well, & that Maurice Cowling is paler.

Oh yes! The War Chair Election. Cyrano de Bergerac (la Gowing), the Grand Electress, is a key figure in the proceedings.

Please write soon.

PS I see someone has proposed Mao's widow as Chancellor of London University.

The Kingsley Club is a Worcester College dining society named after the dissolute brother of the novelist Charles Kingsley. He was an undergraduate of the college but did little or no work, much preferring the pleasures of the flesh. That year's Ford Lecturer was Owen Chadwick and his subject relations between Britain and the Vatican in the Second World War.

To Trevor-Roper, 23 February.

Many thanks for your letter of the 8th which I should have answered much sooner, but I have been assailed with chores, and have only in the last few days been able to get back to work on a book interrupted since June last, and to start digesting the immense amount of new material I acquired in two visits to Paris in July and December, in the police records and _not_ chez Favier. I can gradually see the book taking shape. I have no 'Party line' and have never had a general idea in my life, but I find documents generally tell me their own story.

Thank you too for the information about D'Arcy Osborne, the hero – and he was indeed just that – of Owen Chadwick's delightful lectures (the audience has actually been _increasing_ throughout the term, surely the greatest compliment to be made); and the audience is a pretty odd mixture: mediaevalists like Jeremy and Sandy Murray (do you know him?), Jesuits and Benedictines, Catholic priests, ex-Ambassadors, the President of St John's, looking more and more like Thomas à Becket at the high altar, fairly ancient ladies in buns, some very pretty girls in smart hats, Menna, sitting well away from her husband – the New Era is about to open at the Queen's – Beryl Smallie sitting well away from Menna, various tieless PPE-looking characters, some Anglican divines, a bevy of College chaplains, etc. etc.) The lectures are to be published by the C.U.P. I can see how Osborne, as a descendant of Danby – 'The Botanic Gardens'? – could be interpreted as English history. I much enjoyed the description of the Hired Agent, Mgr Pucci, passing information to Charles-Roux and d'Ormesson, kneeling down. A position much favoured by XVIIIc seducers and clandestine lovers. Of course, yes, I know Leeds Castle from my Tunbridge Wells childhood. I believe now it is used by the Foreign Office.

Last week I dined in Ch.Ch. as a guest of Hugh's. A most agreeable evening, thanks to the presence of Dmitri Obolensky, who was able to inform me about a Magdalen contemporary of mine, Galitzin. There were some ladies present, research fellows. I think Hugh did not approve of them, and made that plain, even AUDIBLE. At High Table I was placed next to a Cambridge theologian, a Tonbridgian like Owen, now a Professor of Theology. Hugh alarms me; he is talking of suing The Standard for some nasty piece about him in a gossip column. I am sure he would be MOST unwise to go to court, it might cost him thousands, he might lose the case. Perhaps he will listen to words of moderation if they come from you. He quotes your case against Lord Chalfont, I tried to point out that, in that, you were on unassailable ground. I fear Hugh is a hot headed and impulsive man. That is what is so nice about him. I do hope he sits it out and avoids publicity. Anyhow, I much enjoyed my evening, and his new room is very magnificent.

Norman Stone tells me he too is getting married (remarried, he was at one time married to a beautiful Haitian creole, of a family mainly exterminated by Papa Doc) on 21st March. There must be some collective folly inducing EVERY Cambridge historian to enter wedlock on the same day.

Eagleton has made a tiny bid to be a McCabe, but he has gone unheard, apart from a small bleat in the Oxford Times.

Of course this College approves of Murdoch, he is, along with Quaker Sainsbury, one of our most generous benefactors. He was at one time a Wuggins man.

Merton have asked me to a grand lunch on 7 March organised to keep the Third Year historians happy. I had lunch there on Friday and was impressed by the urbanity and the excellence of the food.

War has been FROZEN; so the elections are off for the time being – a pity, as my friend John Keegan seems to have been doing quite well. Perhaps my chair will be FROZEN too? I hope not, it is a nice chair, though I would not be too happy if it were to become the Oxford Chair of Habsburg Finance.

There does not seem to be any news. I went to Richard Brain's farewell party, the Warden was there, looking remarkably spry. This was in a bizarre room in Pembroke.

We have lost Mr Carter, the SCR steward, who has been with Worcester since 1924, save for War service in the R.A. He was a remarkably RUDE man, and his rudeness was well aimed and always delivered from a standing position to the back of one's neck. Actually he at once approved of me, for, at lunch, I asked for <u>wine</u>; so that I could never put a foot wrong after that. He was 72 but insisted on carrying on with lunches. We have rather a good portrait of him, by an Eton master.

I have to go to America at the end of March. I am dreading it, as I have not been in an aeroplane for years and years. Still, they are paying me well. I am going to Brandeis, to talk about Vichy, and to Harvard, to talk about Thermidor.

Your presence in Oxford has been reported. I very much hope to see you when I come to Cambridge (for one of the multiple weddings) on 21st March. Some time I must introduce you to the <u>Baron of Beef</u>. It was Jack Gallagher's headquarters, and Robbie goes there at weekends. Also a lot of people from Newmarket interested in horseflesh.

I saw James in a hurry outside the Sheldonian, carrying some shopping bags. He was rushing off somewhere.

The Left seems to have run out of graffiti.

Best wishes to Xandra.

Rupert Murdoch, the press baron, was an undergraduate at Worcester College, Oxford. So was Tim, Lord Sainsbury. Both were very rich and gave some of their money to their old college. James was Trevor-Roper's stepson, James Howard-Johnston, a Byzantine specialist from Corpus Christi College, married to the novelist Angela Huth.

To Trevor-Roper, 9 March.

I read your review of the IMMENSE Choiseul and the mysterious castle to which Rohan B refers is that of Ray-sur-Saône, near Vesoul. It belongs to the Marmier family, descendants of Kings of Antioch, the present Marmier is the Comtesse de Salverte, her husband is an amateur historian who will not allow anyone to see the papers relating to Choiseul. Rohan has been to the castle, and, owing to his stutter, was so long at the main gate that the butler actually let him in. He got a cup of weak tea, saw the refectory, and that was all. I have actually had a drink (not tea) with Mme Salverte, after Sunday mass in Ray. But then I knew someone in the village, and she was not aware I was a historian. Antoine, the Louis XV specialist from the A.N., once spent a fortnight in Ray, at the local inn, to which the comtesse goes every evening in order to play bar billiards with her <u>manants</u>. Antoine even learnt bar billiards, played with the comtesse every night, buying her rounds of drinks – she is not expensive, she is quite happy with <u>le gros rouge</u>; but it was all to no avail. He never got beyond the drawbridge. The château is <u>vachement medieval</u>, on a hill above a bend in the Saône. One of the de Salverte boys went to Cambridge, after Downside. Perhaps a historian from your present university might manage to earn his entrée, he could certainly get a drink, but not a sight of the papers. I think the lesson of Choiseul's career is that it is better to belong to a small court, like that of Nancy and Luneville, than to a big one. It was rather like originating from the Duchy of Bouillon.

On the 22nd I am depositing an <u>enormous</u> ms in your College Lodge. It is not a bomb but an illiterate work by an American which the CUP will not publish. It has to go back to Bill Davies.

The Inaugural was beautifully rehearsed and very Gallic. I am bound to encounter Barraclough at Brandeis. I do believe he was in Merton in some capacity when I was an undergraduate. For a man so large, he is very mobile.

PS Ever since Backhouse, Merton has had a Chinese Connection (via Sun Yat-sen). I met a young Chinaman historian, Third year, called Bobo Lo, when I had lunch with the undergraduates on Saturday.

In the spring of 1981 he was invited by Bernard Wasserstein, who had a chair in history at Brandeis University, to come and give lectures. This invitation was augmented by Simon Schama, who was at the time a professor at Harvard. This meant that for the first time in almost a decade he had to get on an aeroplane, something he loathed. Needs, however, must and there was no suitable ship available even though he much preferred travelling by sea. Whenever he went to France he liked to take the ferry, claiming that much the best was the one that ran between Newhaven and Dieppe.

The trip to the States seems to have been a success and at the beginning of April he wrote to thank Wasserstein for his part in it.

I got into Heathrow after a perfectly comfortable flight, part of it spent watching a film of quite unusual inaneness. England was looking very green, but now it is quite Arctic. I find myself thinking with affection of Brandeis, even of Steinbergers, of Waltham, of the Silver Bullet, and the young man in the cowboy hat who drives the 1.35 from Roberts to Boston . . . Here Benn is benning & everything is boring & predictable.

To Trevor-Roper, 9 April.

I greatly enjoyed Brandeis, despite all the rather unbeautiful names on the buildings such as Goldfarb, etc. But Barraclough remained invisible. I really wonder whether he actually <u>exists</u>, as few people there claim to have seen him or even <u>heard</u> him on the phone; on the other hand, he is listed as having an address in Boston. Harvard I did not greatly like, at least the place, Cambridge; every square was crowded with earnest students SITTING DOWN in the dust and protesting about this or that, mostly somewhere called El Salvador, and there were horrible <u>boutiques</u> full of Mexicans, and more students on the banks of the Charles River playing (atrociously) guitars, and listened to by barefoot girls. The Faculty Club was rather more agreeable, I had lunch beneath a portrait of Frederick, Prince of Wales (Monster); and there was a lady at the next table wearing an enormous red hat that would have done quite well at Ascot. American students are so terribly <u>literal</u>, they made me feel utterly flippant; perhaps I am.

I went to a Balliol Gaudy on Saturday for 1900–1930. The Chancellor was there. I sat next to a Mr Smith, who came up in 1917, and who is the son of A.L. Smith. In fact we sat right opposite his father's portrait, which comes before that of Pink Lindsay. He said it was a very bad portrait, that his father would never have stood with his hands in his pockets, or worn a cardigan that did not match his coat. I think he was the Master's 9th or 10th child. Later I had a talk with the Chancellor, who seemed to be under the impression that I was Quentin Skinner and who talked to me most learnedly about Machiavelli; I did my best, that is not very well. He told me that before he gave away the Wolfson prizes in 1979, he had to read a boring little book about the Paris sewers and corpses, not at all 'the broad sweep of history'. I agreed meekly, not revealing that I was the historian of sewers and corpses. I think this was diplomatic. I left him, well after midnight, in full flow on the subject of Biafra. Tony Kenny told me later that he took him off to the Lodgings at about 2.30 am. At dinner, he gave a magnificent and tearful speech. All in all, a very good occasion. What I noticed was how <u>good-looking</u> were many of those old men. Class, I suppose. Before lunch I watched the boat race with Stacy Colman, a former classics master at Shrewsbury who was at one time (in the 30s) a Mods Tutor at Queen's. He is a rowing enthusiast; in fact the school Boat Club have named a boat after him. He used to row in the Balliol eight with Bill Coolidge, the homosexual millionaire and Balliol benefactor.

I was very pleased to see that horrible man Irving properly clobbered in the <u>TLS</u>.

I shall be coming over to the Fens some time this month to unload on the CUP an immense <u>pavé</u> which they are not publishing, it is no good. About 1500 pages in typescript, it is called inappropriately <u>The French Revolution in Miniature</u>; and as the man is incapable of a joke, this is not a joke. It is in fact a study of a single Paris section. I shall drag it back to the Fens on the bus.

On the 30th I am to attend a military wedding in the Guards' Chapel, followed by a reception at St James's Palace – one of my St Benet's Amplefordians, now in the King's Hussars. I shall enjoy the occasion.

No other news from here. Felix Markham was at the Gaudy, full of complaints about being neglected, no one coming to see him, etc., I was not oversympathetic.

Oh, yes, I hope E.P. Thompson was kept out. You must tell me about the BA meeting. Thompson is regarded in the US as the living Buddha.

Next month I shall send you Ronald Blythe's collection called Places. It contains a piece about my Cobb grandparents in Colchester. I hope you find it entertaining. Actually I think it is coming out in the Guardian as well. Essex is giving me an honorary degree; if they give me a hood to go with it, I'll wear it in your chapel in November.

Best wishes to Xandra.

Hubert John Forster Smith, son of A.L., was the second son and certainly not the 9th or 10th as Cobb suggests. He was a hockey blue and for many years Land Agent to Lord Astor and later the National Trust. Stacy Colman (1906–93) had a long association with Shrewsbury but was also briefly headmaster of the Church of England Grammar School in Melbourne. Bill Coolidge (1901–93), the Balliol benefactor who rowed in the same boat, became an Honorary Fellow of the College. In 1955 he established the Pathfinder Trust as a result of which eight Balliol men a year were able to spend the summer vacation in the United States. Coolidge derived his considerable fortune from inherited shares in a famous soft drink company and could not unreasonably claim to be an authentic Boston Brahmin, on nodding terms with the Cabots, the Lodges and possibly even God.

To Trevor-Roper, 21 April.

I am greatly relieved that the Blessed Edward See the Wounds has been kept out of the BA. But what a peculiar argument by Keith Thomas! I doubt whether many people read those memorial pieces in the red volumes.

It is very good of you to have supported me with the Beefsteak. I had a phone message some time back from that ex-Jesuit, Peter Levi, asking if I were interested. It was not exactly the patronage I would have desired, but I said: thank you indeed, please go ahead. I was also told that I was being sponsored by Noel Blakiston, whom I like very much, and John Jolliffe, a friend of Maurice Keen's. I am so seldom in London it seems rather silly; but there are so very many nice people in that prestigious club that I found I was tempted. But there is no reason really why they should have me, though I hope they do.

I could not make Cambridge before going to Brandeis, as I had a lecture on Belgium (or rather, on Leopold III) to finish before I went there. So I think I'll bring the unpublishable <u>pavé</u> over on 6 May and leave it, like an enormous bomb, in Peterhouse porter's lodge. Will Xandra and you be in Cambridge that day? I'll ask Bill Davies if that date suits him.

I am glad you trounced the trendy Bishops. I must say I like the sound of the Archbishop of York. Would that HE had gone to Canterbury. The only bishop I ever met, Mortimer, the father of my pupil, I liked. But he was not at all trendy, wore lilac gloves to induct young clergymen, and kept a <u>prodigious</u> drinks' tray. He did all his sermons on whisky (Haig as I recall).

Alas, I am not invited to the Chichele. I think your host must be Simon Hornblower. Or could it be John Sparrow? I hardly know anyone in that place, apart from John Sparrow, and 2 former Balliol pupils, the one dull and bureaucratic, the other nice but dotty. I was sent for by Mr Duck when Derek Parfit was taking Schools, he was having a fit, lay on the floor groaning and making dreadful vomiting noises, after tipping over his table, the ink went all over a Somerville pupil of mine, also a P (Miss Pinder) and there was much distress in the M to Z room, presided over by John Cooper, who looked more than startled. I took Parfit by the arm and walked him round and round the quad outside. His parents, both doctors, had given him two lots of drugs that had contrary effects. Still, he did get a First, and then became a Moral Philosopher. From the age of 8, he was the great rival of Michael Prestwich. He once asked Menna, when 9, what was the most important battle in modern history. Apparently it was somewhere called Mohac or Mohacs. Menna failed.

Fame. Fame! I have been mentioned (in a footnote), in an inaugural lecture by my opposite number in your University, Beales. He has quoted from my Gallagher piece. Poor Jack! His lecture reminds me that I have never given an inaugural. Too late now. But I could always make up for it with a valedictory.

I spent part of the holiday looking for Blair Worden. SEH was closed. He lives next to LMH, in a house in which Anne Whiteman used to have her room. Very odd. I failed to find him. Apart from that, the holiday has been bearable, thanks to the Arctic weather, there have not been the usual holiday crowds of semi-naked hairy people heading for Port Meadow. A cold spell for a Bank Holiday is a great boon.

I have just read, for review in <u>The Spectator</u>, a book about the French elections. What appalling people Giscard, Chirac, Mitterrand and Marchais are! Apparently Giscard has monarchical pretentions and goes to meetings with a leather blotting pad carrying a fleur de lys and an imperial eagle. He is supposed to be descended from Louis XV, his wife actually <u>is</u>. Maybe he is related to Rohan Butler's tedious hero. Mitterrand too has monarchical airs. I expect Ministers will soon have to walk backwards when in the Presidential Presence. I am told the most formal of all monarchs is Baudouin. The father of a pupil told me he was taken into the presence of le Roi des Belges by a man in <u>l'habit à la française</u> carrying a chandelier of lighted and guttering candles, although it was midday. Anyhow, by comparison, I find even Mollet bearable.

What will old Max be Lord of? Is he a Liberal? I very much fear the Owenites will eat into the Conservative vote and so let in the awful Foot.

There are too many books to review. I should be writing. Perhaps I shall be able to next month, which is that of Owen Chadwick's and my birthday.

PS Of course the Chancellor MUST stay on.

To Trevor-Roper, 1 May.

I am <u>delighted</u>. I have been asked to lecture once a week by the History Board of your University in place of Blanning, so I've chosen next term. I've left the day for them to choose. I shall try & get a bed in a College for whatever night I stay weekly. It is a wonderful excuse to go East regularly, & I'll improve my knowledge of Hitchin, Luton, Letchworth & other interesting places on the route of the bus. I won't be coming over on the 6th, as I had forgotten that I lecture here on Wednesdays, but I'll certainly be over later in the month. I'll let you know.

Yesterday I went to a <u>superb</u> wedding in the Guards' Chapel, & an equally superb reception at St James's Palace (where I encountered yet another portrait of Frederick, Prince of Wales). It was attended by the <u>fine fleur</u> of Ampleforth & Downside.

They have elected me to the <u>Beefsteak</u>. Very many thanks for your support. I'll go there for lunch every now & then, when I am seeing publishers & that sort of thing.

I am extremely glad about Cambridge. I wonder where I'll have to give my lectures? Cambridge will get quite sick of me what with pulpit appearances & lecturing ones. Do you think I should lecture in a <u>gown</u>? I suppose not, as I am not a member of the University.

To Trevor-Roper, 8 May.

I travelled up to London yesterday with your host for the Chichele Dinner on the 13th. He sees you possibly in the role of the Prophet Daniel and fears that you may be assaulted by the author of <u>Choiseul</u>. Indeed <u>Choiseul</u> itself, weighing several stone, could make a lethal weapon. But I expect the evening will be peaceful. I had a delightful journey, as I find Isaiah a marvellous conversationalist. Perhaps you will be lunching in Merton that day? I hope you will, as I always go there after my Wednesday lecture.

My Cambridge lectures next term will be at 10 on Wednesdays, so I will be staying Tuesday nights in the Fen Capital.

Last week I was visiting a blind friend off the Iffley Road and was confronted by a yellow and red LABOUR poster of James's. I had no idea he was of that persuasion. Wolvercote at least has stayed Conservative.

At the <u>Spectator</u> lunch yesterday I met Maurice Cowling's friend George Gale.

Hoping to see you on the 13th.

On 4 June he wrote to Martyn Lyons expressing a wish to visit Australia where Lyons was now installed as a professor. Sadly the visit never materialised and he never went to Australia. Sandwiched between references to his Honorary Fellowship at his old college, Merton (which seems to have mainly involved unexpectedly good meals), and the detestable heat, he struck an unaccustomed note of paternal domesticity. 'We have a new Cobb, William, born on 4th April. He is an adorable little thing, and I am much enjoying being a father again at 63. De Lesseps started a new family, which eventually reached 9, when he was 70.'

Cobb was presumably referring to Ferdinand De Lesseps (1805–94), the man responsible for the Suez Canal. On 6 June he wrote to Trevor-Roper.

I heard an amazing Hexterian paper from someone called Arno Mayer at the German History Seminar. Your successor was there. We were both easily convinced that Mayer was/is a fraud. He is at Princeton.

We have been invited by Robert Blake to have dinner with Lord & Lady Soames the day before Encaenia. Asa has been sighted in Oxford several times this term. His wife I sighted yesterday wearing a white trouser suit, as if she were about to play cricket. Perhaps she was? The Worcester ladies have won something in a boat. Mercifully all the dreadful plays going on in College gardens have been more or less washed out.

To Trevor-Roper, 30 June.

It was extremely pleasant to have had tea with Xandra and you the other day and to have seen how well you are both under the tonic effect of a permanent East Wind.

I have read – with delight – your lecture on Carlyle. What an odious, boorish, craggy, brutish man! Though I must say I do find parts of his <u>French Revolution</u> quite inspired, especially the evocation of the brutishness of the Crowd (ex-Mob). Whatever was the matter with him? How could ANYONE turn against the XVIIIth century, when, clearly, it was so infinitely superior to the following one? He sounds an archetypal Fascist. All this nonsense about Life Forces, <u>L'Élan Vital</u> as it would be with that quack Alexis Carrel.

I am also reading – for review in the <u>Sunday Times</u> – a collection of pieces by Laurence Stone. At least he seems less keen on Models than he used to be. But he <u>does</u> pontificate, and he pontificates by numbers (generally, one to four, every now and then, one to six). At least I find myself in excellent company, yours actually! It is nice to be told that we both write well and that our works are entertaining to read! I shall have to write my piece soon.

At the Blakes' supper, I was placed next to Mary Soames. She was absolutely charming. We found we had a shared interest in Dieppe, a shared hatred for Leopold III, and a sort of regard for that rogue, the Comte des Flandres. The Regent from 44–50. She told me she used to play ping-pong with him in the Royal Palace. I think she was quite surprised to have met someone who had ever heard of him. I believe he is now nearly bankrupt and has had to ask his nephew to bail him out from the Civil List. All in all, we had an absolutely splendid evening.

I get a degree from Essex next week. If they give me the hood, I shall wear it when preaching. But, alas, it is not a DD.

I have got to give a lecture at some silly festival called the Romantics. I don't LIKE the Romantics!

PS At the Balliol Gaudy on Saturday I sat next to Michael Pratt. He arrived late, puffing and blowing. He is still unmarried, and as purple as ever. He has written a history of Sicily.

To Trevor-Roper, 2 September.

Since I got back from Shrewsbury we have had Jeremy to supper, and so have had more news of Oriel. Jeremy referred to some candidate with a name like ZEMAN, a mathematician, I think, from Warwick. There is a very trying historian of that name, a Czech I think, but it cannot be the same. If they had any sense, they should get Maurice Keen, even though he <u>is</u> from Winchester. But I don't suppose they'll have any sense. Jeremy seemed pretty gloomy; but I expect he'll be seeing you in Scotland this month and will be reporting on the present state of play. Meanwhile, I am much looking forward to seeing you on 2 October, first in Merton, then in that gloomy place that, for one evening at least, will be illuminated.

I have just read an old novel by a Balliol Snell Exhibitioner, <u>The</u>

House with the Green Shutters, published in 1900, and that I picked up in a second-hand bookshop in Shrewsbury. It is <u>not</u> a flattering account of life in a small Scottish market town. In fact it reminded me above all of Aberystwyth. I wonder if Xandra knows the book? It is really very powerful and has some interesting descriptions of the University of Edinburgh.

I am plunged more and more in the history of Vichy: a sordid and distressing period, in which the French come out rather badly . . .

I was sad to hear of the death of James Griffiths, an affable if rather lonely President of Magdalen who always used to make Jack Gallagher and myself most welcome.

In 1984 I have to retire. Where to? I shall have to go prospecting in North Essex and Suffolk.

Warmest greetings to Xandra. It will be nice to see you both in a month's time.

PS Don't you think I should preach about the World Council of Churches?

To Trevor-Roper, 8 October.

Last Friday was a delightful occasion. There were so many old friends at the party in the Mure Room, overlooked by a leering and sardonic-looking Mure (his bust used to overlook High Table in the Hall, Robin Harrison had it expelled to the Rose Lane buildings); and the dinner was splendid, especially the Chancellor's speech (of which in fact I cannot remember a single word, all I recall is that it was tremendously witty and apt).

I make my academic debut in Cambridge on Wednesday. I have been told NOT to wear a gown, apparently lecturers don't; but I have decided that I WILL wear a gown, as I always do here. I don't know what sort of condition I'll be in as my <u>social</u> debut in Cambridge begins the night before in a Cambridge barracks, with a regimental dinner with the Royal Greenjackets, in which one of my nicest Balliol pupils, Charles Vyvyan, is a Major. (His father, Michael Vyvyan, known as 'Electric Whiskers', is a Life Fellow of Trinity and has a Czech mistress – her enormously enlarged photograph fills a whole wall of his room in Nevile's Court.) Curiously, Michael Vyvyan is the literary executor of that truly awful man, R.H. Tawney. Anyhow I am much looking forward to this dinner. I have only attended such functions as a guest of John Keegan at Camberley. I have applied to St John's for luncheon rights every Wednesday. It used to be my sister college when I was in Balliol. I am not very tempted by my present sister college, St Catherine's, though I have a nice pupil there, Chris Bayly.

I hope you are amused by my wicked piece on Thermidor in your festschrift. Encounter are publishing it in their December number, but they want to cut out the beginning and remove all those calendar girls. I have objected to this and have said they must do the whole thing or nothing at all. There is a silly misprint: 'impossibilities' for 'impossibilists', on p. 281. I think the piece might have some topical interest and I very much hope that, though rather frivolous, it is worthy of the collection.

I returned to Merton on Saturday, for a Gaudy. I was placed among my fellow-matriculands of 1935. These consisted entirely of a parterre of very well-fed looking country parsons, prospering in Merton livings. They all had very pale, watery blue eyes that gave a bizarre impression of holiness and dottiness. But I must not make anti-clerical remarks, given my two preaching engagements next month (the other is at Univ, the Sunday before Peterhouse). I don't expect it will be graced by the presence of Lord Goodman (an Old Roman God in John Sparrow's anagram). The only contemporary I knew was Arthur Peterson, and he does not speak to me, as I could not get on with his boring brother, Alec, one of the most ragged masters at Shrewsbury, who having failed completely as a teacher, characteristically went into education, ending up as director of that place in Norham Road. Arthur was in charge of fire engines under Herbert Morrison. He was headboy when he and I managed to persuade the headmaster to get rid of the Revd Hoskyns-Abrahall, for suspected popery (he had a prie-dieu covered in mauve silk in his study). He is now Bishop of Lancaster. Shrewsbury, catering for Irish Protestants and Liverpool Unitarians, has always been a Low Church school.

I don't seem to have any news of interest. I do not know how the Agony of Oriel is proceeding. I see the Seton-Watson brothers have written a book about their father.

How nice it would have been to have met Backhouse at a Merton Gaudy.

I seem to be more concerned than ever with Vichy. I have reviewed two books about the period for the <u>Sunday Times</u>, a third for the <u>Spectator</u>. Meanwhile I am being denounced by the Welsh Nationalists. This gives me great pleasure.

Warmest greetings to Xandra, and hoping to see you both before too long in <u>your</u> University.

Geoffrey Mure (1893–1979) was a Fellow at Merton College, Oxford, and was Warden of the college from 1947 to 1963. Robin Harrison (1900–c.1970) was his immediate successor (1963 to 1969) as Warden. He was an ancient historian but had spent the war working for Lord Woolton at the Ministry of Food. Alec Peterson ran the Education Institute at Oxford. He was an early advocate of the International Baccalaureat.

To Trevor-Roper, 20 October.

I am glad you enjoyed my naughty, anti-revolutionary piece in your festschrift. I certainly find myself in very good company. Tomorrow I make my second appearance towards the top of the House of Glass, an extraordinary building, a sort of glass House of Cards, the cards of which look as if, having been dealt out, they might slip off at any minute. Caius seems quite a friendly place, though I have already been captured for an evening by Christopher Brooke. I see, in the <u>TLS</u>, that you have been denounced by some dreary African as a 'racist', though in what context I do not know.

I will give you a ring one of these Wednesday mornings.

PS Warmest regards to Xandra.

To Trevor-Roper, 9 November.

Who <u>is</u> John Vincent? I have an idea that he was once a Fellow of your College, and that he was involved in some way in the Garden House fracas of some years ago. I am puzzled by his review of your <u>festschrift</u>. What DO I have in common with Lord George-Brown? I did not think I had ANYTHING in common with Lord George-Brown. I don't drink NEARLY as much as he. And I was not aware of imitating old Brogan. It all seems one of those closed Peterhouse jokes. Perhaps you will be able to throw some light on these dark places when I come and preach on the 22nd. I am working at this moment on my two sermons, drawing inspiration from the book I have just been reviewing, a seasonal theme, by the Regius Professor of Ecclesiastical History in this University. I shall come with a message, if not of joy, at least not of gloom.

Dinner tomorrow evening with Christopher Brooke(!)

Last night I had drinks with a South African who was a schoolboy at Charterhouse. He has the warmest recollection of you, because, so he tells me, you came to give a lecture at the school on the subject of the Founder, whom you described as an utter scoundrel, Oppressor of the Poor, a crook, a manipulator, a toady, a Whited Sepulchre. As a boy, he absolutely loved it. It is a very necessary exercise.

Friday I saw John Sparrow, he was ticking off young men and women for walking on the grass outside the Camera. He pointed his umbrella at them and made them come over to get their wigging. I wish old Mercurius had been there.

John Sparrow says he has lost his memory, but that he has got his car back. Deep gloom and dense fog over Oriel.

To Trevor-Roper, 30 November.

Thank you very much indeed for your hospitality last week-end. Xandra seems in splendid form; of course, Fenland is enormously invigorating, as healthy, I should say, as your native county. I was very gratified to share a page with you yesterday. I am getting more and more involved in Vichy and have been roped in to give a talk on it at St John's (Cambridge) tomorrow afternoon. This will be my last visit to Cambridge, for a time at least, but I have expressed willingness to do more lectures Michaelmas 1982. It is a good excuse to have regular visits to the better half of England.

I do not feel very warmly towards Kenyon.

On Wednesday I dine with your successor in Oriel. Perhaps I'll be told what is happening there.

Eric Christiansen is getting married. Do you know him? If you did, you would find this news quite surprising. Or perhaps it is not.

To Trevor-Roper, 31 December.

New Year greetings to Xandra & you. I expect you are now in

Melrose, though not, I hope, snowed up. I am hoping to see you on the 5th, when no doubt the Guru Thompson will be trundled out again. But he won't get in! I managed to get in an allusion to Peterhouse in last week's TLS (in which your Dean & Chaplain mauls some awful Cambridge Marxo-Theologian).

Still no news of Oriel. Or am I out of touch?

I am still plunged in the equivocation of Vichy.

I see that one of my historian colleagues has got a CBE.

I wonder just how old Postan really was.

1982

To Trevor-Roper, 20 January.

Thank you for your letter from the white wastes of Melrose. I hope Xandra & you are now safely back in Trumpington Street. We were 3 days without hot water & the snow has been coming through the roof of what is supposed to be my new study so I've been living among buckets. It may console you to learn that in the middle of last week, Oxfordshire was the coldest place in Europe: -20C (Moscow was -16); it certainly felt like that.

I started lecturing today on the Thermidoreans. I had been going for about 15 minutes when a girl put up her hand & said, 'Professor, you are supposed to be lecturing on Paris Collaborationism, it says so on the Lecture List.' And so it did. The boobies at the Press had put my lectures in reverse order: the Collabos on Wed; the Thermidoreans on Friday. It made me feel all back-to-front and back-to-front I'll have to remain for the rest of the term.

I'm coming to Cambridge (Pembroke) on February 8th. Could I call on Xandra & you at 11-ish on the 9th for a coffee? I would very much like to see you both.

The new Provost of Oriel has a Christian name that begins with a 'Z' which induced one of my colleagues to propose, at lunch today, 'from Asa to Z'.

I am glad Owen Chadwick has been knighted. But what is the form? 'Professor the Revd Sir O.C.'? And does his wife become 'Lady C.'? When I saw her at the BA party, she thought not.

Oh dear! I have killed poor Louis-Philippe in the wrong place. I have sent grovelling apologies for my mistake. Best wishes to Xandra.

PS I've had an indignant letter from Heffer's re my TLS piece on the Shell Guide.

To Trevor-Roper, 22 April.

I have been sadly negligent in my correspondence. But nothing ever seems to <u>happen</u> in this provincial backwater – so unlike the deep intrigues & great events that characterise the Fenland. What <u>is</u> there to report? That Michael Pratt breezed through, red & breathless, on the way to some country house victim. Oxford is <u>dormant</u>. We are not even Falkland Islanders. I am <u>engrossed</u> (as a commoner) in a struggle against a foul & corrupt alliance of OUP and IBA (Crime in the arm of Death) who want to inflict on poor Wolvercote a 220-foot radio mast. John Patten has been a great help; he's a good MP. But the mast has quite kept me away from <u>les Îles Malouines</u>. (What <u>has</u> St Malo to do with that bleak place?) The <u>Times</u> seems to have taken leave of its senses. Perhaps it will soon calm down.

I am to contribute to Owen Chadwick's <u>festschrift</u>. My piece has to be about <u>religion</u> so I cannot trundle out more of those girls of the revolutionary calendar.

I did not get to the BA Elections owing to work in Paris. I hope 'Charisma' Thompson was banned once again.

I am looking for a pretext to come to Cambridge next month. I have discovered the areas known as 'the Kite' including 2 <u>wonderful</u> pubs, <u>The Elm</u> & <u>The Free Press</u>, the former kept by a <u>vast</u> Frenchwoman who speaks bad English and is rude to customers she doesn't like. Like North Oxford it is 'the other Cambridge'.

Recently I met a Girtonian (1930+) who remembered my eldest aunt, Jane Swindale, the first of the 8 children of my maternal grandfather, a country GP, who was Garden mistress there for years & years. She died in Cambridge aged 91, preserved by the East wind.

I think I can get Trinity to invite me for something next month. Greetings to Xandra.

PS Give me news of the <u>outside</u> world, of Syndics, McCrums & all those exciting people. We are deep here in the Slough.

John Patten was MP for Oxford from 1979 to 1987, although boundary changes meant that from 1983 he represented the west of the city and Abingdon where Cobb ended his days. He was enobled as Baron Patten of Wincanton in 1997 and although also a Tory Catholic politician is not to be confused with Chris Patten, his contemporary and a pupil of Cobb, unlike John, who was a graduate of Hertford College.

To Trevor-Roper, 20 May.

I am 65 today. I don't really FEEL it; but there it is. Owen Chadwick is one year ahead of me. I was very gratified to see myself included in the <u>Sunday Times</u> birthdays though I have not made it yet with the <u>Times</u>. It did have Aylmer recently, even a drawing of him, bringing out his Cyrano-style nose. (I suppose people from Winchester get in automatically, they are so High-&-Mighty. The poor Queen having to go to that awful, self-satisfied school!)

A letter from Hartmut, who has been examining a Cambridge thesis on Schacht, the work of one of your Research Fellows. Hartmut tells me the young man's mother was Borman's secretary from 1938 to the end of the Bunker. She escaped from the Bunker through a sewer and later married an English Intelligence officer. Apparently the young man only discovered this about his mother a couple of years ago. Did you know this? Last Friday I listened to a very good paper at the German History Seminar on the military opposition to Hitler by a German Professor who has written a biography of Beck.

I have NO news. Nothing happens in the swamps of the Isis. John Sparrow, I am told, drinks more and more; and Fellows have to take it in turns to drive him back to Iffley at night, as he has lost his driving licence.

As I am an OAP, I am going to get a Railcard and start travelling all over the place, to places I hardly know, like Scotland and Cornwall, as a demi-historian.

I do feel our Government is making rather a fuss over the Falklands. As I am having lunch in the H of C on Tuesday with Chris Patten – a former pupil and I think no great friend of Mrs T – no doubt I'll learn more.

The TLS have sent me the last volume of the memoirs of a French novelist, Louis Guilloux, who died last year in his 80s. Flicking through it, I was amazed to discover a footnote to '(1) L'historien Richard Cobb'. I turned rather anxiously to the text. Mercifully, it seems that he liked me very much. An odd sensation, as if being addressed from the other side of death. We met in July 1966, and stayed up talking, mostly about one of his novels, till 3.30 am. I hope I get off as lightly in any other recollections in which I might figure! Anyhow, I have spent much of today reviewing a silly American book for the Guardian.

Why is Jack Plumb getting a successor? I thought he could go on and on, like Warden Bowman.

I rather hope the Pope doesn't come. I don't really approve of ANY Pope. I became a historian after reading The Rise of the Dutch Republic, a book with sound, magnificent prejudices, at my prep school.

Warmest greetings to Xandra, and please give me news of the great Fenland world, we are so provincial here.

Louis Guilloux was born in St Brieuc, Brittany, and spent all his long life there, writing Breton novels and having an eponymous prize created after his death designed to foster 'the ideals and values of the Breton writer'. Cobb would have approved of that sort of provincialism. He sounds less certain about Warden Bowman, who was Provost of Merton College from 1904 to 1936 and must have seemed likely, particularly to a man born more than a decade after he was first elected (Cobb was born in 1917), to go on for ever.

On 26 July 1981 he typed, on a Worcester College postcard, to thank Worden for one of his parties. He loved the party, which elicited lots of capital letters. The occasion was 'SUPERB'. It attracted 'EVERYONE'. But it was the setting which appealed to him as much as the conviviality. 'I loved that wild Gothick garden,' he wrote, 'and the house was a peculiar mixture of High North Oxford and Vienna. I was reminded of the place I stayed in Vienna, Cottagegasse, in 1935, with Felix Salten and family before I was expelled from Austria for pro-Socialist activities by the Schusnigg police.'

On 15 December he wrote a letter to Bernard Wasserstein beginning with an apology for missing Wasserstein's wedding the previous month. He had been involved in a 'major domestic crisis'. Had he attended the nuptials it would have been his first Jewish wedding, although in 1937 he attended the reception after the wedding of 'a lovely girl called Annie Lindhamer' whom he had met in the front quad of Merton while an undergraduate. On that occasion, however, he was not asked to the synagogue. Annie Lindhamer died in Auschwitz in 1943.

Memories of his visit to the States were still, evidently, fond but he had not yet received the $300 promised by Harvard for his talk there. He had written to Simon Schama to complain but had at the time of writing received no reply.

Towards the end of January he still had not been paid by Harvard and noted in a letter to Bernard Wasserstein that 'a significant silence has fallen on Simon'. He had heard that Schama had been in Oxford the previous December and conceded that he was 'a bit cross'. On a political note he was irritated with the 'bloody' Poles, whom he described as 'The Irish of the East', and thought the Soviets were displaying 'marvellous restraint'.

On a brighter note he had finished a long chapter on collaboration in Paris which he was calling 'French and Germans'. He seemed happy with it. 'I am pleased with my chapter,' he wrote. This ran to no less than 40 Worcester College postcards. He said that he would be typing the cards on to paper over the next few days.

In June Bernard Wasserstein received a reply to his slightly barbed greetings to mark Cobb's 65th birthday. The experience had proved 'painless so far' and mainly involved cheap train journeys using his 'magic Railcard'. He had been to Sheffield, which he liked, comparing it to Lyon. He had still had no money from Harvard and was in a state of capital-lettered 'DESPAIR'. He was also consumed with envy because the Foch Professor of French was getting the red ribbon of the Légion d'honneur and he was not.

Later that June, the 24th, he wrote to Bernard Wasserstein.

I saw Simenon in Lausanne on Sunday. He told me that in 1942 he had a visit from a member of the <u>Police aux Questions Juives</u>. 'Your surname indicates that you must be a Jew. It is derived from Simon.' His mother had to dig out the <u>certificates de baptisme</u> of his 4 grandparents in Belgium & in Dutch Limburg. The policeman was not satisfied. '<u>vous</u> sentez <u>le Juif</u>'. S said he did not know <u>what</u> he smelt of. A <u>horrid</u>, sinister story.'

On 29 June he was fretting over the delivery of his manuscript and had rung the publisher. He had sent it on sheets of small Basildon Bond paper and was worried because his publisher's secretary told him that the manuscript had gone to an outside reader, something he had never encountered in his dealings with the Oxford University Press. He was anxious that quotations in French should remain in French and should not be translated. He had provided a glossary and considered that this was sufficient.

In July he wrote to thank Worden for another of his annual parties and on 1 September he wrote to Bernard Wasserstein accepting an invitation to take part in a conference at Brandeis on the Jews in Modern France. He had also taken Wasserstein's advice, whatever that might have been, and had, as a result, finally received a cheque from Harvard for his lecture. It came with two apologetic letters. He was also doing a piece on the Oxford University Press for Richard Ingrams at Private Eye for a series on 'Great Publishers of Today'. He swore Wasserstein to secrecy as he still had two books due to be published by them.

On 9 November he wrote to Wasserstein worried about money, with the Inland Revenue apparently demanding tax. His publishing schedule seemed to be up to speed but not all his publishers' requests pleased him. 'The publicity lady asked for a recent photo of me. I thought <u>not</u>, it would not help sell the book, though if they like, they can have one of WILLIAM with one of his teddies.'

1983

On 15 March (The Ides), alongside a scrawled 'Zeldin's book is awful,' he wrote buoyantly to Bernard Wasserstein, 'A good day'. The post had contained a cheque from the BBC for a repeat of a talk on Simenon, a nice letter from Geoffrey Elton, now elevated to the Regius Chair of History in Cambridge, and a handsome-looking author's copy of his new book on the French and Germans. What's more the weather was clement.

Nine days later he wrote again to Bernard Wasserstein, wondering how much money he should bring for his impending visit to Brandeis University. He thought $200 in cash would probably suffice and he also confided, 'I have bought new trousers & will be buying a new sports coat in order to improve my appearance.'

On 26 May he wrote congratulating Bernard Wasserstein on a happy event, 'Very good news about the birth of your DAUGHTER. There will be a suitable present for her from William's parents when you and Janet are over here this summer.' His recent birthday was noted in The Times, causing him to remark that he was finally 'FAMOUS'. Meanwhile surgery on his tiresome fingers was successfully complete.

I now have TWO hands again having had the stitches taken out of my right hand at the Nuffield yesterday. The right hand, at last uncovered, looks vaguely familiar, like an old friend who has been on a trip and who has come back. My left hand is proposing to welcome him back. The fingers seem to have retained their grip. I tried them out on a pint glass of Guinness yesterday, and they passed the test.

To Cobb's chagrin it seemed unlikely that he would be able to attend Worden's annual party in 1983. On 30 June he typed from the Godstow Road house to warn him that a christening in Shropshire might take precedence, as, in the end, it did. 'Agreeable,' he wrote in a later letter, 'but your party would have been more so.' He remembered Worden's links with village life in Huntingdonshire and remarked: 'My sister, who seems to have any amount of Churchill lore, tells me that young Winston and his sister(s) were at one time in Hemingford Abbots during the war.' He had also been fielding a host of letters from his old friend Hugh Trevor-Roper, recently translated from a lifetime in Oxford to the Mastership of Peterhouse. He wrote:

I now have an enormous collection of the Lamentations of Hugh from the Depths of the Fens, his Ovidian exile. But he seems in in fact to be in very good spirits. I have told him that he is very fortunate in his enemies (as fortunate, indeed, as the splendid Norman Stone, who did such a marvellous job on that old horror Carr – I contributed the information about the sand shoes worn without socks).

A month later, on 29 July, he wrote above the whimsical strapline, 'Tibbles Professor of Feline History', to Bernard Wasserstein, celebrating yet another party, this time in honour of his new book on the French and the Germans.

What a splendid party! Though it was a pity I arrived late, the fault of a Soviet watch. I think I can remember most of the people who were there, though I have a sort of feeling that John Patten and Raymond Carr were there and maybe they were and maybe they weren't. I had a fearful hangover yesterday morning, and it worsened when I saw a mad-eyed caricature of myself staring at me from the middle of the book page of <u>The Grauniad</u>. John Rosselli's generous text did much to restore me, and there have been nice reviews in <u>The Listener</u> and <u>The Spectator</u> so I feel the book is really doing rather well. I hope my speech was not too long and too rambling. I must say they are VERY nice publishers, fancy getting TWO parties out of one book!

At about the same time Wasserstein sent him a postcard of the Queen Mother purporting to be a personal message from her. This seems to have crossed with one from Cobb which was virtually identical to the above, fretting again over the presence or otherwise of Raymond Carr and John Patten, worrying that his speech was too long and rambling, aghast at the picture of him in the Guardian and reflecting on the character of the various reviews that had appeared on the book. He is caustic about John Weightman ('a dull dog and one of those London people who can never resist having a dig at Oxonians'), grudging about George Gale ('half mad') and 'delighted' by Norman Hampson.

On 6 August he wrote again to Wasserstein, suspecting the worst from David Pryce-Jones:

I imagine it would be very hostile as I took him to task in <u>The Sunday Times</u> for the innumerable mistakes in French in his <u>Paris in the Third Reich</u>. As he is half-French – his mother is a French Rothschild – I felt that he might have done rather better, he wrote me a very aggrieved letter saying that all the mistakes were the fault of some poor female copy editor; ever since, he has been ever willing to pounce on any mistakes of <u>mine</u>. I think his review was in <u>The Sunday Telegraph</u>. He strikes me as rather small-minded and venomous.

Later that year, it was Cobb's turn to host a party. This was to celebrate his book about growing up in Tunbridge Wells and he wrote, 'A week before Beastly Bastille Day, 1983', to warn Worden about the venue and to lament, once more, his absence from Worden's own party. Maurice Keen had reached fifty recently – on 30 October – and Cobb gave him a bottle with the comment that sixty and seventy were much to be preferred.

On 11 December he wrote to Heald, who had recently published a book on Old Boy Networks. Cobb offered a caveat based on his time as a tutor at Aberystwyth.

I wish you had asked me about WELSH Networks. There are two you don't mention and of which I am very much aware. One is the EEC permanent bureaucracy in Brussels, peopled by ex-Aber pupils of mine led by Hywel Ceri Jones. There is literally a Welsh enclave rue de la Loi. The other is in University administration. I doubt if there is a University in England that does not have a Welsh Registrar, Deputy Registrar and Assistant-Deputy-Registrar. Again I have watched my former Aber students as they jump through one hoop after another, it is an entirely self-perpetuating hierarchy of which the career of the present Registrar of the University of Nottingham is a perfect example (incidentally it was he who, as Registrar of Essex, got me my honorary doctorate there). First, DAR at Aber, then AR at Salford, then AR at Nottingham, then R at Essex, now R at Nottingham, the next move will no doubt be to Manchester, when the present R (also from Aber), retires. Another Welsh network is, as you mention, the medical one, but above all in hospital ADMINISTRATION, Registrars etc. The Welsh have a marvellous capacity for looking after one another.

I think Networks are far more powerful in France than here, partly because there is more POWER about. Incidentally, the papal encyclical forbidding Catholics to be masons is dated 1827 or thereabouts. In the eighteenth century, the Grand Master of the Grand Orient de France was the Comte d'Artois, Louis XVI's brother.

Cobb did, however, think Heald had been 'unkind' to his 'dear old School' (Sherborne). However, he told Heald to look out for his own book about 'the Salopian Matricide'. When this did finally appear Cobb dedicated it to Heald, in a spirit of conspiratorial anti-public school establishmentarianism.

Three days later, on the 14th, he wrote to Bernard Wasserstein summing up 1983 in well-satisfied tones, not least because of the encomium from Isaiah Berlin in the Sunday Times.

Long Live Isaiah! How <u>right</u> they were to make him an OM, how right they were to give him the Erasmus Prize (at the banquet he sat between the two Queens of the Netherlands, the current one and her mother, I bet you have never sat between two Queens). Also my little French book must be out by now. Incidentally my French publishers <u>les editions du sorbier</u> are quite desperate to do <u>French and German</u> in translation, they tell me they have written to Tom McF several times, but have not had a reply. Could you not activate him, unless, of course, he has given it to Fayard? The book has recently been in the news in Paris so there is no lack of interest in an eventual translation.

1984

To Trevor-Roper, 19 January.

VERY MANY HAPPY RETURNS for the day after tomorrow, 21st of January (which is also the date of the execution of poor old Louis XVI, not that he was at all old, I mean it affectionately, for he was not a bad fellow, just a bit devious, and with a perfectly FRIGHTFUL wife, I hate all the dreadful Habsburgs, and Vienna is the most dreadful place I have ever been to, worse even than broken down Sofia). CONGRATULATIONS ON THREE SCORE AND TEN. And thank you for your wonderful letter from Melrose, which I'll answer soon, at the moment I am wrestling with a brand new lecture course about the Third Republic, about which I do not know very much, though I did live under it for a few years, and once knocked down M. Pierre Laval in a rush to catch the last metro at Rond-Point des Champs-Élysées, by the statue of Clemenceau. I excused myself humbly, addressing the white-tied mongoloid-looking gentleman as M le President (there are so many Presidents in France).

Actually, Blair & I have great hopes of seeing Xandra and you at Blair's dacha on the evening of your birthday, that is what we are hoping.

Yes, alas, on the scrap heap for me, though it seems likely that I'll be going to the US for a term at a place called Rochester, NY, near the Canadian border. It could be quite agreeable, and perhaps they'll give me a DD, though I think I am due one here, having been invited – or about to be – to preach at Eton, in the very presence of the Blessed Henry.

We have a new Professor-Elect to succeed the Chichele. My election committee, I mean the one for my succession, meets, I think, on 14 September.

I think I should become a Tory MEP. But how does one do that? No, I think it would be dreadfully BORING, the price of French turnips etc. Not for me. My father, when he retired, wanted to go & preach to the Heathen, but Chavasse, the Bishop of Rochester (who I suppose was a successor to the founder of my gentle College), told my father one gave the BEST, not the worst years of one's life to God. So we are in the worst! And my father, after retiring from the Sudan, went to live in Tun. Wells and became secretary to the local branch of the CMS. I would quite like to be a DEAN. Wells would do. Perhaps I should pay another visit to the Republic (South Africa) and give more talks on French Protestantism to the Afrikaaners of the University of South Africa (Pretoria). I am sure they'd have me back. Oh well, I'll look around. Perhaps I should be on a Royal Commission on Pederasty.

Hoping very much to see you on your birthday, greetings to Xandra.

To Trevor-Roper, 4 March.

I have taken a very very long time to reply to your splendid letter from Melrose on the subject of the Undertaker, the Baron – of whom there is a most improbable picture – drawn long before his Ruin – in today's Sunday paper supplement – and the rest of the junto. It is a victory message that has given me every possible pleasure. I am afraid that the last time I wrote to you, I congratulated you on your birthday at least a week late, this from something that Blair had written and in the belief that Xandra & you were to be present at a supper party at Blair's dacha somewhere near Northants. Alas, you were not there; but we did our best to console ourselves, in Blair's dining room there is a pulpit which inevitably drew me, at a late stage in the evening, to its lofty height and from which I preached a sermon in French in the Jesuitical manner of the RP Riquet, formerly of Nôtre Dame. Some time earlier in the evening I seem to have spilled what looks like soup over my trousers. And I only saw you very briefly at that splendid occasion in Balliol.

There has been much news from here. I have a SUCCESSOR, and just the one I hoped for: our Trinity friend, Norman Stone. I am DELIGHTED though the presence here, on the spot, of my favourite drinking companion (vodka) may not be too good for my health. The electors – good men, I think – have shown wisdom. I BELIEVE the chair was first offered to Keith Thomas, who turned it down, but this may be idle rumour. I am told there is much FURY in your present University. I will no doubt hear more, having been invited to a Feast at Cromwell's College by my opposite number on the 17th. Can I pay you a visit for coffee on the morning of the 18th? Then there is the New Warden of Merton; good news, too, I feel. What is more, Jack McManners's chair has been frozen for a year, so you will have the Undertakers with you a bit longer, bad news your end, good news though this end.

Yesterday, in the Broad, I encountered Major the Viscount Morpeth, in Master's hood, uniform, 4 large medals, two from Oman, one from the UN, and a brilliant red cap with a gold rim to its peak, so we had a drink in the KA before he went off to take his grandma out to lunch and I to Merton for lunch with the historians. George warned me about Bayham. Apparently one has to take one's own lunch with one, if invited there, preferably a picnic basket. There was also some talk of Camden's Boy not being too popular with the worthy tradesmen of the Royal Borough: bills overdue, rude words, &ca, &ca; so I think I may delay my visit to Michael's Seat. I have already had a further visit to his fief, having given a talk to the Lower Sixth of Tunbridge Wells Girls' Grammar School. I reached the place on the stroke of eleven in the morning, and, being under 8 stone, was almost swept away by an <u>aglomerat</u> of young girldom as they swept impetuously down the narrow corridors of this Edwardian building. I finally reached the Common Room, shaken but not crushed under female foot. A very frightening experience. But the girls were in fact nice, CORRECTLY DRESSED and with hair in apparently natural colours. One, called Imogen, had chosen my book as her Form Prize. Well done, Imogen!

On the 13th I am venturing into Foreign Parts. I have got my visa from their Consulate, 9 St Cross Road. Yes, I am to speak to the little gowned ayatollahs of WINCHESTER (Aylmer College); I fear they will lapidate me for FRIVOLITY. I am being prepared by Maurice Keen, who is one of the Brethren. So if you hear no more from me, you will know that I have been lapidated.

I am to be raised to literary summitry, in fact a giddy pinnacle, having been asked to be this year's chairman of the Booker Prize. I fear that this will result in my being in disfavour with pretty well every publisher in England, though I am hoping to retain some favour at Chatto's.

I have decided to ignore my retirement and to go on lecturing in my own subjects in the Faculty (<u>Menna</u> is doing the same; <u>Menna</u> is now deep in the celebrations – but what is there for good French Protestants to celebrate? – of the second centenary of the Edict of Fontainebleau). I have few other retirement or non-retirement plans, though the new Warden, if he has ANY decency, might set me up in a convenient Merton living somewhere in Otmoor. I do not think I'll be idle.

Has Trinity a new Master? There has been talk of Sir Dimitri, the new Knight, moving east. I hope he doesn't, as I find him amiable and would miss him. Now, with Norman going, I fear my last link with that magnificent College will be severed and that is indeed a great pity.

This has been a hard term. New lectures to get up and give, far too many outside Talks (next term I hope to be going to your old school) and I have got much behind in my correspondence.

Yesterday Balliol was electing a new Pennington, I mean a new Tudors and Stuarts man. I do not know whom they have got. Thursday I was at the Sunday Times, correcting a proof. What an AWFUL building! No wonder they have so much trouble there. I would expect a defenestration every hour, but I don't suppose the windows open.

Warmest greetings to Xandra. As you see, great events have been taking place in your old University. Norman & his wife are having lunch with me in his future College on Friday; it won't be a GOOD lunch, but I thought I had better break him in gently. We'll have to make up on drink.

I have had a solicitor's letter on behalf of a lady in Bournemouth who expresses anguish because, in my book, I call her late father a gypsy. Is that such a very bad thing to be? I have mollified her with a grovelling letter.

Please write again & forgive me for my long silence, I have been hard pressed.

The judging of the Booker was proving irksome and he wrote to Worden on 29 August 1984: 'I have now read 83 novels and am beginning to wilt ... I shall have to watch my Ps and Qs at the Booker Dinner. I think the only solution is not to drink anything till I have announced the winner.' He confided to Worden that he could not remember the later stages of either the recent faculty dinner in Balliol or Worden's own 'wonderful' party in Norham Gardens. 'I think on both occasions I made a speech, but I have no idea what they were about.'

In a letter to the Daily Telegraph he wrote:

Chairing the Booker Prize panel was perhaps an unusually uncontentious experience in that I liked my fellow judges, there were no rows, and we had no unusual difficulty in settling on Anita Brookner's *Hotel du Lac*.

However, I retain a certain resentment against the publishers, who inundated us first with bound copies, then with proofs, and finally with Photostats of proofs.

Still, I encountered the work of many novelists of whom I had never heard and whom I would not otherwise have read, such as Angela Huth. I have, therefore, not found any necessity to bother with Proust.

The other judges included the authors Polly Devlin and John Fuller, the Labour MP Ted Rowlands and the Literary Editor of the Financial Times, Anthony Curtis. Some thought a worthier winner would have been Julian Barnes's 'Flaubert's Parrot' or J.G. Ballard's 'Empire of the Sun'.

Hugo Brunner was an editor at Chatto and Windus as well as an Oxford grandee who lived in the north of the city and became Lord Lieutenant of the county.

165 etc. THE FIRST OF OCTOBER 1984 (I ceased being a Professor at midnight.)

Dear Hugo,

You were so kind with the offer of the Reform on the 18th. In fact it won't be necessary, we change at Bucklebury House after our meeting and are transported from there collectively to the Guildhall. I am going to have to hire a DJ, Margaret won't let me appear in my 1935 Peter Robinson outfit, she says the frays would show up on Telly.

I addressed a cohort of mostly octogenarian ladies in T[unbridge] W[ells] on Friday. There was a nasty weasel man, a shopkeeper I think, who asked why I gave such a sordid view of the Royal Borough, why had I not mentioned the Agricultural Show? And so on but I said my book was not a Chamber of Commerce hand-out and ALL the old ladies were on my side, I confounded the creature. I also got in maximum publicity for the next book. The Baron was there, as well as his nice neighbour. The Baron is a bit lost, he is selling the shop and is looking for a job involving books. It was LOVELY waking up in the morning to look out onto Calverley Park in the beautiful September light. And I made several jokes on the subject of Scott-Page.

I did not see The Times today, it was not sent, so I don't know whether Craddock had an apology. I am going to the US Embassy on the 25th for Tony Powell's prize.

The Bowl is full of roses.

21 October, to Hugo Brunner.

Thank you, from both of us, for your kind postcard. My WEEK OF FAME (which could so easily have turned into a WEEK OF SHAME) is now safely over, and I can now get back to writing and lecturing. At the dinner I ate hardly anything, drank very little but was amply compensated by having been placed next to dear Isaiah, who was in wonderful form, especially about that extraordinary place All Souls. Margaret was lucky, too, she got on very well with Jim Prior and with a charming ex-Ambassador. I was glad about Anita. Bill Webb told me off quite roundly, Derwent May was HORRIFIED by my frivolous references to Proust and Joyce. I am sending my second speech to the TLS, they might publish it, and I am doing a piece for the SPECTATOR about books that I liked and did not make the short list, starting with Bainbridge and the marvellous Jacobson.

Let's meet for a drink soon. Friday I am taking part in the installation of the Warden of MERTON, lunch to follow, a very grand affair.

23 OCT 1984 [rubber stamped] but typed 165, Godstow Road, Wolvercote, Oxford, 22 October 1984, to John Roberts.

Dear John the Elect,

SUCH a shame, but I'll have to miss the best part of your installation, the knocking on the door, your admission, the Keys, the chapel, the bells ringing. The thing is I have NOT retired, and from twelve to one on Fridays I lecture on the dear old Revolutionary Government, in the absence of Colin who is off for the next two years. But I WILL make the Savile Room by one and of course the splendid lunch. I have asked the Sub-Warden to present you my apologies for not being at the first part. It is SUCH a happy occasion, an <u>antipasto</u> for your actual arrival. I have seen quite a lot of Merton – at lunch – lately and I have come greatly to like Robert and the younger Fellows (I have always liked the older ones, have even become more tolerant of the Dean of Degrees: my opposite number). I still have a room in College and will be going on lecturing. Wuggins very kindly made me a SRF. So I am pretty pleased about everything, especially about my Successor, my favourite Cambridge drinking companion, who will, I am sure, support me at the College Buttery. Also IMMENSELY relieved at having seen the Booker thing right through without any great mishap. We have an elegant short list and Anita's book has an eighteenth century grace and dryness. A great triumph too over the Media, who all rooted for Ballard (Blackwell's even gave him a whole window).

On the 14th I preached at the College of the Blessed Mary. Perhaps Mark was in the congregation. The microphone fell off my neck with a loud clatter just as I had started, and I had to scrabble about on the floor of the pulpit to retrieve it, re-emerging like a jack-in-the-box, a bit of comic relief at least for all those good-looking boys dressed in black and white, the KSs in white. The service ended in trumpets. I knew Anderson and his wife from their Shrewsbury time. Lord Charteris was gentle and charming.

Now that I have a bit more time I really must get down to see JBS.

HAIL TO THE ELECT.

Love to Judith.

Love from Chairman Cobb.

PS I had lunch on Thursday with Tim Heald, who sent you his greetings and good wishes and wanted to know whether, as Warden, you would go on WRESTLING, I assured him you would, every day, at 7, before a morning run round the Meadows.

That Christmas Balliol College produced a Christmas card which featured a photograph of the dinner held on Friday 17 February to celebrate the 90th birthday of the Chancellor, Harold Macmillan.

126

Cobb sent it to a number of his correspondents. The one to Heald came with a letter which exulted, 'Is this not a SPLENDID example of crass Balliology? I hope you can pick me out, sitting on the Extreme Right, <u>comme de juste,</u> *looking at the menu without my glasses. I am one down from Jasper.'*

To Richard Ingrams he wrote later, 'I had meant to send you a Balliol Xmas card, a photo of the dinner for Supermac's 90th, in which I can be seen NOT falling into my soup, Richard Brain suggested I send it; but then I got engulfed by Christmas.'

He wrote to David Gilmour from Wolvercote on the 30 December. 'I had the good luck to be in Brussels myself on the 4th,'

. . . and met there old Deschriver, Minister of the Interior in the Pierlot-Spaak Government and as such responsible for the <u>épuration</u> of the <u>inciviques</u> (as they called the <u>collabos</u> in Belgium) of the autumn and winter of 1944. I sat next to the old boy, a charmer, at the dinner given us by the Belgian Ambassador in the middle of the Thames! – on HMS Belfast – and he proved an absolute mine of information. I have 2 graduates working on modern Belgian history and intend going on with it myself.

He then repeated his account of preaching at Gilmour's old school, and also the Charterhouse stories. He evidently liked Axel von dem Bussche. He was 6 foot 8 inches and, according to Cobb, had tried to blow up Hitler (and himself) when the Führer was to inspect a new model of an officer's greatcoat. 'Axel is VERY good value. I suppose he is a Prussian – like Hartmut and all the BEST Germans. Yet another example of the superiority of Protestantism.'Axel 'the crypto-Hitlerocide', Cobb and Tim Hilton had originally met at a St Antony's dinner where they had been put together at what Cobb called 'the naughty boys' table'. Hilton later recalled:

At first we did not know what to make of him. Then he gave much praise to Marshal Timoshenko, after whom I am named. So that was okay. Then it became apparent that he was the man who had tried to assassinate Hitler, on the grounds that Adolf had sullied the high traditions of the German Army. You can appreciate that RCC and I then hung on his every word. In 1943 Axel, a highly decorated young officer, was deputed to show the Führer a new style of army overcoat. Into its pockets Axel placed two hand grenades. His plan was to detonate them as he grasped Hitler in his arms, thus committing suicide at the same time as killing the tyrant. Anyway everything went wrong, the grenades didn't go off . . . can't remember the details. What I do recall is that Richard and I thought that we needed a special round of drinks. Axel liked this idea so we went on and on at the bottles. Count Axel was much stronger at this business than RCC and TH. He was really quite an impressive chap. Then Richard slid from his chair, lay under the naughty boys' table and went to sleep. Count Axel von dem Bussche told me this was a common way to end the evening when German officers dined together, and no doubt he was right. Axel and I were friendly for a while and corresponded. He had a very formal sort of handwriting, learnt no doubt in some Prussian gymnasium.

NB. Axel's attempt on Hitler's life is not to be confused with that by Claus Schenk von Stauffenberg, which was in the following year.

To Trevor-Roper, 17 December.

I have been no correspondent at all, for the last 6 months. My only excuse is that I had to spend the summer READING NOVELS (86 in all), then had to prepare a lecture, in a series organised by your successor, on the July Crisis of 1914 seen from France, a talk for the German Historical Institute in Paris, in French, a sermon at Eton (in English followed by the laying-up of the Standard of the Blues and Royals) plus my usual stint of lectures. Only now am I beginning to breathe. I did achieve SOMETHING as chairman of the Booker, I managed to keep Martin Amis and Angela Carter and something something de Teran off the shortlist and manoeuvred so that Ballard did not get the prize to the FURY of the media, the critics and Ladbroke's. So I have done a little NEGATIVE good. I have also been to your old School to give a talk on French Calvinism, the True Word, la Bible Martin, etc., out-Menna-ing Menna. I stayed with an AMAZINGLY drunken Housemaster – we started on the sherry at 3pm – who washed his

128

socks – I counted 16 pairs of them drying – in the wash-basin of his bedroom. This <u>seemed</u> to be School House, anyhow it faced onto the statue of the Founder, the scoundrel you once lectured on there. I was taken to the Master's Common Room – three rows of port-wine faces (so my host was not an exception) entered through a door with a wonderful notice: NO BOYS ALLOWED BEYOND THIS POINT, quite right too, since they were swilling down the armagnac on the other side of the strictly guarded frontier. More drinks after I had talked about Calvin and his sucessors with the Housemaster and his enormous DOGS (no wife, never had been one; but he seemed to get on very well with the BOYS, he was a Cambridge man, possibly even from PETERHOUSE). By the way, a Belgian Baron, quite nice, who lives in Tunbridge Wells, in a lovely Septimus Burton house, and helps sell my book, is DETERMINED that I meet this awful man who dresses up as an SS to get himself thrashed. But I have managed to take avoiding action. Charterhouse: yes, I loved the statue of the Victorian Headmaster holding a Toy Chapel in his hand. So Wingate was a Carthusian – that I did not know. Nor that the school now contains two Bismarcks and one Bethmann-Hollweg, there were some of each apparently before 1914. I wish I could have stayed longer. I did observe that the History Library should be called after you. Perhaps they will take up my suggestion.

James I have seen 3 or 4 times, he even came to my 1914 lecture. We had a visit from George when we were on holiday in Whitby. He was sad, deeply worried about his parents, the estate, money; but we managed to cheer him up a bit. Have you seen the current number of the <u>Tatler</u>? If not, you must rush out and buy it in Melrose, there is a most AMAZING photo of Lord Michael holding a glass at a dance.

I must stop. People keep on calling in, Etonian pupils of the past. My Successor is more or less invisible, he gave one lecture in the 1914 series and has impressed everybody on the Faculty Board beneath the portrait of Queen Anne (I miss Her) by his Gravity. He is regarded as utterly RESPECTABLE, even something of an Elder Statesman. How fortunate he was to have avoided the All Souls Club. And in Worcester, installed in my old rooms – I am now installed in a tiny room overlooking the Lord Asa's garden – he will be forced into a puritanical mould, there is no BED, no DIVAN, none of the comforts of the Trinity Zeppelin. Norman is now generally regarded as a man UTTERLY austere, a Glaswegian Gladstone. I suppose we were expecting something a bit different. At the moment he is believed to be in Buda, or in Pest (whichever is the more respectable of the two halves of that bifurcated city that I have never visited).

I am just back from lecturing in French at the German Historical Institute in Paris about Occupations. A solemn lot, but nice. We have here in Oxford this year a rather wonderful German, about 6ft 6, with one leg, called Axel von dem Bussche, who seems to have had one of many goes at Hitler. But how can I tell YOU anything about this? I know NOTHING about the Germans, save that I like my friend Hartmut. Please write to me, forgive me for my long silence and give Xandra my best wishes in this cold season. I shall be coming to the Fens next term for some Feast in St John's. I hope you have all the JUNTO in full flight. By the way, why not get the Cardinal the bishopric of SHREWSBURY, they are BEGGING for someone.

After the familiar scrawled 'Richard' at the bottom of this letter Cobb has written in brackets the legend 'No longer the silent'.

1985

To Trevor-Roper, Twelfth Night.

Your letter of 23 December has had the happy effect of raising me from my bed, where I was laid quite prone with an unusually vicious liver attack, something that recurs every now and then ever since I caught a nasty form of hepatitis in Paris, shortly after my demobilisation, an illness provoked, I imagine, by the liquidity, in the literal sense, of my War Gratuities as applied in various Parisian bars. I am now feeling much more cheerful, partly, I suppose, because I am NOT in Peterhouse. I, mistakenly, thinking it was for the pleasure of my company, for my beaux yeux or whatever; but it was for nothing of the kind. I was invited to spite Dom Knowles. He had me placed in the Dom's room, on the right, in the main quad. The wardrobe was full of the Dom's clothes, both civilian and monkish – the civilian ones were a bit on the LOUD side, the sort of thing one might associate with the Baron – not mine, of whom more later – but your <u>resident</u> one. The elderly scout eventually took me into his confidence, pointing out to me that, every further night I stayed in my usurped rooms, the poor Dom would be dossing at some uncomfortable hostelry, perhaps the Cambridge equivalent of the Seaman's Home in St Giles. So I got out forthwith, writing from Oxford to thank Pecksniff (for Butterfield LOOKED like Pecksniff) for his rather double-edged hospitality. One of Butterfield's sons teaches at the Peterhouse Annexe, University College, Dublin – but I don't THINK he is a teetotaller though, like all in the History Department there, he is careful NEVER to drink Powers, but ALWAYS to drink Jameson, Three Swallows, or Paddy. Powers, like Bushmill's Black Label – the nectar of my old Master, Sir David – is a PROTESTANT whiskey. Desmond Williams and Kevin Nolan – who also had a spell in Peterhouse – drink MOSTLY Jameson. They are men of DEEP religious conviction. Incidentally, I am glad to see that Xandra's daughter-in-law is also of a deep religious conviction, but I think she should write to the jolly, red-faced Bishop of Oxford rather than to <u>The Times</u>. I had supposed James to be some sort of BENNITE, but I suppose that can go with Deep Religious Conviction (DRC).

The Baron: Nicolas van Branden de Reath. He MAY be bogus; but there are an awful LOT of Barons in Belgium, they are increasing all the time, the King can make them whenever he feels like it. The Baron's father was literary editor of <u>La Dernière Heure</u>, quite a decent paper. The Baron was taken as a small child to England by his mother, also a Belgian, who sent him to Downside (probably a fairly pederastic place, frequented by <u>le gratin international du monde pédale</u>, if you will excuse the vulgar and cruel French expression). When he was about 20, he went to live with the author of a number of quite good studies of architectural history, including one on Decimus Burton's Tunbridge Wells. He died in 1983, a week before my book came out; and the poor Baron, now aged 40, is a bit <u>désemparé</u>. He has sold the bookshop he had in Chapel Place and at which he promoted the sale of my book to the local feudals: De la Warr, Sidney, Hussey – Michael, of course, got a FREE copy from me. Yes, the Baron does get into most of the noble mansions scattered along the Kent & Sussex border, though he has not yet made Eridge, though George and MICHAEL have. He is a nice, inoffensive creature who is probably going to have to sell his quite beautiful house, 11 Calverley Park, and go & live in London. I have stayed with him a couple of times without anything unseemly happening and seem to be quite safe there.

Von Bissing was not a bad chap at all. He was a relatively MILD Military Governor of Brussels during the First World War, managing to keep the Flemings at arm's length. He was succeeded, in 1940, and in the same capacity, by his NEPHEW, General von Falkenhausen, also a decent and honourable officer, who managed to keep the Gestapo out of things in Brussels until July 1944, when he was dismissed as Governor and recalled to Berlin. He was tried in Brussels after the war, was acquitted, and then married, in some pomp, his Belgian mistress. Of course, in 1940, he turned up with all his uncle's <u>fiches</u> about Belgian suspects, most of whom were then re-arrested. It was the same in Roubaix, where I was stationed for some time: General Baron. Whatever, 1914–18, was succeeded in 1940 by General Baron, HIS nephew. I hope you were all nice to young von B.

I am reading an immensely BORING biography of King Leopold III by one of your colleagues in the Upper House, Lord Keyes. L III, it would seem, was a combination of Louis IX, Louis XII, Henri IV, <u>Le Roi Chevalier</u>, and the XIXth c Shaftesbury. He stood up for the Underdog. (I have no time at all for ANY dog, and have written three letters to <u>The Times</u>, protesting about their pro-Dog propaganda, signing myself as Secretary, Oxford Branch, <u>pro-cat</u>, affiliated to <u>l'Union Féline Mondiale</u> headquarters in Siam, but the paper has not published ANY of them, obviously Douglas-Home is in the pay of Cruft's; but HA! I have a former pupil in Spiller's Dog Foods and he has agreed to put some effective and terminal ingredients in ALL their packets as they go out from their manufactory in Reading: REVENGE for the SIXTEEN times I have been bitten by those smelly animals.) He was the Greatest Friend of Admiral Keyes, &ca &ca. I am to do the hagiography for <u>The Spectator</u>.

I suppose it is snowing in Scotland, too. My young pupil, David Gilmour, tells me he is going to LIVE IN SCOTLAND, he hasn't been exiled for any <u>offence</u>, and he is to live in West Lothian; and I am so ignorant of Scottish geography I am not sure whether this is on the East or the West Coast or in the Highlands. But it is a LONG way from Twickenham where he lives at present. Yet his father is a gentle kindly man. And his two brothers and his sister have been allowed to go on living in England.

I must stop. Alas, there is NO retirement from testimonials.

I will come and see you the day AFTER the Cripps Feast in St John's which is on Friday 22nd March. Best wishes for 1985 for Xandra and you, and MAY THE RIGHT PREVAIL. I am going to Blair's party on 19 January.

On 14 February, Cobb wrote to Hugo Brunner.

Your pretty card arrived a day or two ago & made us both envious, me in particular, as I have been gasping with asthma, waking up at 3 or 4 in the morning and having to rush downstairs to get my pump. Mountain air would clear away the miasma of the Valley of the Isis. Still, we'll be off to Whitby on the 30th. I am a bit better now and have been working on various additions to <u>Percy House</u>. I SHOULD be reading theses, but have decided to give myself the luxury of getting back to a bit of writing. I have just been to my sister's and my brother-in-law provided me with quite a lot of new material about his father, including Bodley Head contracts. Tomorrow I am having the Penguin man, Martin Soames, to lunch in Balliol. Monday I went to a Virago party for the launching of their second-hand bookshop, given by Alexandra Hilton. I gave them a copy of my OUP book (I'll be dropping one in at 26 in the next few days). Elizabeth Knight is laying on a publication party at the Morgue on 17 September, & I have asked her to ask you, Richard B, Richard I, Ronnie Blythe; it might be quite amusing, as I believe Nero is likely to be at it. Anyhow, I look forward to seeing you at RI's birthday party on the 25th. I can only go there if you can give me a lift, M cannot go as she'll have Lucy in tow.

I have read with DELIGHT <u>Boys Together</u> by John Chandos. It is absolutely WONDERFUL on unreformed Eton in the golden days of Dr Keats, pretty good too on the wild era of Shrewsbury under the unpleasant Samuel Butler. John Nicoll gave me a copy. I'll bring it for you to read.

I expect you'll all come back from those lovely Alps feeling absolutely FULL of vigour. I have dreams of Les Mayans-de-Sion, in the Valais.

More delightful letters from Tunbridge Wells. I am making a last visit to No. 11 Calverley Park on the 24th. Monday I had a voice test at the RNIB, reading out extracts from ACE. I think they are going to let me do the whole thing, in a series of 3-hour sessions. Tracey has sent me more nice reviews. William had a wonderful time at my sister's, looking at tigers, beautiful wild cats, ocelots and owls with huge yellow eyes.

See you soon, love to Mary Rose.

PS John Whitehead, the former Town Clerk of TW, died ten days ago aged 97. His death was announced in the paper. Two days after the funeral, his house in Calverley Park was burgled, ALL the silver was removed. I suppose these wretches keep an eye out for the Death columns.

Elizabeth Knight, who was married to Robert 'Bob' Burchfield, the rugby playing Kiwi who was editor-in-chief of the Oxford Dictionaries, was the publicity director of the University Press who used to throw rather good parties at the Press's London HQ in Dover Street.

1986

On 8 January he wrote to David Gilmour still in a state of excitement and worry about lunch at White's Club. 'The place where there is a full length Duke of York in red is it not?' he asked, adding that he was delighted that Gilmour had managed to get hold of Edward Mortimer ('le grand Edouard'), who had evidently been sending him spoof letters offering decorations 'which I richly deserve'.

He was also still concerned about Gilmour's imminent departure for Edinburgh:

I have told Lord Dacre about your impending banishment to northern parts. I thought Xandra might help you with <u>les indigènes</u> as she is one herself. I suppose you'll have to become a Calvinist. When you are up there near the Arctic Circle you will be able to reminisce, as did the enormously verbose Louis-Philippe, once back in France, about 'mon cher Twick'.

165 Godstow Road. To John Roberts, 22 April.

It was very good of you to have phoned the College Secretary asking her to give me the sad news of dear John's death. I got her note Saturday morning just as I was leaving for London for a tour of pubs with Nicky, my eldest. I was to have gone to see John in February, but Jean rang up the day before saying he was too ill to see anyone, so, in the end, I did not get to see him. In the autumn he wrote me such a brave letter, how he was using all the time remaining to him to re-read all the great Russian classics. I can see so clearly that impressive leonine profile and the floppy beret. He was the nicest of all Francophils and would have so much loved to have been made Director of the British Institute in Paris, he would also have loved a bit of recognition from the French, the red ribbon and that sort of thing. Anyhow, the Dutch did the right thing by him: Commander of the Order of Orange Nassau ('I am now a Coon' he wrote to tell me.) He left the Order in a bus in Amsterdam, the efficient Dutch police retrieved it for him. What an UNSELFISH man he was, always doing things for other people, so that he never really got his own work done. I remember how he used to wheel out Richard Pares to see the cricket in the Parks. In Marseille he got to know, through Guiral, a French surgeon, Dr Caustre, who was hospitable to him. Some time later he learnt that the surgeon's eldest son had been killed potholing. He took the plane to Marseille to attend his funeral. Typical. He was a man who made splendid gestures. You must be very sad. I am, though in a way the news comes almost as a relief, he must have had so much pain.

How is Jean going to cope? I gather she is in a pretty poor state herself. Oh yes, are you doing an obituary for <u>The Times</u>? I do hope you do, no one could do it better I don't think JSB was ever in <u>Who's</u>

<u>Who</u> for some reason, so I do not even know his dates, I know that he came from Bedford and that he was at school there, and that his mother lived to a great old age. I don't know whether he was an only child. I must write & tell Mme Meuvret and Bert Goodwin. Do let me know about the Memorial Service. Will it be in Keble? I'll be away in Paris from 28 MAY to 6 June, otherwise here all the time. I hope you give the Address.

Did Mark tell you I had PREACHED at Eton?

I have a copy of my new book for you; I'll give it to you when I see you. It is about Merton, among other subjects. John Carey tells me that the tiny College next door is getting Keith Thomas as its next President. I much look forward to seeing you & Judith installed in Merton Street. Robert and others very much hope that you will make Merton less <u>Whiggish</u> and more pleasure-loving, MORE WINE, MORE BRANDY, later Guest Nights etc.

The new French Ambassador has just written to say that <u>I</u> have the <u>ruban rouge</u> as a Chevalier. So I call myself LE VIEUX CHEVALIER.

On 13 May he wrote to Tim Hilton and his first wife, Alexandra, apologising for a no-show the previous day. He had been up until the small hours in Cambridge after giving a paper at Sidney Sussex and although sticking to wine, unlike other drinkers, he woke feeling fragile and then drank too much Abbots Special ('ALWAYS fatal'). The rest of the letter concerns arrangements for a future meeting together with chance sightings of mutual acquaintances but in his PS he wrote:

I have just read a WONDERFUL novel, <u>Place des Angoisses</u>, by Jean Reverzy, set in Lyon, all about the doctors of the Place Bellecour, it was given me by a Lyonnais who liked my little piece about his city, now out in translation, <u>les tours de france de monsieur cobb</u> (sorbier) which has had a rave review in <u>L'Express</u>. I do like the French hostility to Capital letters, I ALWAYS call it <u>le comité de salut public</u>, you MUST read this marvellous medical novel, it's GREAT.

On 1 July he wrote to Richard Ingrams, inviting him to a party to celebrate his ruban rouge in the Balliol Fellows' Garden: 'It would be lovely if you could come, even if only for the Perrier,' he wrote referring to Ingrams's abstinence and sneering at the mineral water company's claims about the natural effervescence of their product. 'My FOOT. They run currents through it.'

He was still fulminating away about the awfulness of cricket, complaining that at Shrewsbury the previous weekend there were 'FOUR cricket matches going on, some 50 Flannelled Fools. Or <u>would</u> it be 100? How many are there on each side? Fifteen? A deeply depressing sight.'

He had also been to Paris and was irritated when, as the Folkestone train was about to leave Victoria, 'a disagreeable voice announced: "There will be NO buffet car on this train. That means there will be nothing to eat or drink on this train." And he then repeated the announcement twice more, with a gloat. Good old BR!'

On Sunday 21 July 1985 he wrote to Hugo Brunner:

Guess whom I met at the <u>Spectator</u> party Thursday last? Yes, you have it, the redoubtable lady herself, surrounded by a frightened group of sycophants. She had dangerous, remorseless eyes, those of a <u>mafiosa</u> (if that goes into the feminine). I told her I'd called on Tracey on my way, next time, she said, why did I not call on HER? Not bloody likely. I also met Woodrow Wyatt, VERY nice, an old Worcester man. And Richard Ingrams plus Lovely Daughter and hosts and hosts of others.

Good old Claire (and Sean) see Summer reading in today's ST. I have written to thank her. I have also had a rave letter, headed 'Fan Mail' via Balliol, from All Souls. ALR, no less! He has greatly enjoyed my 2 Chatters, F and D and <u>Promenades.</u> Gosh! He does not exactly hand out testimonials (save to himself). I can see I'll have to visit him at the mansion near St Austell. Actually, I quite LIKE him, he adores CATS.

Have a good time in the CH.

The 'redoubtable lady' was, of course, Mrs Thatcher. Woodrow Wyatt was the original champagne socialist, a bon viveur and millionaire.

On 16 August he wrote to David Gilmour, who had just moved house – and country. He was still greatly exercised about this. He had, unsurprisingly, no idea of where 'Lothian' was, described Scotland as 'The Outer Islands' and was concerned for Gilmour's survival there.

You will have to make a close study of the natives. Can you understand them? I have had a picture pc from a place called Auchtermuchty or something, anyhow the seat of Laird Angus McIntyre. There are a whole lot of refugees from Oxford staying with him up there. But you are MILES & MILES from White's. You'll have to come back. Is James Douglas-Hamilton a neighbour? I would not know, having no idea of Scottish geography, it is a country that looks as if it been torn out of a paper. I hope it is not TOO gloomy and dour.

1986

At the beginning of the year, on Twelfth Night, he wrote to David Gilmour, rejoicing in the fact that the previous year he had two new books published in English, two in translation and had been praised by 'the most improbable people viz. Julian Critchley and Gerald Kaufman', and was writing a new column for the Times Higher Education Supplement, mainly positive but about to go darkly negative with one or two articles devoted to those he had hated, who would be mainly Irish save for the usual suspects.

I greatly enjoyed and admired your book on Spain reading it in the Spring, as we were supposed to be going to Madrid & Barcelona (by train) at Easter but then I went down with a vicious bout of pneumonia, as bad as the spot on the lung I had in 1939, and, in the end, we went to Lyme Regis instead, a bit of a come-down. We NEARLY bought a cottage in Whitby in September – I am a North Sea enthusiast too – but were put off by the surveyor's report, so for the moment we won't be moving to North Yorks, but we'll be having another prospection there this summer.

*Apropos of strange places he told Gilmour that his original read-
ing of The Leopard was in a French translation while ...*

... stuck much of the day in a pretty grim hotel in Sofia, Boulevard
Russki, waiting much of the day for a phone call from a beautiful
Bulgar (female) who had VERY long eyelashes. My bedroom had a
view of the hideous building of the Central Committee. I got myself
drunk on rose brandy, with the result that my hands, indeed the
whole of me, started sweating Attar of Roses, the whole room was
impregnated. And EUROPE, I mean civilised Europe, seemed miles
and miles away, and I went into a great sort of Italianate nostalgia. I
DO NOT RECOMMEND THE BALKANS. But Maria Peneva WAS rather
beautiful. All this happened before I turned up, chastened, in Balliol.

*On 19 January he wrote to Heald saying that he had just written
an encomium on his behalf for the Senior Tutor at Balliol. The college was looking for some sort of Creative Artist in Residence.*

I have just written proving that you were – like your referee – a
Creative Artist. I also said that, again, like your referee, you were not
exactly weighted down with gravitas, being, on the contrary, very
buoyant, even in rough waters. I pointed out that we both write
detective stories, I mentioned that you were known in Balliol as Il
Yokello di Dorset and that you were in fact a Dorset Imperialist.
I affirmed that you could – and had – put your mind to the most
varied subjects – Real Tennis, Travel, the Army, Schools, etc. etc. etc.
– save perhaps Theology and Philosophy. My enthusiasm was so
unbounded that I think they simply MUST take you. Damn. I have
sealed it up now, I forgot your nimbleness as a karate expert. Never
mind. Lightness of touch runs right through my piece.

   I think it might help your candidature if (1) you grew a beard, (2)
wore sandals, (3) wore CND, AA, Greenpeace badges in both lapels,
(4) insisted on having a nut omelette cooked for you, (5) avoided the
compromising company of Maurice and myself. You would have to
talk about the Third World, Oxfam and Mandela, etc.

Heald did not get the job.

To Trevor-Roper, 10 February.

Please forgive me for having been such an APPALLING correspondent, and that over a matter not of months, but of years. I am
sure I have excuses but I cannot remember what they are: writing too many books, answering too many letters from residents
or former residents of Tunbridge Wells, dealing with indignant
Salopians, writing in fellow sympathy to Julian Critchley after we
had both been CANED by a silly man called Charlesworth in a
rotten journal called the Salopian Newsletter read I suppose by
vieux salopards, singled out by the LORD HIGH CHANCELLOR for
having written a book that is 'readable and unedifying'. GEORGE
tells me I am not in Total Disgrace, and I am about to remedy the
situation by presenting Xandra and you with two of my (disgraceful) books. As I can never POST a book, I'll take the bus and deliver
them through the letter-box of your Lodgings. I dare not show my
face in your College, because my PERSON (personne physique as
they say in French legal language when they hand one a warrant)
is in dire danger there. I must tell you what happened. Last week
I went, in all innocence, to give a talk about Maupassant to the
Boys at Eton. All went well till after the talk. Then several of the
Masters (Beaks in local patois) went back to where I was to stay for
the night. A bachelor establishment called innocently (and HOW
I was deceived) the Corner House, almost under the very gaze of
the Blessed and Benevolent Henry. Indeed, I could feel the protec-
tion afforded by the near presence of that Best of Monarchs. Fool,
fool! We sat drinking some Hun wine, then my hosts left one after
another, and I was left with a young Master, quite a good looking
young man, too, who had stayed some time previously in Tunbridge
Wells. It seems that there had been a Public Reading of one of my
innocent works called A Sense of Place, and the young man concluded that j'en étais. Nothing could have been more untrue. I fear
I suffer very much in a more conventional direction. Anyhow, left
alone with him in the Corner House, he insisted on KISSING me
goodnight, something I had been spared even when M. Jacques
Viot gave me my croix though I had then been kissed by a redoubtable moustached Greek lady, now French, the Rector of ALL the
Universities of Paris. You can imagine WHAT a relief it was to get

back into my Guest Room and slip the lock! The young man turned up at breakfast the next morning in a silk dressing-gown. Later I told my host what had happened, well, NOTHING, mercifully, HAD happened. But I had felt the dangerous smoke of Petrodrovecsian Sin all too close. It is not the sort of thing that should have happened to me at any time, much less at my present advanced age and confirmed status of Respectability. I am not sure that I DARE move East, even to drop the books through your door, they might be lying in wait for me opposite, the other side of Trumpington Street. What AM I to do? Please advise me. I thought I was so impeccably respectable.

Anyhow, what HAS been happening in that place opposite? George told me you had scoured the stables and that the Wicked had been CHASTISED.

I glimpsed James in Merton chapel on Saturday. A service for Michael Wallace-Hadrill, an address by Dick Southern of which I could hear only a few words, the acoustics were so bad.

Next year DV – if I REACH it – we go for five months to South Carolina. I have never visited the Deep South. It seems a unique opportunity to get an Honorary DD, which I thoroughly DESERVE, though I do not want one from Runcie.

Woe Woe! What a world of Sin! I shall have to go to Bayham for an elevating week-end with Michael Pratt.

Oh yes, I am SO glad you liked Paul Slack's book. I had a great struggle to get him elected to a Research Fellowship at Balliol some years back. Christopher Hill said he was only interested in counting corpses – just what I do in one of my books – and the others too wanted to elect a GHASTLY man (now, I'm glad to say, in KING'S CAMBRIDGE). I had to send a telegram summoning Maurice Keen out of the fleshpots of the Oyster Bar in Cork. We won the day by a majority of one.

I am supposed to be retired, but I seem to lecture as much as ever. What IS sheer bliss is to miss Faculty Board and College Meetings.

I have been invited to Foreign Parts, to give talks in Edinburgh and Glasgow for the 40th anniversary of the Institut Français d'Ecosse. I shall take the opportunity to look up my old pupil

141

James Douglas-Hamilton. David Gilmour also lives somewhere up there, in West Lothian, but I don't know where West Lothian IS.

Do you think I'll be SAFE in South Carolina? I'll have Margaret and William with me, of course. Anyhow, it is a VERY long way from Peterhouse.

Many many greetings to Xandra. George will soon be a Colonel, CHARLES (the son of Electric Whiskers of Trinity) already IS one, as well as being Commandant of the Greenjackets.

I must stop. My two pints of Guinness at the local await me.

PS I have read in translation a book about Speer by Matthias Something. What a crafty devil the fellow was.

The book on Speer which Cobb had been reading must have been 'Albert Speer, das Ende eines Mythos' by Matthias Schmidt. Trevor-Roper had read it some years earlier and felt the author 'spoils his case by overdoing it'. In his seven-page letter of reply Trevor-Roper goes on at some length about the iniquities of his opponents in college and reports mischievously that everyone on the spot in Cambridge is merely a cipher for the sinister Professor Vincent of Bristol, who is really the spider at the centre of the web. It is he, not the Master, nor the Fellows of Peterhouse, who really pulls the strings. Actually Trevor-Roper seems to think that he is victorious but he is nervous of seeming complacent.

On 28 May Cobb wrote to Michael Hodges from Wolvercote and thanked him for a card from Venice. 'I have never been there. Should I go there? At least it must be fairly empty of Americans just now. I haven't been to Italy for over twenty years. I don't MIND the place, but they eat so few potatoes, and I cannot bear a potatoless meal.'

On 7 March he wrote to Hugo Brunner:

It is March 7th, my father's birthday, & you must be in Hong Kong, having delicious Chinese food – possibly even DOG done very tastily with pineapple – and seeing what must be quite an amazingly crowded place. I had to put off Joseph Hone for lunch, a couple of days ago I had to hand in my lower dentures, and had been existing on scrambled egg and baked beans. But I did in fact get them back yesterday evening. Anyhow, he'll be coming some time in April. And I shall look forward to seeing you at Balliol Buttery today week at 12.45. I enclose my fifteenth piece ROSES ALL THE WAY, for the THES, a slight foretaste of Sofia plus Vienna Two. I shall do a sixteenth, on a nice German-Swiss called Alfred Rufer, next week.

I had nice letters from Jeremy and from Christine. Frank Norman can wait for the moment. Christine says Carmen LIKED Rebecca West, well that fits, Monster to Monster, etc.

The current number of Private Eye has the story of the Eton Kiss. I hope it won't make me unpopular in that community. Of course I suppose Richard was bound to use it, once I had told him. I had a letter from Maurice Keen today, he says he had never been kissed on trips to Public Schools, but once had his bottom pinched, I think at his old school, Winchester. Ah well.

On the day before Waterloo Day he wrote again to Michael Hodges to confirm a lunch at Brooks's and enclosed a card asking Hodges whether he had ever been to the scene depicted. 'Some of the entirely GHASTLY Mitfords are buried in the churchyard, but you don't have to look at them.'

On 11 April he wrote to Blair Worden. 'The French have given me the RUBAN ROUGE. I am very bucked, I'll wear it on EVERYTHING. I had a letter from M. Viot, the new Ambassador.' The letter was signed, with much love 'The Old Chevalier'.

On 24 April he wrote again to Worden:

John Carey did not really get the point; he does not understand – nor I suspect, approve of – Public School Boys, their essential frivolity and their taste for hoaxes. Still, as Professor of English he must have read Cranford and there is a VERY frivolous and rather characteristic Salopian in that – a more convincing one, I feel, than the rather unbelievable hero of A Tale of Two Cities. I think John is a bit of a Puritan (like a good many of the Fellows of my old College).

On 3 May, Cobb wrote to thank Richard Ingrams for his enthusiastic review of 'A Classical Education'. 'WONDERFUL. SUPERB piece.' The title was his own idea of 'a sick joke' and was based on Edward Ball's first remark to him when he arrived at the barrier of the Gare Saint-Lazare in Paris. Beryl Bainbridge had also praised the book in print, unlike the Telegraph reviewer, who complained that it made him sick. Cobb's comment was that in that case he must have 'a very disturbed stomach'.

'The day after the glorious first of June', Cobb wrote to express his disapproval of a book Heald had just published about cricket grounds in Britain. 'I thought it was Cricketer who went for all the Cardus stuff. It was quite a shock to discover that you too were a cricketophil.' He recalled turning his deckchair away from the wicket whenever his father took him to Maidstone or Canterbury and opined that the beastliness of the game was so quintessentially English that it would survive even under a left-wing dictatorship. It was as incomprehensible as the English love of dogs. 'I have been bitten eighteen times to date, the first time in the High Street, Tunbridge Wells.'

On 2 October, on new rather smart printed Godstow Road paper, he typed to Heald, 'This is getting ridiculous, there must be a Conspiracy, Cricketer and you taking over the entire Book Page of the Times! You are both quite dotty about that boring game.' He was very worried that Labour might get in, provoking a civil war and possibly even forcing him to stay in South Carolina, which he was about to go as a Visiting Fellow. He thought Mrs Thatcher a good thing, unlike the publisher, Anthony Cheetham, who had been attracting hostile publicity. 'I think he equals, in my Hate Category, S.K. Holland and Martin Walker.'

On 19 September he wrote from Wolvercote to Bernard Wasserstein thanking him for his letter sent just over a week earlier. Cobb had news of Wasserstein's brother David, who had evidently taken to hiding behind a red beard:

My successor has been spending the Summer either in Pest or in Buda, I suppose brushing up his Magyar. I met Maurice the other day at lunch in Balliol. He had an amazing Pole from Cracow in tow, the Pole was a mediaevalist working on the Teutonic Knights. Maurice seemed to know all about them.

I thought you would like a portrait of your old friend 'Bomber' Harris. The GPO is currently doing a series of RAF types including Dowding, a Spiritualist, who used to communicate with those who had Passed On from his huge house in Calverley Park, Tunbridge Wells. I am glad you went to the Spa. I used to take dancing lessons there with the idiot son of Austen Chamberlain who had a tongue that hung out.

On 1 October 1986 he wrote to Richard Ingrams and wondered, by the by, whether or not Ingrams knew a place called Etchingham:

My uncle, a Chelsea GP, had a cottage there in the 30s. He had a virulent – and admirable – loathing for his neighbour, Rudyard Kipling, and delighted me as a schoolboy by telling me of a scene at Etchingham Station when Kipling tried to jump the queue to buy a First Class Return to London. 'I know you are Mr Rudyard Kipling', says the ticket man, 'but you can wait your turn like everyone else', my uncle chiming in with 'Hear, Hear'.

Harold Macmillan, Chancellor of the University, died that year. Oxford Chancellors, like Popes, reign until death and their successors are elected in a process almost as arcane, by an electoral college composed of as many of the University's Masters of Arts as turn up on the elected day or submit their votes by post. The two most likely successors were two other Balliol politicians, Roy Jenkins and Edward Heath.

1987

Cobb wrote to Blair Worden at St Edmund Hall on 10 January. The letter was typed on pink paper which, apparently, had no significance and was part of a gift which Cobb was attempting to use up.

There were attempts to put his name up for the Chancellorship but Cobb would have none of it.

No golden robes for me. I would go for (i) Carrington, (ii) an intelligent DUKE – there must be one or two – or even an EARL, (iii) the King of Spain (the beadles and marshals of the Back Bar of the King's Arms are in favour), (iv) an American millionaire. I have strong NEGATIVE views: no politician, above all not the BORING HEATH. Our friend Hugh would be fun, but as Isaiah says, his candidature would be killed stone dead. Anyhow, I hope it all leads to a lot of fun and not too much rancour.

In South Carolina for five months he was homesick and wrote to Blair Worden in mid-February telling him so and disparaging his students at Chapel Hill for their liking for 'CANT' and their love of 'Moral Issues'. 'Oh for a bit of cynicism,' he laments. 'There are car stickers: "I (heart symbol) Soweto" (Oh do you? Well I've <u>*been*</u> *there & don't, it's a dump). I took a pro-Botha line with my graduate class, they were* <u>*stunned*</u>*. Still people* <u>*are*</u> *friendly & I like this place better than the jungle of NYC or the* <u>*massive*</u> *bureaucratic architecture of Washington.' He found the presence of the American Army and Navy reassuring and he was glad to be in a city where Kinnock and his Labour colleagues in Britain were not news: 'My girl students are FAT & wear lilac socks. The boys are fat too & wear basketball boots. M. keeps on thinking we are back in Johannesburg (where at least the girl students, mostly Jewish, were elegant, slim &* <u>*not*</u> *in lilac socks). Still I feel* <u>*safer*</u> *here than in SA.'*

Lectures, however, were, alas, intellectually and academically unstimulating. 'More or less 5th Form stuff,' he wrote, disparagingly, 'with much use of the blackboard.'

On 7 April he wrote from Columbia to Hugo Brunner. 'In my mail sent on by Worcester & reaching me today a sad little note signed "Naseby" (?) from Deal telling me of the death of Edward Ball on 29th January. I feel <u>*sad.*</u> *The end of a* <u>*long*</u> *chapter in my life. Please tell Richard I. next time you see him.'*

At the beginning of July, Cobb, adapting himself to Jeremy Lewis' persona, wrote of a weekend spent mainly at the International Bar in Dublin in 1960. 'The Bar seemed to be entirely full of braying young men from Lancing and Sutton Valence, just the sort of

146

schools that had at an earlier time filled the ranks of the Black and Tans. I expect there were plenty of OS bloodies there too. Shrewbury used to be much favoured by the lesser Ascendancy families, after all, it IS the nearest major Public School to Holyhead.' He had, in Lewis fashion, met a man in an Oxford club who introduced himself as 'Scruffy': Cobb maintained that 'he was wearing two overcoats, both of them heavily stained, one on top of the other, as though he had given each a turn for lying in a gutter off the Four Courts.'

He was grateful to Lewis for making him laugh with his book of self-deprecating, accident-prone memoirs. 'I detect in you', he surmised, 'a fellow-sufferer from the Malevolence of Objects. On entering the Army I managed to break, in several pieces, an object I was supposed to assemble, and which after I had broken it up into little bent bits, I was told had been a bicycle pump. I scored the lowest mark available. My life has been a 70 year war with objects.'

Cobb was appalled to learn that Lewis had been educated at Malvern. 'Indeed an AWFUL school, all the more so because my AWFUL cousin, Jack Deed, who played cricket for Kent, a Gentleman of course, not only went there but was for years a Governor of the place.' Deed had 99 innings for Kent between 1924 and 1930, scoring 1863 runs at an average of 22.72. 'I once gave a talk there and stayed with a rather gloomy housemaster, a historian from Wadham, who gave me HORREUR muesli for breakfast.'

Five days later, on 20 July, he wrote to Lewis adding a thought on teachers:

Schoolmasters live for ever. In today's THE TIMES, there is an obit of Dr Grundy, poor fellow; back in the 30s, he endeavoured, in vain, to teach me German. We called him 'Hitler', a bit unfair, he smoked a pipe, which Adolf didn't, but he DID have a moustache.

Someone should write a book about BAD Public Schools.

On the same day, 20 July, he sent Worden a typewritten letter thanking him for his annual party which he described as 'SUPERB'. He *enjoyed meeting A.N. Wilson 'looking as always rather <u>louche</u>'. He would have stayed longer but had he done so he thought he would have fallen off his bike on the way home.*

To Trevor-Roper, 28 July.

I have had indirect news of Xandra and you both from Blair and Mad Morpeth, and more direct news from James. So I know that you are still in the Fens, and that you have acquired a house in Didcot (not, I hope, with a view of the Power Station?). I am very glad you are returning to the Thames Valley (though the Cam is MUCH healthier) and it will be nice to see you both again. At the moment I am engaged in clearing out my room in Worcester. I think I'll be giving most of my History books to Balliol. I don't think I'll be writing much more History apart from a little squib for the OUP entitled <u>The Irrelevance of the French Revolution</u> to come out in 89. At the moment I am writing some more autobiographical pieces for John Murray. I am a bit cross with George for having written that letter to <u>The Times</u>, it could have been damaging to Mrs T (whom I quite admire) and he must be QUITE mad standing as a Liberal in Easington; what is more he appears to be LIVING in Easington.

I was in Tunbridge Wells twice recently and heard many stories about your old favourite, Michael Pratt, and his dislike of ever PAYING for anything.

Last week I had my obituarist, Philip Mansel, to lunch in Balliol. He told me he was doing both you and me for the <u>Independent</u>. I did point out that there was every possibility that we both might outlive the <u>Independent</u>.

In what state have you left Peterhouse? What of the Baron, the Cardinal, Croft, et al? How are they all going to be under the reign of the Blessed Henry?

I have a second Dupuytren, my right hand is closing up again. Fortunately, I am left-handed. But I don't know how I am going to manage buttons, ties, shoelaces, etc.

I had hoped to see Xandra and you at Blair's superb party. Alas, no luck.

Dr Hill, according to rumour, is down among the Aussies.

I spent a semester, from January to May, at Columbia, South Carolina, an experience I much enjoyed, though my first year pupils were quite MASSIVELY ignorant, including a contingent of close-cropped US Marines. The South has a strong military tradition, there are <u>ten</u> war memorials in the grounds of the State House, some of them to wars I had never heard of, including one in 1847 between the US and Mexico. We went to Atlanta for a conference; in the Greater Atlanta telephone book (Southern Bell) there are 283 Cobbs, including one, a black lady I reckon, called Magnolia. North Atlanta and Marietta are in Cobb County. In SC I got on quite well with the elusive Herzstein. I very much liked Charleston and Savannah. All in all, a pleasant trip. I had not eaten shark before.

On my return I became SEVENTY. I find it MUCH more distinguished than being 69. I even had a birthday party.

My pupil, Edward Mortimer, was invited by SE M du Machin de la Chose des Portavions to the French Embassy for the Bastille Day party. But I was <u>not</u> invited. Perhaps my fault was having got my red ribbon from his predecessor, Jacques Viot. So I feel sulky. Not that 14 July is something to CELEBRATE.

James and My Successor are both keen that I should meet Princess Margaret, I am not sure why, they seem to think she likes Salopians. I think My Successor has the matter in hand. He does not seem to get on awfully well with Your Successor.

If I had been here for the Chancellor Election, I would have voted for Robert Blake. I asked Blair to put me on his list, but he wouldn't. Anyhow, my ONE concern was to keep out Heath.

Warmest greetings to Xandra. Will you both be missing Cambridge?

PS I have asked Peter Fraser, the Acting Warden of All Souls, to send you a copy of my Address at Robert Shackleton's Memorial Service last December. I had never greatly liked RS in his lifetime, but, going through his notebooks etc. with Taylor's Librarian, and talking to old BNC people, including my young cousin, John Cobb, a doctor, I started feeling quite warm towards him. He was such a LONELY man and there was something rather engaging about his craving for honours, gongs, medals, sashes, gowns, dinners etc. It was an extraordinary occasion, certainly the only time in my life I am ever likely to speak from the pulpit in the presence of the Archbishop of Canterbury! Blair told me you had not had a copy. I was away in the Deep South when they were sent out by All Souls.

Shouldn't Robin Briggs be VC of Essex (the only University at which I have an Hon. Degree)? Can't you tell them to take him on, he is very much a LOCAL?

On the same day, 28 July, Cobb wrote to Lewis beginning with more news about Lewis's book which he had been reading to a blind friend on the south coast. Unfortunately the Independent had given it to someone else for review and he was trying Auberon Waugh at the Literary Review instead. Failing Waugh he intended to ask Richard Ingrams at Private Eye. While on the coast he had made observations.

Some Dutch engineers – a good choice – are building some vast sea wall to protect Seaford and Bishopstone from the angry elements. Apparently both places face WEST and get the full blast of the westerly gales. I thought how beautiful Seaford, was looking out on that lovely golf course in the fold of the Downs, lovely that is save for all the silly golfers dragging their little wheeled toys behind them. Surely that must be the SILLIEST of all games. Seaford seemed to be crammed with noisy Italian teenagers shrieking like parrots.

I have been having a most bizarre correspondence with a Mrs Moon, of Dorking (Surrey). Her father was hanged in Strangeways in 1936, after murdering his wife (her mother) and the nanny. That makes it a very middle-class sort of murder I reckon. She had been reading my little book about Edward.

Only a day later, on 29 July 1987, Cobb wrote to Lewis with more thoughts on the malevolence of objects.

The last time I travelled TWA, my supper, encased in some sort of steel mesh, ended upside down in the lap of my neighbour, an

American lady who was very nice about it as she dabbed the remains of Chicken à la King from her beige corduroy skirt. Indeed I have NEVER managed to penetrate the containers airlines encase their food in.

Early this morning, as I was getting out of bed, three shelves of books slowly and quite deliberately threw themselves on the floor. How I felt for Anthony Eden's father, when, on a day of pouring rain & hoping to hunt, when the glass had pointed boldly to FAIR, he picked up the bloody OBJECT and threw it down the steps, shouting, TAKE THAT YOU FOOL. I could go on about typewriter ribbons, spools etc. How right French is to favour the reflexive: les lacets se delacent. MY shoelaces UNDO THEMSELVES at least six times a day, choosing their moments with care, eg, on returning from Seaford, on a crowded escalator in Victoria, BOTH lots, perfect timing. I can sympathise with your encounter with the curling film on the steps of the bus, I know ALL about that sort of thing, furthermore, having no hips, I am constantly having to hoist up my trousers, while the shirt comes out in the front, life in short is one long STRUGGLE. Naturally when I went in to the Palace for the State Banquet for Giscard, my white tie had to fall off into my consommé. This year I spent five months pushing American doors that you had to pull. So I DEEPLY SYMPATHISE and KNOW ALL ABOUT IT.

On 13 August he wrote to Lewis, using a typewriter ribbon so faint that it was barely legible. The reason was terror of another losing fight against the inanimate. He didn't dare change it, having as he put it 'been through that sort of thing before'. He had also had an unpleasant skirmish with a publisher's wrapping: 'Thames and Hudson sent me a picture book yesterday. I went at the wrapping with a sharp knife, horrible grey stuff fell out all over the floor, and the book itself still remained inviolate. Some sort of a JIFFY bag, the latest horror in OBJECTS.'

Three days later, on 16 August, he wrote to Lewis again. The typing is much more legible and it emerges that he had fought a successful battle with the machine. 'I am quite LIMP and have palpitations, the result of changing the ribbon on my new typewriter, one of cunningly fiendish construction. It took me 2½ hours to carry it through, I had to lie down to calm down. So one soldiers on. I once threw a typewriter downstairs, and the damned thing had the cheek to survive.'

On 22 August he wrote to Lewis again, still enthusing over his book and another by Ruth Dudley-Edwards:

VERY good on the sinister Pearse. The father was a church stone-mason from Birmingham, Charlie Burgess (Cathal Brugha) was a Yorkshire commercial traveller. The semi-demis are ALWAYS the most fanatical, some sort of historical law. The PNB, the pro-Nazi Breton collaborationist party, was made up largely of <u>Gallos</u>, that is French-speakers, many of them not even Bretons, who had made a point of learning Breton in their twenties (a bit like the Liverpudlian Saunders-Lewis). Actually the only place I have ever really felt ALIEN has been in Southern Ireland. But then I am incurably ENGLISH, no Celt in me at all. I used to stay when External Examiner in the National University, in Stephen's Green Club. I remember a bedroom on the back which had a door which did not seem to lead anywhere, I opened it, at 3 am, when much the worse for wear, it opened on to a VOID, four storeys down. I closed it hastily and put a wardrobe against it, a close shave.

To Trevor-Roper, 16 September.

I am so glad that you are at last away from the <u>mafia</u>, for years & years, so it seems to me (as a regular to the Fens, to the <u>Kite</u>, & to the <u>Free Press</u>), there has been a blight on Peterhouse, perhaps it goes back to <u>Butterfield</u> (responsible, certainly for the Irish connexion), perhaps even further in time. I associate Peterhouse with one of the most destructive & quite the cleverest of Balliol undergraduate historians (I am told he knows all there is to be known about Bede), Patrick Wormald, an Etonian, whose father (not a bad chap, however) was a Fellow there. When I see you in Didcot (I hope next month) I'll tell you more about Patrick.

Maurice Cowling, who was at school with Robbie Robinson, looks like a conman (Bowra would have called him a <u>Card</u>). I have never read any of his books. There <u>is</u> a nice man – I think with a

Jewish name, & not a historian, anyhow <u>he</u> found something I had said – or written – funny, & wrote to me to say so, so I approved of him. I know, & like, young Harold James. Is he going back? I do feel <u>Merton</u> deserves a more amiable sister, though Merton itself has a Methodistical streak which I attribute to Roger Highfield, a Magdalen man, whom I have spotted, wearing a Merton blazer, finishing lunch (alone) on the terrace of <u>Au Pied de Cochon</u>, near the Odéon. Anyhow, I hope we can meet for lunch in Merton, some time next month.

I think really there is only <u>one</u> viable college in Cambridge, & that is Trinity; of course, I have been corrupted by Jack, by Avril, & by 'Electric Whiskers' (Michael Vyvyan, the father of my pupil, Charles, now a full Colonel & in the MOD & rather more popular with the PM than George).

George came to stay with us in Whitby. We are worried about him. His parents seem to have cut him off, & he lives in a world full of fantasy & good intentions. He travels light & doesn't wear pyjamas. I somehow feel he is not fully imbued with the House Spirit of W.H. Smith. What will become of him? He knows everyone (Michael Pratt included), but does that help? Yet I think, beneath all that bluster, that he is quite shrewd. He needs to be. Perhaps, in time, the advent of a Good Woman might do the trick, persuade him to wear pyjamas (in Whitby he swam in the sea, 3 times, in his pants), to buy a second suit & a second polka dot bow tie. I think he would be rather a good MP, especially in a family fief such as Hexham, quite a lot of his soldiers voted for him in Easington (I am taking the £2 bonanza offered to OAPs in November by British Rail to visit him there). His brother Philip seems to have sided with the Earl (George always refers to his father, bleakly & almost impersonally, when talking to us, as the Earl of Carlisle).

Friday I see the surgeon & will then learn the imminent fate of my right hand (I am left-handed): either another Dupuytren + skin graft, or 2 fingers amputated. (I am not keen to see these go, they've been with me ever since before the Russian Revolution, &, once <u>fingers</u> are lopped off, what next?) In my vanity I am continuing to lecture this coming term (on France 1936–45).

Blair & I are <u>equally</u> concerned that you manage to place <u>BRIGGS</u> as V/C of Wivenhoe Park; it is more than time that he left the Old Souls' Club & the Isis Valley.

I don't suppose we are likely to meet the Princess. My Successor comes & goes in a Mysterious Way. I gather he is not much in favour with <u>your</u> successor (seen only in profile on a medallion) owing to his lack of assiduity in his attendance beneath the portrait of Queen Anne.

I am relieved to learn that one can not libel the dead. Otherwise I would have been in trouble over what I wrote about a former chaplain (of popish tendencies) of Shrewsbury School.

Please give Xandra my warmest good wishes. When you are fully settled in at the Old Rectory, I would like to pay you a visit. I have never been <u>to</u> Didcot, only <u>through</u> it. As for a pub in Oxford, I find the Back Bar of the KA quite agreeable; it is frequented by retired Fellows of Merton, active Fellows of BNC, the VC's mace-bearer, the Head Porter of Merton, &, every now & then, by our good MP, the Geographer from Hertford. They have a <u>prodigious</u> range of beer, including my favourite Hook Norton. There is a trying Resident Bore, a Liberal (of course) & bearded. But, I have a louder voice than he. I am sure the ideal formula is to meet there a bit after midday & then go to Merton for lunch at one (my friend the Historian of the World who looks more & more like a Roman Senator is quite often at lunch).

Alas, I have to remove masses of books from my room in Worcester. I am giving most of them to Balliol, it is so <u>near</u>, starting tomorrow.

If I moved to the Fens, I would live <u>much</u> longer & wd make young Mansel <u>wait</u>; but Margaret won't & William starts tomorrow at a new school in Oxford, so I am deprived of the East wind & will not acquire the red & blue faces of the Girtonians (my aunts included).

PS I did not pick up a DD anywhere in SC.

On 21 September he wrote to Richard Ingrams.

We were in Wallingford last week, getting William his uniform for his new prep school in Oxford. We had lunch in the Wine Cellar place, there were two amazing old Queers with fruity voices at the nearest table, some femmies, and some left-wing spotties dressed like Andean Indians but, alas, no you, no Mary. At the shop they said you were both on holiday in Greece, or somewhere equally unpleasant (I have the DEEPEST loathing for Papandreou).

Do you realise that this May I reached 70? Yesterday, I watched myself on the Secombe programme on ITV, and thought I looked it, I also looked BENEVOLENT (which I am not).

On 24 September he typed a two-page letter to David Gilmour. He had been re-reading a piece Gilmour had written about him for the College Record. Cobb thought it 'FABULOUS' and 'VERY VERY funny'.

Meanwhile he hoped Gilmour would enjoy his next book:'It is to be published by your fellow-Scot, John Murray (Byron's publisher), next year, at the moment it is hovering between two titles, the rather feeble ELDERS & BETTERS and, as I feel, the better A PRIVATE VIEW.'

He was hoping to meet the King of the Belgians, and was contemplating a dinner party for Gilmour and his wife, Sarah.

I am in a Good Mood having finished a Second Thoughts for <u>The Independent</u> which I now read instead of <u>The Times</u>. My obituarist – also that of the Lord Dacre – for the Indie – is Philip Mansel, who went to your school, wrote a good book about my No. 2 Hero (No. 1 is the great Sir Robt. Walpole) Louis XV!!! I hope Philip does me proud. It is terrible really but in my 71st year, I <u>still</u> observe <u>with great interest</u> female anatomy.

HURRY UP AND MOVE SOUTH.

To Hugo Brunner, 27 September.

It was so nice seeing you last week with Melencholy Roger, <u>un homme qui a épousé son siècle</u> and one of my favourite Fellows of Balliol, along with Young Green (the chemist), Les Woods (of many domiciles), Jasper the Wise, and my own nice Successor, Colin (whom you may have met), indeed as nice as my Other Successor. Not to mention Maurice, though suffering a bit from being an Old

Wyk or whatever it is. I quite forgot to talk about E & B, though I am sure there are no problems. What I AM wondering now is what to do next? Shall I write up the two Vienna pieces and then see whether they would not go with my eighteen or nineteen THES pieces, of which, I think, you must have a fairly complete collection? Or shall I try them out as a small book on their own? I am now fairly free to get on with more writing, having caught up on 4 reviews, all sent off last week, though I have to read the revised version of a thesis by an NZ graduate.

I spent eight minutes as 'President' of the Wolvercote Local History Society, making I think appropriate noises, then beating a discreet retreat back to the pub. I do hope something can be done with Margaret's little ms. Anyhow, you'll be seeing her this Wednesday. She is very much looking forward to that, and I do hope you can give her some advice. By the way, please do not mention the translation of <u>A[rmées] R[évolutionnaires]</u>, she does not know about it and would not approve, any more than I do. I do <u>wish</u> John Nicoll had never come up with the idea in the first place. I feel it is a betrayal of my own effort, which was directed primarily towards a FRENCH readership. It was easier to write in French in any case. I just hope there is little publicity over the translation, it is something I hope will be little noticed. I have done absolutely nothing to promote it in any way.

I have had a nice letter from Richard Ingrams. He says why do I not invite myself to one of the Eye lunches, held on alternative Wednesdays? But how am I to know WHICH is the alternative one?

Yesterday I was walking on the towpath by the Thames at Richmond with Nicky and we were passed by an academic-looking threesome: a lady and two men; the lady said to me, when overtaking us: 'It is Professor Cobb, is it not?' I replied that I thought it was; but I have no idea who she was, save that the face seemed vaguely familiar. Nicky was impressed. I had the Baron to lunch on Friday – a bit the worse for wear, his mother having opened bottle after bottle of wine the previous evening. She does sound rather formidable.

I would be SO pleased if Penelope Lively got the Booker. I had to fight HARD to get her on our Short List in 1984.

In September he typed to Lewis with news of the death, in Teignmouth, of Olive Limbury Buse, aged 100. The moral, according to Cobb, is that one should never overdo it and generally take it easy, making a possible exception for winter sports, which were never a Cobb thing. He had spent Saturday lunch drinking in a pub in Richmond surrounded by RAF types of his own generation – 'old chaps in BLAZERS and whiskers'.

On 6 October he wrote to Lewis:'le 6 Octobre' is …

…the first volume of Jules Romain's boring and pretentious 20-volume roman fleuve, Les Hommes de bonne volonté – à ne pas lire as Le Canard used to recommend in its book reviews.

When I was a child, there was a convent school in Mayfield run by an order of French nuns, they had come over in 1905 as a result of the Law of Separation. The Mother Superior was always French, but the teaching nuns were, I think, English. Is this where your daughter goes?

He wrote to Blair Worden on 15 October. 'I'd <u>love</u> to come to dinner on 3rd November. I hope to have <u>two</u> hands by then. At the moment I only have <u>one</u>, having broken my right wrist. A minor inconvenience as I am left-handed; but I cannot type …'

Four days later he wrote, in similar vein, to David Gilmour: 'Sorry about this,' he apologised, 'but I have broken my (right) wrist so cannot type. I seem to be very breakable.' He ended his letter: 'Sorry not to write more. Difficult' and signed off with love from 'Richard (Fragile)'. He wrote to Gilmour again on All Souls' Day this time signing himself, 'Richard – Fragile, Handle with care. PS Do you want to be Headmaster of Shrewsbury? The job is going & may lead to Higher Things. Reintroduce the Birch. Have you read Alan Massie's "<u>One Night in Winter</u>", Brilliant.'

On 25 November, he wrote to David Gilmour again.

Actually I really never <u>have</u> read Proust, apart from <u>Pastiches et Mélanges</u>. If I get a long prison sentence, I might wile away the time reading him; meanwhile, I much prefer Boudard (whom I hope to see in Paris shortly). I don't like reading things that are complicated, <u>vachement intellectuels</u> or about ideas.

On 8 November he was able to write to Worden about Brunner:
'Hugo is to be the next High Sheriff of Oxfordshire. He'll have to
wear Court Dress and give lovely parties.'

To Trevor-Roper, 30 December.

I was very grateful to George for having brought us together again,
though without Xandra, at the Sorbonne, with Our Mutual Obituarist.
(I am beginning to think that I'll have to go back to <u>The Times</u>, or at
least take it with the <u>Independent</u> if I am to keep up at all with the
latest deaths, for I have not seen anywhere else an obituary of Ralph
Leigh; and indeed on the day after we met over lunch, so a neighbour
tells me, a review of mine of some awful Marxist book on the French
Revolution – a Canadian Marxist to boot, there is some General Law
which makes Canadian Whatevers more boring than any others, perhaps something to do with Maple Leaf Identity – came out on the
book page of <u>The Times</u>.) And now I have to do Dame Veronica's
essays for the same Philip Howard: alas, not nearly such an agreeable
undertaking as doing yours for Bron, and it is difficult for me to do
her without comparing her unfavourably with you. I found her much
given to ponderous statements of the self-evident, and her collection
consists largely of Occasional Pieces written during the first half of
the 1940s and that bear the unmistakeable marks of those tired, jaded
old warhorses – historical Minivers – of ABCA, BW & P, MOI, Bush
House – the Dame must surely have been underground?

Is that why she was made a Dame? Was it for War Work, contribu-
tions to the War Effort, etc? She does go on so much about Germany,
German History, Luther, etc. Please tell me when and why she was
Damed. It is bad luck on her that her collection of mostly ancient
pieces – the most recent is dated 1978 – should have come out at
much the same time as yours. You write elegantly, you are a joy to
read, she, alas, is often pretty heavy going, especially when on such
themes as History & Morals, Historical Truth, Progress, and so on. I
want to be as nice as possible about her, because I have been told
– I think you told me – that she is a nice person, I imagine, pretty
old. The ONE essay of hers I really liked was on Gibbon, but then
the subject is irresistible. How TERRIBLE most of the seventeenth
century people are! When I was seventeen, I was all inflamed for

the great Duke of Newcastle, the greatest benefactor of your most recent University, but then I got deviated into the French Revolution. Excuse this long parenthesis, this sentence has got out of control.

Our host, George, what IS to become of him? He might be a good MEP, if MEPs matter. But, as you say, what is most needed is the Good Woman. He would be quite a challenge: sleeping in his underclothes, the ancient suit, the ancient bow tie, the strange clumsy gestures. As he quotes one of the girlfriends of Our Mutual Friend, Lord Michael Pratt, of the latter, 'Michael is very nice, I like him very much; but he is rather ugly, I could not marry him,' and George would need to be taken firmly in hand, cleaned up, maybe it is too late. No, I don't think it is; after all, take my own case, I was in my mid-40s when I got married. There is still hope for George, but NOT in that ridiculous Party(ies).

I gave two of my sons book-tokens for Christmas. My eldest bought with his The Last Days of Hitler, which I thought showed both discrimination and promise (he is 24 or so). On a rather different subject, I have recently read, for Yale, in page proofs, my old pupil's marvellously entertaining book on Trebtitsh Lincoln (I think I have almost certainly spelt the first part wrong). It is a story ALMOST as extraordinary as your book on Backhouse. Indeed, there are vague parallels, for TL was, for one session, Liberal MP for Darlington, with the backing of the rather naïve cocoa millionaire Seebohm Rowntree, The author, Bernie Wasserstein, expresses his thanks to you in his life of this resourceful scoundrel. I read his proofs with the greatest pleasure: a read almost comparable to your book on the ex-Mertonian.

Which brings me to another villain, Goronwy Rees. Do you think I can write about him WITHOUT getting involved in all the spy stuff? Isaiah seems to think I cannot. At least Goronwy, unlike Wright (whom I have no wish to read), can write. If he was a Soviet agent I can only conclude that the Soviets are poor paymasters, for all the time I knew Goronwy, he was desperately short of cash, running up debts at his newsagent &ca. I found his undoubted villainy rather attractive and he had a spurious charm and a winningly liquid smile, even the very blue eyes smiled. Isaiah tells me he denounced, as a Soviet agent, Robin Zaehner ('the Prof'), the closest friend of the Rees family, who backed me (no doubt fatally) for a Senior Research Fellowship at All Souls in 1956 (I was short-listed with Frank Spooner,

Aylmer, Pears, a philosopher and Stern, an Arabist who got it, beating Spooner by a head). What a bit of luck I <u>didn't</u> get into that rarified place! I would not have liked it; and a few years later, I got to Balliol instead, and had PUPILS. But I always liked Zaehner though perhaps he was bad company for me, as he did drink an awful lot. He had a fixation, too, on one of the Directory, the boring La Révellière-Lepaux. I cannot think WHY.

Of course Cowling HATES all Public Schoolboys, he has a fixation about having been at Bishop Latimer, and is desperate to be a gentleman. I am sure he is well received at Newmarket (as a bookie which is what he looks like). Does ANYONE read his strange books? I think Peterhouse will always be an unhappy place, it seems to be built into the rather florid architecture. In future I shall avoid that end of Trumpington Street. Cambridge is full of Danger Zones, there is that awful place Caius (Gonville AND Caius) with its pepper pot and its dreary Master, Wade (who was at school with me). Actually I rather LIKE Elton, though I am not sure whether I like Thomas Cromwell; and Jack Plumb has always been civil to me. There are some nice young historians: my friend Blanning (of S[idney] S[ussex], but NOT a Puritan). Tombs, Chris Andrew, Bayly (ex-Balliol) and of course there WAS, living in Trinitarian splendour in the Zeppelin, My Successor here, accident-prone Norman.

Well, if <u>you</u> don't move to Lambeth Palace, I hope someone soon <u>does</u>. What about the London man? Is he not Sound, an Enemy of Enthusiasm? Runcie presumably cannot stay. Of course they should not retire them at 70, far too young. York, Durham and Canterbury all need to be purged. Dryden, my favourite poet, hardly the right adjective, he is the ONLY poet I have ever read (Pope excepted). I am so ignorant of that period that I had not known that he had gone over to Rome (always a bad move). Just as I gave up <u>The Times</u> to get away from Rae, I gave up <u>The Sunday Times</u> to get away from Raphael and Steiner. It is hard to know which papers to read.

In a fortnight I hope to have my Dupuytren Mark Two straightened. It is a distinguished ailment, though I have beaten Mrs T by having had it twice. Anyhow I must do as much writing as possible in the next fortnight, starting with this long overdue letter to you (I got your SECOND letter the day after our meeting at lunch). Do come to the back bar of the King's Arms, some time soon. I tend to go there on Fridays at midday, often meeting there My Successor and some of the more relaxed Fellows of BNC and Merton (my old College under the Historian of the World has become more relaxed, less austere, more pleasure-loving. I was recently in your old College and was talked to by Alban Kreilsheimer).

Some time I want to visit Xandra and you in your Rectory.

There was no intrinsic merit in writing my <u>pavé</u> originally in French, all the source material was in French, all the people were French – one or two Belgians – and much of the book was written in France, and I chose my own printer (in Gap). Still it is indeed gratifying to have SOMETHING in common with Gibbon.

New Year Greetings to Xandra and to yourself.

On the last day of the year he wrote to Lewis congratulating him on his introduction to Roy Fuller's memoir of life in a building society ('to make a Building Society sound not just interesting but enthralling is a remarkable achievement'). He had met Roy Fuller with his son, who had been a fellow judge of the Booker Prize, at a party at the American Embassy to honour Anthony Powell, to whom he had written in order to congratulate him on his Companionship of Honour, which Cobb thought should have been the Order of Merit since he was so much more deserving than 'that trendy miserabilist, Gram Grin'. He meant another Balliol novelist, Graham Greene. He was also in Margaret Drabble's new 'Oxford Companion to English Literature'. He was obviously pleased and even more so because, he thought, Hugh Trevor-Roper was also included but Christopher Hill and Eric Hobsbawm were not. He had not, himself, purchased a copy but 'looked through it once in the OUP shop'.

1988

On the first day of the year he typed a long letter to Blair Worden, starting with a celebration of the entirely fictitious news that Hugh Trevor-Roper had become Archbishop of Canterbury:

I expect we'll all be invited to that splendid place south of the river . . . he is about the best theologian going, very sound in the true eighteenth century sense, and an Enemy of Enthusiasm. I think Hugh plans to send Runcie off to the Falklands and he is purging Durham and York as a top priority. We can now look forward to sermons both erudite, elegant and SOUND. Do you think Hugh will wear lawn sleeves? I believe what actually clinched the matter with Mrs T was Hugh's very high-powered DD from that US University. I wonder what his plans are for the Dean of Peterhouse? Should there not be a Bishop of Cambridge? I really don't see why Ely should have it. That big church with the clock outside it would make a perfectly adequate Cathedral.

On 16 January he typed a letter to Bernard Wasserstein in response to a piece in The Times about Trebitsch Lincoln, the subject of Wasserstein's latest book. 'I am delighted that a bit of what I wrote about the book is to go on the front jacket. FAME. In a recent letter, Hugh TR told me how much HE had enjoyed the book, he had written to someone in Yale to say so.'

On 18 January he wrote to Hugo Brunner:

Wonderful lunch and after with Isaiah. He talked and talked. According to Isaiah, Goronwy was always so anxious to PLEASE that he would go to bed with anyone, of either sex, who showed an interest in him. Evelyn Waugh seems to have been one who did. Isaiah does not think he can have been very much use to the Russkys as a spy, probably all he retailed to them was All Souls Common Room gossip etc. of the late 30s. Anyhow, it was a most refreshing talk, and I think I can see my way to the sort of evocation of Rees (as Margie, his wife, always called him). I want to do <u>Goronwy at Plas Penglais</u> or something along those lines, possibly about 5 pages, anyhow I am going to get down to it as soon as I have got the Dame out of the way, Isaiah says I must be nice to the Dame, as she is old and fragile, so I will, though, really, all her wartime stuff was hardly worth republishing (it would be a bit like MY digging out the short stories I wrote in the 30s and early 40s).

I spent yesterday afternoon going through the papers of my Merton contemporary, the poet Christopher Lee. A huge archive, with some big literary names: Leonard Woolf, T.S. Eliot, etc. etc. I have told the daughter she really must keep the archive together in its entirety. Bodley would be the right place for it, if they would take it. It was strange reading about 3 of my own letters to Christopher, most of them about the Poles in Blackpool, some of them quite vivid. I did write an awful LOT of letters during the war years.

So that ties up <u>Elders and Betters</u>, and now to Pastures New.

Isaiah expressed concern over MY Successor. He thinks he is a bit of Goronwy and that he is not carrying out his teaching duties. Actually I saw Norman and Christine in the KA this morning, both in very good form.

Did you see that SPLENDID piece on the murderer, Sean McBride, in yesterday's <u>Sunday Telegraph</u>? Someone called Bruce Anderson, an Ulsterman, so Norman says.

Next month for Tim Heald my talk on 'Murderers I Have Known'.

On 28 January, hand evidently restored, he typed immaculately to Worden about Christopher Hill:

Christopher has always been an OPERATOR. He is DEVIOUS and, as Master, worked through Secret Committees, so that the Governing Body was largely disenfranchised. Very soon after his election, he distanced himself from his principal electors (who included Maurice and myself). I don't think he was very much good as a tutor, he never SAID anything, but his pupils were terrified of his long SILENCES, as hunched up in his huge black leather armchair, he looked at them aesthetically and inscrutably through his half-closed lids (hence the nickname Ghengiz Khan given him by Jack and myself). I think in fact he is a very SHY man who hides himself behind <u>enceinte</u> after <u>enceinte</u> of irony.

C. Hill is not really MY sort of historian. He has IDEAS and he does not really like ARCHIVES, his only book based on archival sources (those of Hugh's about-to-be official residence) was the one on Church finances. Of Collinson he commented, when we were electing his successor, that he 'only knew about ecclesiastical history', to which I replied that history was rather important under Elizabeth. Maurice didn't really want Collinson. I think the Earl was right: there is room for <u>both</u> the proto-Archbishop AND for someone who knows all about Warwickshire (or Kent, or Essex). Of course I simply LOVE archives.

Like many orthodox Commies Christopher has been pretty hierarchical. When I first went to Balliol there was an Inner Circle of huge red leather armchairs, six or eight of them, the resting places of the more senior Fellows. Christopher occupied one of them. Young folk like Maurice and myself were expected to sit on the periphery. It was all a bit like l'Association Marc Bloch of Paris, presided over by Braudel, with Etienne Bloch on his right (<u>pour faire parler les morts</u>, he was the murdered historian's nephew), the <u>professors</u> sat round an oblong table, those of second rank stood behind, ready with the blotting paper, the non-believers were allowed to sit against the wall on uncomfortable gilded chairs, like wallflowers at a dance in the Spa Hotel, Tunbridge Wells. Christopher HATED pleasure. He was in every way a bad Master. In the end I don't even think he enjoyed the deviousness of power. He gave up early. He was pretty hopeless with Old Members and much disliked having to go to the US and Canada, though he seems to have had a soft spot for Strylia (his great friend Streeton was, is, at Adelaide). I was left to deal with the Balliol contingent of S Africa, most of them VERY rich.

In another letter to Worden dated 15 February he explained that Hugh Stretton, by then a Professor at Adelaide, was the only person reputed to have broken down at least three of the barricades Hill was reputed to have erected around his inner self. On 27 March he wrote to Worden again to tell him that his stitches had been successfully removed so that he had two serviceable hands, and ten fingers, two of them 'still very far from straight'. He had also made the speech at the Merton College Gaudy and commented: 'I thought those members of "My Class" looked decidedly antique. Perhaps I did to them. Still, I made them laugh and, furthermore, avoided ALL reference to the Sister College.'

To Trevor-Roper, 7 February.

On the subject of the resident of Easington. I was ironing yesterday at tea-time – I LIKE ironing, find it soothing and conducive to inspired thought while standing up, in fact I do ALL the ironing for our household, there is some sort of mathematical law that I have discovered: the smaller the person, the more the ironing, William 7¾ has twenty times more clothes than I – anyhow there I was ironing, facing the street. All at once I see a well-known figure in the middle of the road, bow tie blowing in the breeze. In bursts George. Straight from Romford (his present residence, rather worse, I would have thought, than Easington) where he is following a course on How To Sell Life Insurance Policies. He was clutching a rather muddy-looking, much-fingered folder which he told me contained a series of dog-eared Courses on how to do it. This, he explained, was just a matter of filling in till he becomes (one) an MEP and (two) an MP. He seems to be in no doubt that (two) would in due course follow (one). How to sell life is two days a week; three days a week, there is some parallel training, but he did not actually get to that subject, having suddenly swerved onto that, always inexhaustible, of mauve-faced MICHAEL [Pratt], Camden's Boy, the grouse moor marksman. George had recently been to the Lordly Residence of Bayham, and had been taken off to Divine Service at the church dedicated to your friend, Ye Martyr. They arrived late, in a small, noisy group, Michael scattering footstools and hymn books before, with difficulty, inserting himself in a pew near the back. The whole congregation turned round to watch the arrival of Lord Michael plus female entourage. Later I took George to the Snug of my pub, frequented mostly by the workers in the paper mill. His presence created a sensation; he was in the middle of telling me how young Lord Dalkeith (I think) was summoned by Lord Stamfordham to meet the King, sharp at 12.29 am. There then followed a very remarkable imitation of the King's somewhat Germanic accent: 'The Princess Mary iss ferry beautiful . . . etc.', ending by ordering the poor young man to marry her, which he dutifully did. The Snug was crowded. The proletarians listened to George in wide-eyed amazement, as he went on about various infidelities etc. etc. George himself was quite unaware of the sensational impact he was having on the WORKERS, male and female. They listened avidly to this loudly delivered chronicle of naughtiness in high places (and high beds). YES, indeed, he has the common touch, might even be ELECTED, but he will have to abandon the ridiculous bi-cephalous (les tigres muselés de Pitt de Cobourg, often abbreviated to pitetcobourg, in the inflated language of the Year Two, in relation to the Grand Coalition) organisation under whose variegated colours he is at present offering himself. It is a pity he CANNOT bring himself to recognise the merits of our good, if over-talkative PM. We asked him to have an Indian meal with us, he would not, having been made ill once while eating a biryani in Oman. While still in the Snug, having finished with the Princess, he gave a graphic account of his farewell encounter with his Brigadier: 'You are not fit to command a platoon . . . much less a regiment . . .' The Workers liked that, too. We last saw him heading down the middle of the road clutching his off-blue folder. Did he turn up later at Didcot?

For once Dr Hill and you are in agreement. The former has little respect for the new Earl's scholarship and told us that he was a fraud. This was when we elected Pennington. Well, of course, Merton too occasionally turns out a Monster, though obviously it cannot compete with its sister college. But what IS this about the Cardinal going off to preach the Word to young Canterbury seminarians? What IS to become of the Baron? Talking of Cambridge, I hope you have read today's Sunday Telegraph; there is an angry letter from the daughter of the late Raymond Williams referring to the Garden House business in which John Vincent was rather directly involved (so I have been told).

Michael Foot Mark One (Spy Foot) has a Dutch wife (his fifth, I think, not his fifth Dutch wife, only the first of these). Michael Foot Mark Two, the Beau Brummel of Politics, has a wife who writes under the name of Jill Craigie. I must have got her mixed up with Miss Plaidy. They both sound as if they came from the same place as Miss Brodie.

Thursday last week I gave a talk in Soho, at the Groucho Club, to the Crime Writers' Association on the subject of 'Murderers I have known' (I have, in fact, only known ten, so I suppose I was a bit of a fraud). I met there Miss Wallace, the daughter of Edgar Wallace, and was able to tell her that I had been at kindergarten, in TW, with her brother (later, she told me, killed at Cassino). On the train home I was greeted, in Scotto-Italian, by My Successor, who clearly had imbibed quite a lot and was unable to switch from Italian, even once he had dragged me off to the bar (where he introduced me to a journalist called Colin Welch, who was so drunk he was unable to speak ANY language). My Successor had been examining a UCL thesis on the Austro-Hungarian Army, and this had set him off on the Italian groove – Magyar would have been more suitable. I managed to persuade him to get out at Didcot (Dacre Junction) and mount another train, and I delivered him up to 13 Thorncliffe Road. I saw him the next day, as fit as a fiddle, in the KA. What is more he had written a letter to the TLS to the effect that I was not a philistine because I had not read Proust. Your Successor will no doubt get used to Mine in the course of time.

Can you, can Xandra imagine ANYONE who would be prepared to buy a Life Insurance Policy from that unencumbered figure in the ancient blue suit? No, I think POLITICS is the answer, also, as you say, the somewhat improbable GOOD WOMAN. George had come to see his cousin, Sandy, only to discover that Sandy is away from Univ most of this Term, looking after HIS Northumbrian estate.

I must stop. It IS Sunday, and I must give my mind to the Lambeth Succession. Warm greetings to Xandra.

I have no idea why Cobb has given his Balliol favourite, Lord Michael Pratt, capital letters. He liked Pratt, the younger son of the Marquess of Camden, which was unusual.

'The new Earl' who was disparaged by Christopher Hill was Conrad Russell, son of Bertrand the philosopher. Pennington who beat him for the vacant Balliol Fellowship was Donald Pennington. Cobb's talk to the Crime Writers was at the invitation of the present editor, who was then their Chairman. Edgar Wallace's daughter was Penny, for many years a stalwart of the organisation. Cobb, for once, behaved immaculately.

On 12 May he wrote to Wasserstein with news of the election of a new Master at Balliol. 'My Balliol spies tell me that there are three internal candidates: Jasper, Colin and Denis Noble . . . they have also looked at a number of external candidates, giving them (and themselves) stupendous meals, seven courses etc.' Cobb seemed more taken with a new image of himself as a 'COURTIER' on the grounds of sitting at dinner next to the Duchess of Kent, first cousin of his publisher and friend Hugo Brunner. A son of hers was reading History at Downing College, Cambridge, where the Master, Peter Mathias, was tutor to Prince Hirohito when he was at Cobb's former Oxford college, Merton.

On 18 May he wrote to Hugh Gough thanking him for his new book.

Philip Howard has asked me to do it for THE TIMES, which I will next week. It is a wonderful opportunity to say nice things about you. Philip is about the only good thing left amidst the ruins of that paper. I did a Diary for them but they stopped it, without telling me, after three had come out. There is an uncouth editor of the Diary page. I have denounced him to Norman Stone and to Richard Ingrams (I have dangerous friends.)

On 30 May he wrote again to Gough. 'CRASH. A cascade of papers, unanswered letters has just fallen off my table.' Of Gough's latest book he wrote:

It is quite indispensable. I had the oddest feeling every now and then of meeting old pals, eg Bias Parent, etc. But WHERE? In the end I found quite a few of them, the Nevers crowd, for instance, in my <u>Armées</u>, some more, Lebois etc., in one of my pieces in <u>Terreur et Subsistences</u>. It was the oddest sensation. I knew the Toulouse crowd fairly well. I was absolutely <u>fascinated</u> by the resourceful Robert, of Rouen: a wonderful story. By the way, was he a Belgian? I am going to give the book a rave, but it will have to be a short one, the bloody TIMES likes compressed reviews. I expect to get it off this week.

'Your editor has not done his job too well.' Cobb counted 64 misprints, accents missing or accents where there should not be. 'RIOM does not have an S, you can either have REIMS (Fr.) or RHEIMS (Engl.) but not both. The <u>chef-lieu</u> of the Marne is not REIMS, but Chalons-sur-Marne (69). It is the MINUTIER DU NOTARIAT, not MINUTERIE (238), which is a light-switch, a mistake made years back by Beatrix Hyslop in her book on the Orleans estates.' Then, in case of a second printing, he lists the page numbers on which

he has found errors. There are six lines. 'Most of them are very minor things; eg Puy-de-Dome with the circumflex, ibid. Chalons, Ferreol without the accent, etc. In my review I'll just say it is a pity such a good book did not get more careful editing. Or, HELL, I think I won't mention it.' Then in a handwritten afterthought he has written, emphatically: 'I won't.'

On 6 June, 'Two Days after the Birthday of George III', he wrote to David Gilmour. Gilmour had invited Cobb to his parents' annual party at their home in Isleworth, Middlesex, on Monday 20 June. Margaret would be preoccupied with looking after William but …

… I will come if I can find my way. I have no idea where Isleworth IS, nor how to get there from Paddington, nor where or what Syon Park is. I am a stranger to London, and recently mistook White's for Boodle's (where I was to have lunch with Brigadier Vyvyan) but Isleworth, Old or New, seems a good bit more accessible than <u>le royaume septentrional</u>.

His new publisher, the allegedly Scottish John Murray, had shown him the pillow on which Byron died. 'It has some very odd-looking <u>stains</u> on it.'

On 11 June he wrote to Bernard Wasserstein purporting to be Euphonia Outram of Cambridge bidding him to gin and tonic in the Balliol College buttery followed by lunch in the Senior Common Room. The signatory was fictitious; the invitation genuine.

On 13 June he wrote to Gilmour once more, worrying, still, about how to find Isleworth. He was obviously hoping to be given a lift by Edward Mortimer but wrote that …

… being driven by Edward Boy is pretty terrifying, but it may be the only solution. My book, <u>Something to Hold Onto</u>, is a bit disgraceful, there is a bit about <u>Gaby la Landaise</u>, a Paris prostitute, Hôtel du Centre, rue d'Aboukir, I used to frequent in the early 50s, till, poor thing, she blew her head off by putting a revolver in her mouth, after having trouble with her <u>Jules</u>. Actually I was really very fond of her. A bit more like that. I suppose I had better return to the XVIIIth century, it is so much SAFER.

He wrote to David Gilmour on 20 June.

I feel sad at having missed the party. I was looking forward to seeing you and Sarah and perhaps Oliver too, if he were going to be there. But I never heard from Edward Boy, I wrote to him in Burford a week ago, and Maurice told me on Saturday that he was off to Ireland. I did not feel like asking the Kennys for a lift, and I could not face the long Tube trip in this heat, not to mention getting back here after changing at Didcot. I particularly wanted to see you as we are thinking of having a winter holiday in Sicily next January, and I have never been there, indeed have never been south of Rome. But I expect we'll meet before too long. Do you ever come up this way? Scotland is such the hell of a way up north and you won't be at the <u>Spectator</u> party. George Morpeth rang up this afternoon, so he will have given you news of me. I don't even know if the Mortimers still live in Burford. Evening trips to London I begin to find pretty hellish at my age, it is so much easier to cross the road and have a pint at my local. Perhaps you'll be at the Gaudy this Saturday? Anyhow I have achieved SOMETHING today, having got off a review for Philip Howard. MY book will be out in September. Then I think I'll write up Vienna 1935 and Vienna 1962, two goes at my most Hated capital. Then my entire book on Thermidor. I believe Balliol gets the revelation, unveiling or whatever of the New Master today. I hope it is not a bit of Midsummer madness. I HATE the Midsummer, it is the most awful season, save those truly frightful months of July and August (which one should always spend in the East Cape. I do get fed up, don't you? With all the fashionable Pretoria-bashing, actually I rather LIKE the Afrikaaners, they are so much nicer than the millionaire progressives of West Houghton, but one dares not say these things in print). George does not want Philip Mansel to do my obit, I don't mind, for I am not likely to read it. George seems to think that Mansel should not write about me, but I cannot see why not. For that matter Catto is to do me for some other paper.

I expect it was a most wonderful party with all sorts of nice people. But there you are: I would have come if I could have got a lift. Come here for lunch some time instead.

Hugo is VERY grand, wears Court dress, is High Sheriff and all sorts of other things, and he is an ideal editor.

On 21 June he wrote to Hugh Gough: 'My review of your book went off to Philip Howard last night, so maybe it will be in Thursday week.' His review of Gough's book did not appear when he thought it would, causing him to write another letter to the author: 'Damn, it isn't in. I went to the newsagent to buy that rotten paper. Maybe it will be in on the 7th. I know Philip will put it in as soon as he has any space, he is good about that sort of thing.' He was also concerned about a suitable wedding present for the Blannings and thinking of an oriental rug from a shop in Summertown. 'When Raymond Carr retired from St Antony's the College bought him a HORSE. But Tim goes coursing on foot, and horses are really pretty expensive, and where would they keep it in Elm Street?'

On 4 July he wrote to Bernard Wasserstein, whose biography of Trebitsch Lincoln he was reading for the third time. He had been to a Balliol College Gaudy and commented, apropos the new Master, Baruch Blumberg, the Nobel Prize winning biophysicist, 'The Master-Elect knows all about LIVERS, it is the part of my inside in which I take the most sustained interest.'

On 7 July he wrote to David Gilmour still regretting the missed Isleworth party.

My two Balliol aristos, George Morpeth and Lord Michael Pratt, both share a sort of magnificent ugliness. Michael has a MAUVE face and waddles. He has a voice that would cut through steel; talking to his late mother from one floor of the mews house to another, he actually made all the little glass and porcelain objects in corner cupboards RATTLE. I was most impressed! Mama had a similar decibel count.

On 20 July, prompted by reading a new book by Denis Hills, he wrote to Jeremy Lewis saying that it ('Return to Poland') had been a wonderful read which he would bracket with Bernard Wasserstein's biography of Trebitsch Lincoln.

But it does not make me want to go to that grey, muddy country, dirty tablecloths, garish churches, greasy ducks and many, many drunks, it sounds a sad place. Why does Denis punish himself in his manner of travelling and sleeping. A broken-down van used to sleep in in the Polish winter! Is it that he has no money? Or is it that, by some Boy Scout survival, he actually LIKES discomfort? One can see why Big Jim had to fly in to rescue him from Idi. A born rebel. Could it be his Public School? It does that sort of thing sometimes. Now I want to read everything he has written. August my most HATED month – asthma, heat, crowds, men displaying hairy chests and tattoos.

His review of Hugh Gough's book finally found its way into The Times and on 23 July he wrote to Gough.

Thursday I failed to buy THE TIMES, having bought it for four weeks running to no purpose. But yesterday I stole it from Balliol SCR. Your book is in good company, the Bywaters-Thompson Trial was one of the great murder cases of the 1920s. I have a bit about hanging in my new book, an advance copy of which reached me yesterday. My uncle was MOH for Lancs and used to have to attend all hangings in Lancaster Gaol. Anyhow I'll write & thank Philip, and now I'll have to review the Harley book for him. When I had my first Dupuytren at the Nuffield Orthopaedic, I noticed with interest my fellow suf-ferers, a mixed lot that included building labourers with tattooed hands, a tractor-driver, the Mother Superior of a Catholic Convent, an organist, a County cricketer, a young oarsman – what they all had in common was that their Dupuytrens were in the right hand (as in my case). The French name for it is <u>la maladie des coches</u>.

On 17 October he wrote to Hugh Gough.

I hope you have a good time in the <u>Pot de Chambre de Normandie</u> (the highest rainfall in the whole of France) & that you have a chance of eating a <u>raie au beurre noir</u> in <u>La Moulière</u> near where the Wicked Witch <u>Jehanne la Lorraine</u> was (so rightly) set on fire. How tedious all this <u>Bicentennaire</u> business has become!

It must be a bit hard on Soviet citizens of my generation who came through the Great Patriotic War, covered in decorations. I feel a residual warmth for <u>le père Staline</u> or <u>Mister Stalin</u>, as Churchill called him. I remember my sighting of my first Soviet officer, booted & with thick gold epaulettes, in Park Lane in the autumn of 1942. I thought then that, thanks to his elegant presence, we would win the War (or <u>they</u> would for us).

On a train between Arlon and Grembloux the other day a huge red Walloon butcher, <u>les mèches collées au front en cedillas</u>, blew up wonderfully about having to pay a supplement of <u>cent septante-deux francs</u> on his ticket. It might have been laid on exclusively for my benefit. <u>Et puis, Monsieur, je vote.</u> I am v. <u>fond</u> of <u>les Wallons</u>.

On 24 October 1988 he wrote to David Gilmour thanking him for another invitation to White's Club in London.

None of these places is easily identifiable from the outside or even from the inside. What really pleased me in your view of my book was your pinpointing the <u>banality</u> of all my subjects. I like writing about banal people, both in real life & in History. I always have.

On the last day of October he wrote to Gilmour thanking him for his latest book, which Quartet had sent and which he had been able to show to Philip Mansel over lunch at Balliol.

Philip had come up to talk about the obit he is doing of me for the Indie, but somehow we never even got on to that rather off-putting subject. I came to History at ten or so through Protestantism and in my old age I seem to becoming even Protestanter and somehow Englisher. How TRAGIC that Edward VI lasted so little. Rex Eduarde, te canamus, pium fundatorem, we used to sing in those distant days on the Sabrine shore. Somerset MUST have been a Good Thing for he got on quite well with Calvinists. Scottish history seems quite fun, I always like to be reminded of the dreadful Beaton being chucked over a cliff near St Andrew's (a bit like Edward Ball's mother, Medaea). George Morpeth's ancestors seem to have been remarkably adept at choosing the wrong side, one of them even planned to marry the appalling Mary Q of S.

He had been asked to speak in Madrid but was disinclined to accept.

I'd have gone to Madrid willingly in other circumstances. I have only been there once, that was in 1960, when I was giving lectures in French on XIXth century diplomatic history to their about-to-be-diplomats. I was put up in state at La Residencia, Calle Pinar, where I had breakfast with Spanish Bishops and German engineers. The young diplomats were DELIGHTFUL, and at the end of my stay, they even provided me with a GIRL who had the surname of Gordon. I decided to stay on an extra two days on her account. If I were to return, it would have to be not as a commis voyageur, but as an emissary of my favourite Frenchman, Louis XVIII.

Meanwhile he would read 'The Prince' every night in the snug of his local and hoped to see Gilmour for lunch at White's. 'HELP, Where IS IT?'
On 3 November he wrote to Blair Worden.

Anthony Powell even told me that first time, New Year's Day, 1970, that I wrote History like a novelist! I do get a bit lost in all his characters. X. Trapnell was someone I used to know, Julian Maclaren-Ross, who wrote some rather good things but drank too much and used to beat his wife with a silver-topped cane. Julian, when on his uppers, which he often was, used, in desperation, to come to Oxford and sponge off the Davins. They were rather proud to be so sponged off by a writer, so I suppose everyone was happy. The Davins are provincial New Zealanders who STILL think Oxford is important. Julian was healthily ungrateful. Tony Powell is very nice, though a bit of a snob, all that Dymoke stuff.

In a letter to Richard Ingrams dated 24 November:

I don't know whether you have heard that the existence of Hall's Bookshop in Chapel Place, Tunbridge Wells, is being threatened by Lloyd's Bank, they want to extend their premises back into Chapel Place, and this would involve the demolition of Hall's, a bookshop that has been on its present site ever since 1898. There is quite a campaign under way locally, and I was rung up by <u>Peterborough</u> (who lives in TW), who put a piece about it in his column in the <u>Telegraph</u> on the 16th. I have now written to the <u>TLS</u>. And I have sent Sabrina Izzard's letter to me on to Hugo, who knows how to deal with this sort of thing. Sabrina's lease runs out next March, Lloyd's having refused to renew it. Lloyd's have three branches in TW and I don't think there is any <u>real</u> need for them to extend the branch that faces on to the Common back into Chapel Place. Hall's is a magnificent second-hand bookshop, with many literary associations. I wonder if the <u>Eye</u> could give the matter a bit of publicity; it is known all over the South-East. Lloyd's must be stopped.

I had to make the speech of thanks at the Society of Apothecaries in the name of the guests to about 150 doctors, FRCPs, MRCSs and that sort of thing, most of them wearing medals. One of the consultants present was described as an andrologist, or something like that. I asked about this word: apparently it meant someone who specialises in testicles.

On the same day he wrote to Jeremy Lewis and mentioned a car crash in Seaford, which he had visited in order to read to a blind friend. 'The car was driven by an 80+ year old lady driver (who walked out of the wreckage quite unhurt), she had mistaken the accelerator for the brake (JUST the sort of thing I would have done, had I ever learned to drive!).'

On the 30th he wrote to David Gilmour thanking him for lunch at White's Club, which he had evidently managed to find. 'I did enjoy lunch in that funny place, in the presence of the Duke of York all in red. Did you not say that you were giving up that Club? I rather hope not, as I do like going to lunch in such places. How could you think of living months and months with that pompous bore, Curzon?'

On 12 December he typed a letter to David Gilmour congratulating him on getting good reviews for his new book on Lampedusa. He had just received a card from his former Balliol colleague Hartmut Pogge von Strandmann. 'We went to his 50th birthday party last month and I gave him a £20 book token with which, as he tells me, he bought your book.' In his card, he adds:

175

Lampedusa's wife is a cousin twice removed of my grandmother. In Italy we tried to see her, but were only to speak to her on the phone (H's English is still a bit creaky), when she was in Rome and we in Palermo. The von Strandmanns are Balts from Riga. A few years ago, H went there with his 80 year old mother and found her house intact. Reading your book a thing that struck me was that L's assessment of English literature was banal in the extreme, how COULD he have regarded Graham Greene as a worthwhile writer? It is very odd, especially from someone who later wrote a masterpiece. I suppose I always feel a bit out of sympathy with Anglophils, whether French or Italian. They always seem to get us so completely wrong (with the notable exception of Valery-Larbaud). The French still consider Charles Morgan a writer of international standing!

1989

To Trevor-Roper, 21 January.

It was nice seeing you and Xandra at the BA, but there is never time really to talk on those crowded occasions. Earlier I had been trapped with Charles Wilson and his Czech wife, the one Jack Gallagher used to refer to as the Bouncing Czech; and then Geoffrey Elton had expressed some disquiet as to the Doings or Non-Doings of my Successor. (I can never quite make out whether he is being accused of doing nothing, or doing too much, and, Monday, at All Souls, Isaiah had compared him, in character, or lack of, to Goronwy Rees. Poor Norman!) Yes, I do agree about the Quakers, a close-knit, dangerous community, extremely self-satisfied, and with a thing about drink. I suffered under one, a very rich, very self-assured American, Miss Cadbury, of the local branch of the Gesellschaft von Freunden, in Vienna, my most LOATHED capital (worse even than Sofia). In the summer of 1935, when I was doing some part-time work in their headquarters in the Fleischmarkt. More recently, I went over to Saffron Walden to talk to a couple about a Merton contemporary of mine, Christopher Lee, a not very good poet, and they gave me lunch, with APPLE JUICE to wash it down: one of the worst experiences of my life (only equalled by dinner with Oliver Lutaud, a Milton Hillite enthusiast, the son of a Governor General of

Algeria, and a French Protestant, who offered a choice between Vittel and Badoit: experiences that are <u>searing</u>. Whatever one may say about Catholics, they do give you a decent drink). The Saffron Walden couple had a huge book, they looked up a name, yes, he was one (rather like a French Communist, <u>oui, c'en est un</u>), meaning that, whoever it was, he was IN, an Elect. Dreadful. The Scots apart from Norman, Alice Wemyss, James Douglas-Hamilton and David Gilmour are pretty unknown to me. I don't know where anything IS in that strange sort of <u>crinière</u>, David, for instance, lives in East Lothian, but I cannot find it, he has invited me to stay there next month. But <u>where</u>? Jews I am rather FOR, collectively, I suppose because I think Israel a Good Thing and Palestinians a Bad Thing. But the people I simply cannot take are the <u>Irish</u>, north and south, and the frightful Kennedys in the US. I was once taken to the Kennedy Library outside Boston, and had to leave quickly. I was so glad that man in the <u>Sunday Telegraph</u> – where I read your WONDERFUL piece on our Great Revolution – had a posthumous go at that retired murderer Sean McBride. Almost as good as Norman's famous piece on E.H. Carr.

I still haven't done the Dame. Instead, I have written a long piece about Mavis Gallant and the horrors of May 1968 for the <u>Spectator</u>. Much more fun than the Dame. I remember denouncing Caute in a piece I wrote in 1969. It seems he has not improved since then. In May 68 Zeldin went over to Paris especially to see a Revolution close up, he must have been disappointed, as there was no revolution, no bodies in the street. I have never been so glad NOT to have been in Paris as then.

I will be in the KA back bar tomorrow week, the 29th, about 12.15, after seeing some Univ pupils then I go on to lunch in Balliol. I think My Successor might be there, but one can never count on that, he is very elusive.

Goronwy Rees? Well, I am confining myself to his time in UCW. Isaiah told me a lot about him, also about Rowse, who, he said, was not only amazingly conceited, but also very nasty, taking a joy in humiliating people. Goronwy wasn't nasty, he was always desperately anxious to PLEASE; anyone and everyone, including, I suppose, the Soviets. And please and captivate he did. He did have some rather awful friends, including a HORRID Ulster poet called MacNeice, one

177

of the rudest, most unpleasant people I have ever met. They used to go to rugger matches together – an extraordinary way of spending a Saturday afternoon – and get drunk. MacNeice lived on the fringes of the BBC and lived mostly in a pub near Broadcasting House. Latterly, I think Goronwy lived mostly off Encounter, I suppose a suitable fate for an ex-Communist. But I don't think he would ever have been a very good Communist, he would not have had the staying power, and he would have betrayed them too.

I see someone has put the Baron up for the BA. I must register my black ball with Ken Morgan.

Yale tell me a sentence of mine is to go on the jacket of the Wasserstein book. FAME. I have achieved fame of a different order; on the HOME BUYER page of the Kent and Sussex Courier, the Tun. Wells local paper, an estate agent has a sales piece about a flat, selling at £63,000, 'situated in a sought after private road, once the location of historian Richard Cobb, who is well known locally for his writings on TW in the 1930s'. Should I not get a commission? A plaque must follow.

Blair tells me the move to Lambeth is not imminent. Perhaps Runcie is to be given another chance. I feel that in Oxford I have been a signal failure. I have never been invited to deliver a sermon in the University church. However, I have made up for that unaccountable omission by having preached, before the Provost, the Headmaster and the Officer Commanding one of the Guards regiments, in the Blessed Henry's own chapel at Eton. Il faut se contenter de peu. Even so I was a bit put out when Albany equated the ruban rouge with the MBE. I wrote and said so.

PS I had not known of Ralph Leigh's death till you told me of it: the penalty for having given up The Times. Ralph used to send me postcards headed with his name, various initials, and a small picture of the Cross of the Legion of Honour. To have spent a lifetime on the frightful Jean-Jacques, WHAT a fate!

On Good Friday he wrote to David Gilmour.

I don't think I am very popular up in those parts just now as I have withdrawn from a colloque that is to take place in Edinburgh at the

French Institute next month. It was just that I started getting utterly fed up with the whole <u>Bicentenaire</u> business and felt very much in need to get on with my Vienna-Sofia book. There have been so many chores: a preface to Bill Fishman's book, a preface to Carlyle's <u>French Revolution</u> for the Folio Society, a preface still to be done for the new edition of Alastair Horne's <u>The Fall of Paris</u>. And I am reviewing, for <u>The Spectator</u>, Philip's excellent book on the Court of France – how good he is on the power of vanity! – and Jankowski's Yale book on Simon Sabiani and the PPF in Marseille, a wonderful study of a ward machine politician who lost his way and wandered into a form of fascism and extreme collaborationism.

To Trevor-Roper, 27 March.

I read with <u>great</u> interest your article on Cambridge in the 30s in yesterday's <u>Sunday Telegraph</u>. I feel you have captured very well the differences between the two places. On our side, yes, a certain saving frivolity, a welcome lack of earnestness (earnestness, in Merton in my time, we reserved for the 'God Squad', the Buchmanies and the October Club, of which Merton had NO members). Of course I suspect there was no lack of earnestness in Lindsay's Balliol, but then I never set foot in the place in all my time in Oxford. Whereas a few Cambridge undergraduates went off actually to fight in the Spanish Civil War in the International Brigade – I think some were killed, including a New Zealand poet – as far as I know NO ONE went from Oxford. I remember a Merton undergraduate who lived in Mob and was secretary of the OU Film Club and a keen Marxist (<u>Groucho</u> not Karl). He was a small, elegant man, with delicate features. HIS contribution to that ideological conflict was to dress up as a woman, I supervised the dressing, very high heels, black dancing shoes, a red blouse, even a <u>mantilla</u>, and an enormous comb in his very black wig (supplied by Mr Germer), also an outsize black leather handbag. The thing had been prepared well in advance: a lady member of the Spanish Cortes was to give an address, in English, in Oxford Town Hall, on the Struggle of the Spanish People against Fascism. There were notices of the talk all over the place, and on the great day the Press was present, so were the Lindsays, so was I, sitting in the back of the Hall. The delivery, in wonderfully broken English and in

179

a contralto voice, was impeccable. The Senorita even took questions. At the end she was roundly cheered and accepted six bouquets of red roses. There was a solid contingent of Merton historians to observe proceedings from the back. I wish I could remember the chap's name, his movements were wonderful, his gestures too. A couple of days later he appeared as himself to the Press and admitted that it had been a spoof: screams of indignation from North Oxford, the Lindsays etc., a Joke in Appalling Taste etc. etc. I thought it was tremendously funny, and I don't think it did any harm to the Republican cause (there was <u>one</u> Franco supporter in the College, Pedroso, later the Biarritz agent for Hispano-Suiza). Somehow I can't imagine such a thing happening in Cambridge at the time, can you? Later the chap was killed in the Oxford and Bucks, I think in Normandy. The nearest I ever got to the Spanish Civil War was teaching Basque children in Tunbridge Wells during a summer vacation.

I think it is the centralism of Cambridge that facilitates the emergence of gurus. Professors seem to MATTER (always a bad thing). Just think of the enormous power and patronage exercised by Jack Plumb and Geoffrey Elton! The only figure in our time who was a bit like that was, I suppose, Powicke and his Oriel seminar. When I had a Term lecturing in Cambridge, I was surprised by the animation that seemed to occur at each stroke of the hour: 9, 10, 11, midday, hundreds and hundreds of bicycles darting through bollards, crossing the town from one lecture to another, suggesting that in terms of teaching, it was much more spread out and less College-based than it would be with us. This may have been a superficial view, of course. But the whole structure of the University, even in Arts subjects, seems highly centralised: something that has been to very much Oxford's advantage, so many Cambridge historians failing to get tenure, moving west to become College Fellows: people like John Walsh (of course it COULD work to Oxford's DISadvantage).

I used to know a Trinity Communist, a New Zealander called Paddy Costello, a friend of Davin's, who was later on Jack Freyberg's staff, then was NZ charge d'affaires in Moscow, then First Secretary to the NZ legation in Paris when Miss Mackenzie was Minister; then Professor of Russian in Manchester. He and his Ukrainian wife were fanatical Stalinists, the two elder children were Red Pioneers and the eldest boy, Michael, is now somewhere high up in the British Comunist Party, I think he represents the hard line wing. Costello is mentioned, though not by name, in a book of essays by Isaiah; he is represented as having tried to persuade Pasternak to toe the Party line. Costello had met his wife, who was training as a teacher, at Cambridge where he read Classics at Trinity. Costello died some years ago, ALL the children, as far as I know, are hard-line CP.

Of course I think Cambridge is a much nicer PLACE than Oxford. For one thing it is on the EAST (that is, the <u>better</u>) side of England, and well away from the horrible, grim, grey, sinister Cotswolds, a place I associate with thatch, tourists and witches. I LOVE the Fens, especially the Bedford Level, and Cambridge is near enough to my own North Essex and South Suffolk. The skies are superb, and Cambridge is MUCH healthier than the miasmic swamps of the Isis (I remember Xandra making just that point one windy day I met her on Trumpington Street). Girton has always had more nonagenerians and centenarians than ANY other College (it is the ride in for lectures, in the face of East wind: the IDEAL combination would be St Felix and Girton, the double origin of a certain sort of weather-beaten face accompanied by plaits or a bun). Ampleforth and Magdalene would likewise be a good recipe for longevity. Both my Girton aunts lived into their nineties. And, of course, as you know, the BEER is far superior (even though some of it is the source of the wealth of that <u>horrible</u> man Graham Greene). Abbot's Special is INCOMPARABLE, and there is no Oxford equivalent to the <u>Free Press</u> or to RSM Wass's <u>The Baron of Beef</u>, Jack G's alternative College.

Of course I am very pro-Cantab just now for on 15 June I get an Hon. D. Litt. from HRH. This was set in motion by a nice man in SS called Beales. I am the ONLY historian there: there are the Lord Chancellor, the Secretary General of the UN, a Professor of Theology from Tubingen (who gets done first of course!) a Scientist, a local man who knows about Black Spots, and a 20-stone black opera singer, I mean SHE is black, not the Opera, she comes AFTER me, I would not do very well on a see-saw with her, for I have never managed to get much above 8 stone. Anyhow it is a very grand occasion and there is to be some sort of grand lunch in Corpus; the evening before I am asked out to St Catherine's, and the evening of the Degrees I have supper with my principal Cambridge friend, Tim Blanning, a VERY sound man, and his wife, they live in the Kite, near the <u>Free Press</u>. My sister will be coming over from Bedford. She tells me she heard Vinegar – George's name for his former Master – give a talk there on Bunyan.

I have just had a spoof card in some sort of German signed Konrad Kujay or something like that. It has an Easington postmark. My wife has had a whole series of pc's, addressed to 'Miss Wingate', which is where she was born. George does not seem very much to enjoy the study of Law. And he has given the Gate House away to his younger brother. A week or so ago the Hero of the Grouse Moor had lunch with me in Balliol; he is MAUVER than ever, now has THREE chins, and is in very high spirits. I sounded him out on the subject of matrimony – THREE of my Balliol pupils, one of them a Brigadier in Ulster – have recently been contracting that Holy State, one indeed, in Balliol Chapel, on 15 April, to a daughter of Lord Sidmouth. I wonder if it is the same family as that of the excellent man who was in Pitt's Ministry in the 1790s and caught all the Scottish and Irish traitors who were then Hanged? Michael told me he did not have matrimony in view for the moment. He would be quite a CATCH, for he is very rich, has Bayham Manor and a bijou house in Coulson Street, and has a very loud voice. There HAVE been ladies in the Entourage. I have a soft spot for Michael and he took a valiant part in the successful campaign to save Hall's Bookshop in Chapel Place, Tunbridge Wells, from the predatory Lloyd's Bank.

I am FED UP with all the <u>Bicentenaire</u> nonsense. I confined myself to a single impious piece in the <u>Telegraph</u> (the paper I now read) at the beginning of the year. But I am doing a series of talks about (against) the French Revolution at Downside, Harrow, Westminster, BEDALES, etc. in the autumn. I LIKE talking at schools, partly, I suppose, because I always feel so glad to have left mine (though I go back THERE quite often, and I was glad to see that, as usual, there was a Salopian in each boat).

This is a long wandering letter. I have been very remiss, but I have been assailed by chores, writing Prefaces, Introductions, including one for the Folio Society for Carlyle's <u>French Revolution</u> (my copy of which, beautifully bound, I won as the Wilkinson Essay Prize when I was in the Classical Fifth at Shrewsbury in 1933). I have also been back to South Carolina, talking about Thermidor, what a good thing it was (I am going to write a little book about Thermidor for Yale) at a conference in Charleston. The high spot of the visit was a superb reception given at the Citadel by the Commandant, the first US General I have ever met, with lots of very polite, smiling, wide-faced cadets in smart grey uniforms with blue stripes down the side: MARVELLOUS drinks and sandwiches. The hotel in Charleston was AWFUL, cockroaches on the table at breakfast, a Banquet (sic) WITHOUT DRINK. My retinue of six and myself left it after soup to go to a bar downtown. I was also in Columbia, looking up old friends. I have become very attached to the Deep South – AND to the GOP. AND to the Cathedral at Columbia (no black divorced lady bishops there). By the way, cannot you get the Bishop of Durham SACKED?

Margaret, my wife, has just bought a house in the Bocage, not far from Saint-Lo. I am going over to see it later this week. It seems a good location, and Normans, both Upper and Lower, are sensible pragmatists. No Robespierre there, but a Corday and a Tocqueville, excellent food and divine <u>calvados</u> (which, in my days of power, I persuaded the SNCF to lay on their Wagons-Restaurants on all their Western Lines).

I catch glimpses of James, generally looking worried, now and then. Your Successor gave a VERY nice dinner in Oriel at the conclusion of the Balliol French Revolution lectures. I have never known him so talkative and unbuttoned, I think it must be the prospect of Yale. He told me what it was like being a half-Jewish boy at Wellington. It really was a VERY nice party. Blair I see every now and then, Jeremy (my obituarist) looking more and more well-fed, MY Successor never, indeed not since last March. I think he must be in Moscow, he sent me a card from Leningrad.

For my Cambridge Triumph I shall avoid <u>La Maison de Pierre</u>. Recently I was guest speaker at a dinner given in a Solihull hotel by the Bicycle Manufacturers of Great Britain, I told them about Ben Howard's famous shop in Trumpington Street.

Our friend George is, I fear, in the T[erritorial] A[rmy] with the D[urham] L[ight] I[nfantry]. But THAT won't give him a living; and when he comes to Oxford, he takes his friends to lunch.

While I was in S[outh] C[arolina], the Society of Authors wrote to me to ask me to sign some collective petition in favour of the horrible Rushdie. I got it too late to do anything about it, but I am going to write to le Fanu to say why I would NOT have signed it. He sounds both an AWFUL man and a very pretentious writer. Mercifully, when I was chairman of the Booker in 1984, there was no book of his. I did at least manage to keep BOTH Amises, père et fils, off the short list, a useful negative achievement I felt at the time.

Warmest greetings to Xandra. I hope you are both in good health. My Dupuytren advances with the slowness of Kutuzov. I have had two operations on the hand and that is about enough.

PS The Observer had some canard about me going to No. 10 wearing trouser clips; but I have never BEEN to No. 10, and have never worn trouser clips: I tuck my trousers into my socks! Such is History made.

On 20 April, below the legend 'a famous vegetarian, well-known bore and lover of Humanity, one hundred to-day', he typed a letter to Blair Worden.

Balliol is really quite an aristo enclave. One of my first pupils was Lord James Douglas-Hamilton, very nice, also a great worrier about Moral Issues: 'Mr Cobb, Sir, do you think Cromwell was a Good Man?' This, in the middle of an essay on the East India Company. I think James was a late developer. Later he wrote a very good book about Hess and his attempted visit to his father. Lord Michael Pratt was VERY loud and VERY clever, is VERY rich, has a mauve face and three chins and lives in state at Bayham. The Viscount Morpeth is dotty, nice, very poor and a Liberal. He travels light and never wears pyjamas. The Earl of Gowrie was also at Balliol. I have just read an EXCELLENT book on Goering, Der Dinke by Richard Overy, a Cambridge man. I can never read too much about the Third Reich. I have also been reading a silly, snobby book by Patrick Leigh Fermor, who, I suspect, is Irish. He likes all the wrong people: the HORRIBLE Austrians, the flashy, fraudulent Magyars, and drools over Cardinals in red or white and silver. This book has revived in me all my healthy Protestantism and dislike of nationalities that go in for dressing up in dirndls and smelly boots, enjoy riding and like horses. I am incurably URBAN. PLF has really set me off on RCC's Guide to Modern Europe, a very different one from that of the dreadful Waughs, père et fils, and the gloomy, Life-Hating, tortured, BORED GRAM GRIN. The TIMES has sent me Simon Schama's <u>enormous</u> book. Simon is on the back, wearing a BEARD. A mistake, he does not NEED a beard.

On 8 May he wrote to Michael Hodges saying that he had cancelled a speaking engagement in Brighton because it clashed with a degree day in Oxford. 'In any case I don't know what I could possibly have said about anything so ephemeral as LIBERTY.' On the 22nd of the same month he wrote again to Hodges.

Last week I phoned through to THE TIMES a rave review of the Schama book. I thought it was very good indeed, and what he had to say needed saying, especially with all this bloody <u>Bicentenaire</u> razzmatazz. I did have some reserves, he is a bit too clever by half, and it was a pity he hadn't used Norman's <u>Prelude</u> and your book. Even so, the book is a marvellous read and is guaranteed to infuriate all the people I most dislike. Revolutions, after all, ARE mostly about killing, random or State-organised. I seem to be becoming something of an English nationalist; but how much better we did, Pitt etc. I mean, than the Paris Crowd! I feel Simon's book is above all an indictment of Paris.

I must say I simply cannot STAND Darnton. I gather that at the Washington do Simon was barracked by the Femms and others and by the sinister L. Stone. When I heard that, I felt even <u>more</u> determined to give the book a rave.

On George III's birthday (4 June) he wrote to Blair Worden.

I do wish Simon would learn that in the end it pays to THANK people. I sent him, c/o Viking, a list of some hundred misprints and one or two howlers, none of this went into my review, I just thought it would be useful when the book goes into paperback. But of course never a word from Simon. He used to cultivate me when he was in Christ's, even more when he was in for BNC (I was trundled in to tell the BNC scientists that he was the right man). Once in Harvard, he got me over from Brandeis to give a talk at his Centre (Center) and it took me TWO years to get my $200 fee paid, in the end I had to write to the Dean of Arts. Yet my Jewish friends assure me that Simon had very nice parents who told him all about the importance of thanking letters and that sort of thing.

And again to Blair Worden on 7 June: 'There is NO cathedral in Caen. It is in Bayeux!'
   He wrote to Hugh Gough on 21 August.

This awful heat goes on and on and I get more and more depressed. At least at Saint-Pierre-du-Fresne the good old <u>pluie normande</u> kept the long, uneven orchard of Margaret's cottage pleasantly green. We got back from there on Friday, to find Oxford parched and beige. Some time last month, fiddling with the knobs on William's TV, I had the extraordinary surprise of suddenly being confronted with YOU & NORMAN sitting up on a sort of rostrum, and answering questions in a quiet and reasonable manner, quite unflustered, as if you had both spent a lifetime on the media. I was most impressed, especially when I thought of the sort of spectacle I would have offered, as if I had been an elder version of Wedgie. That is why I ALWAYS avoid restaurants and cafes that have mirrors and I'll only do interviews with radio.

   On the Telly your baldness was a positive advantage, it gave you a look of academic ponderation and reasonableness, but you could not really compete with Norman's eyebrows, his secret weapon, which he used to great effect ... I'd love to see him on a programme with Denis Healey.

The Hampsons came over for a crab lunch and Cobb was able to discuss Hampson's TV appearance. Cobb wrote to Gough.

I told him about the effectivess of his eyebrows à la Healey but suggested that your cranium gave you the lead on gravitas. On <u>voices</u>

you were equal, both having the immense advantage of possessing regional accents, a trait which the public associates (wrongly cf Bullock and Wilson) with honesty. I fear my TW accent would get me nowhere: a CLASS voice.

On 19 October Cobb wrote to Hugh Gough after speaking at a meeting of the Royal Stuart Society in the private quarters of the Jesuits in Farm Street near the Connaught Hotel in London.

'A rum lot, pretty mad and very much old Recusant snobs,' but a French member of the order, Father Charles-Roux, brother of Edmonde the poetess and son of the Director-General of the Quai d'Orsay in the 1930s was …

… WONDERFUL, a CHARMER: buttoned up <u>soutane</u>, the red ribbon six inches thick, beautifully curly white hair, manicured hands and a very suave manner. The Js are indeed wonderfully WORLDLY. He won me over from the start by saying I was <u>bilingue</u>. I just love to have my French praised. Well, I AM vain.

When the Reich was collapsing and Laval was in Sigmaringen, he was offered a Luftwaffe fighter plane to take him anywhere within a range of 800 km. The pilot suggested Dublin, Laval hesitated and finally (and fatally) opted for Barcelona in the belief that Lecquerica, Spanish Ambassador to France in 1940 and Spanish Foreign Minister in 1945, would look after him. In some ways Laval was very naïve. He believed in L's honour as a Spaniard, etc. Well, as you know, he landed in Barcelona, was shut up in a villa, and, after six weeks, was flown into the US Zone of Germany, and the Americans then handed him over to the French in Baden Baden. Franco had done a deal with the French Provisional Government: you re-establish diplomatic relations with us, we'll hand over Laval (though not directly, so that Lequerica could argue that he had not in fact broken his word, a piece of casuistry). Gosh, if he HAD flown to Dublin there would have been quite a to-do. One thing is SURE, <u>Dev</u> would <u>not</u> have handed him over, and de Gaulle would have been fuming. One of the great might-have-beens of History. As it was, a number of Flemish VNV and Mordrel, the leader of the PNB, the pro-German Breton movement, did find refuge in Dublin in 1945. I don't think we, I mean the British, would have made a fuss about Laval, but de Gaulle would certainly have.

I do love this time of year. October is the best month, the beastly summer is safely over, coal fires are on the way, and at the moment a westerly gale is blowing up, soon the leaves will have gone, the Meadow will be deserted, the sea-birds will be coming in, and already there is a nice bit of rain. July and August should be abolished, they are hateful months, bad things always happen then. William likes the autumn too and in the summer he always insists on wearing his blue school mac, an act of defiance to the sun. In the 30s I used to wear a black overcoat in the summer.

On 29 October he typed a letter to David Gilmour:

I have been writing away recently about my perceptions of Europe, 1930–1935, prep school, then the History Side at Shrewsbury; and I'll be carrying on from 35 to 39, then come to my disastrous experience of Vienna in 1935. (Alas the quite beastly Habsburgs seem still to be with us!) The book should have some unity as it is entirely about my perceptions of Europe from 1930 to 1962, where it stops. It is full of prejudice, mostly anti-Catholic, anti-Green Fascism. And, of course, anti-Irish.

Over drinks at the Royal Stuart meeting a seedy man with a wet moustache collared me, you may not know – I didn't – he said that my great great grandfather, le comte de Stacpoole, was ennobled by Louis XVIII. I asked him if he were related to (that idiot) Alberic, oh, only distantly, he said airily. It does seem very very very odd that anyone could find a word to say in favour of the awful Stuarts, but there you are, well there ARE lunatics who think George III was a Good Thing.

I feel very sorry for poor Lord Aldington and I hope the pseudo-Count and the twit from Church Road, Tunbridge Wells get clobbered. I cannot for the life of me see why we should have bothered about people who FOUGHT AGAINST US in Italy. It is all extremely unfair as if my generation were being put on trial by some Russian twit.

Both the Liverpool cathedrals are hideous, but they are hideous differently, the Popish one looks like a coffee machine, the Anglican one looks like a runny version of the <u>Tour du Beurre</u> of Rouen.

By 19 November he was breathing poorly and signed his letter to Worden, with love from 'Richard, the Wheezer'. A few days later he wrote again, 'I hope to be back on form by then' (he was looking forward a couple of weeks to a proposed meeting, in the King's Arms):

Lately my asthma has been giving me <u>hell</u>, waking me up at 4am and that sort of thing. But I have been to see a consultant in Wimbledon and I am to get a second inhaler and all sorts of powerful pills, so that by next week I should be more or less back to my loud and frivolous self. As you say, breathing IS important! I suppose I should go and live in my birthplace, Frinton-under-Sea, or Skegness, or even ... Cambridge. I am just back from Cambridge where, as always, I drank far too much Abbotts Special, the nectar of Suffolk beers, which, as you know, are the best in the country. I have also been given a Sidney Sussex tie and soon I am to get rights there. Thursday I breakfasted in the Hall, Oliver (the Huntingdonshire Gentleman) looking down at me from the wall, rather disapprovingly, he would have been even more disapproving if he had a notion of my hangover. His head is buried somewhere in the College garden. Anyhow I'll soon have a port of call in those frabjous parts.

Ludlow is a LOVELY place. I always buy my shoes there. We go quite often to stay near Clun. I was in Shrewsbury recently looking through numbers of <u>The Salopian</u> for 1935 and 1936. I was interested to discover that 30 boys from the school attended some sort of six week course in an estate near Hamburg in 1935 with 30 German boys; and later a NAPOLA group came on a visit to the school, also the dreadful Rolf Gardiner, who gave a talk on the Baltic States. Alas I fear we are going to hear quite a lot more about the Baltic States, not to mention the sinister Ukraine. I am a bit alarmed by present events, there seems to be a vacuum in East Germany, and vacuums are dangerous THINGS. Perhaps there will be an 1849; but it does not seem very likely.

PS I have been re-reading some Simenon and am now rather

tempted to write a book about him, or rather about his books. I always welcome any excuse to write a bit about Belgium and the Platteland. I LIKE flat places and one of the most attractive parts of England is the Bedford Level. I really must get to know Lincolnshire a bit; I have never been to Boston even.

1990

On 21 April he wrote to David Gilmour. 'Yes, it seems I am becoming quite modish in Italy.' The Italian publishers Adelphi were doing two of his books and one was 'Death in Paris', which he described as 'my own favourite . . . an exercise in miniaturism'. The French were to do 'Still Life' and 'A Classical Education', which was 'even better'. There had also been a Book at Bedtime on the BBC in Britain, but he had missed the readings because he was in Normandy at the time. In Spain he was due to give a paper on Thermidor and another on the French occupation of Belgium between 1794 and 1812. These were to take place in Zamora.

I had to look it up on the map as I have only been to Spain once, that was back in 1960, Zamora seems to be right up near the border with Northern Portugal. Raymond Carr has got me involved in this outing, the theme of which seems to be that the French Revolution was a pretty bad thing for all concerned, and I can certainly go along with that. So maybe there will be a Cobb Renaissance in Spain, too?

He was looking forward to 'a nice long train journey from Madrid to Zamora' and to the younger Spanish historians of whom Raymond Carr spoke highly. Besides he had recently returned from one of his frequent lectures in public schools. The latest was at Downside, the Roman Catholic public school in Somerset where he 'met some quite charming Spanish boys, all of them with lots of surnames strung together with two or three 'Y's.'

He was about to become a grandfather, which seemed particularly strange as William, his youngest son, was still only ten, which seemed young to become an uncle. This led him to further *reflections on age and decrepitude – via Tim Garton Ash, who 'has grown a (red) beard (a bad sign) and seems very keen on Havel and all those Czech gesticulators. He is best on the Poles – he has a <u>Krakowiaka</u> wife'; a lunch between Norman Stone, Gordon Craig and the Prime Minister, 'putting her right on the subject of the Huns (Krauts, les Chleuhs, les Doryphores, Tedesci, Niemcy etc. etc. etc.)'; references for four former pupils, all of whom were applying for the same Balliol fellowship; an impending lunch at Alastair Horne's where he was to see John and Judith Roberts; and an over-indulgence in the French subjunctive together with a reading of Julien Gracq's 'Un balcon en forêt', which he recommended fervently.*

A lot of my hair seems to be falling out. I am developing a tonsure, strange nobbly bits of the top of my head are emerging as from an archaeological dig, and I have taken to wearing a cap indoors as well as out. I think it is due to the rather powerful pills I take at night for my breathing. I find too that the back of my head – invisible, at least to myself, a minor blessing – feels very cold when I am sitting near a door. Maybe I should try a wig? There used to be an excellent wig-maker, Mr Germer, in King Alfred Street, when I was an undergraduate. It is now a Health Food Store. Do you think they make wigs in Spain? There must be a surplus of silky <u>senoritas</u> hair. I shall look around.

His next John Murray book was mainly on 'European themes 1930–1963' but also included 'a few swipes at Lithuania, at all times the most troublesome of the three Baltic States (and, because Catholic) enjoying a wide lobby.' After that he was planning Simenon and Brussels from 1880 until the present day, both of which would afford plenty of opportunity to spend time in Belgium, which he described as 'Le Royaume' and of which he was increasingly fond. He and Margaret were 'thinking seriously about living permanently in France, now that we have a house near Villers-Bocage. I think with Kinnock in power there would be a fairly massive emigration, and I find myself a pretty natural <u>émigré</u>! Anyhow we are taking a few advance measures with that in mind.'

On 14 May Cobb wrote to Blair Worden:

The best news of all is that MY man, Martin Conway, has got the Balliol job, the Successor to My Successor. WONDERFUL. Good old Balliol. I am just back from Spain where I had not been for 30 years and where I had an absolutely SUPER time (Madrid, Zamora, Salamanca) talking about Thermidor and going down very well with retired Army officers and members of the <u>Partido Popular</u> (which is pretty well to the right). I went round with Raymond Carr, it was like travelling with royalty. Raymond is quite rightly a National Institution; and the Spaniards are marvellous hosts, in fact I think they are about the nicest people in Europe. Alas they do not love the French!

Gilmour got a similar letter:

I had an absolutely <u>fabulous</u> time. I have never encountered such hospitality . . . Zamora was fantastic: a dozen lovely Romanesque churches and those marvellous Flemish tapestries in the Cathedral. More Romanesque churches in Toro, also in one of them there a van der Weyden! I suppose it was all taken from Charles the Bold. I went everywhere with Raymond Carr, he was treated (quite rightly) like a National Institution. He had rather a magnificent looking thing in red and gold, surmounted by a large crown. I think he got it from Juan Carlos. It made my little <u>ruban rouge</u> quite paltry and Spain did not really seem the place to wear a Napoleonic decoration! But, MY, how they HATE the French, I was struck by the intensity of historical memory.

Carr spoke apparently fluent Spanish in his 'unmistakeable wheezy accent' and Cobb's talks found particular favour with elderly army officers.

In Toro I noticed with interest (and some surprise) that the main street was called Calle Calvo Sotelo. We were received there by the <u>alcalde</u>, a man with a peasant face sculpted out of wood. Some of the women were fantastically beautiful and the children were <u>enchanting</u>, so unlike French <u>lycéens</u> and <u>lycéennes</u>. But then Zamora is delightfully provincial. So too was Salamanca. I came back quite overwhelmed (and with WADS of pesetas). I shall be back there this year or early next. I was amazed to hear that Serrano Suner was still alive and that he was busy writing his memoirs. I travelled in luxury First Class by el Talgo from Madrid to Zamora. Raymond and I were driven all over the place, to within sight of Portugal and all the way from Zamora to Madrid at remarkable speed, with some VERY close encounters with vast lorries. Well, there is still time for us to get to know Central Spain better, I have NO desire to go either to the coast or South or anywhere near the ghastly Basques and Catalans. And I have a fine bronze medal given by the President of Leon y Castile which I am sure is much the best part of Spain. How very much nicer Spain is than Italy! And what a SUPERB language! And the girls! Oh my goodness!

He left Oxford that summer, adding a PS to a letter to Hugh Gough, dated the 10th: 'We will start looking for a house in Whitby early next month. I do not miss Oxford <u>at all</u> & wonder how I ever managed to spend <u>30 years</u> in that inbred place. Whitby will give me a new start (at 75).'

In September he wrote to Blair Worden. He had been speaking at his alma mater, Shrewsbury, and had exchanged thoughts on Worden with his contemporary from St Edward's, Oxford, now the maths master, and had been up till 1.30 in the morning drinking with the head of History and the Arts mistress at the Golden Cross. 'Shrewsbury has most flexible closing times.' He was much looking forward to a forthcoming visit to Worden's college in Oxford when 'I will be wearing, for the first time, my new wig, off-red and discreet.'

Worden had been robbed on a French railway train:

Dear me, WHAT a disaster! But you must not blame the SNCF, it has all the marks of the bloody, thieving Catalans, one of the really abusive pseudo-nationalities along with Basques, Lets, Lats, Esths, Slovaks, Ukrainians, Quebecois, Irish, Manx, Flems, Armenians, Kurds, Serbs et al. I had a similar experience, but got off lighter (literally). Travelling on the old Orient Express from Paris to Sofia to meet <u>une belle</u>

<u>Bulgare</u>. I had dinner in the Restaurant car with a very well-dressed good-looking American. We had a <u>lot</u> to drink, then he suggested we go back to his W/L for <u>more</u>, he got the attendant to produce a bottle of Soave, then he became INSISTENT, I pointed out to him that it was nearly thirty years since I had left the Sabrine Shore, no use, finally I had to make a hasty retreat, in my haste leaving behind in the predator's W/L my new red pullover in angora wool bought for the snows of Wytocha. When I woke up in or near Venice, I went back to retrieve it, ALAS the train had divided at Milan, red angora had been carried on with my Would-Be Seducer to Florence, and, in Sofia, I FROZE.

To Trevor-Roper, 15 September.

Today I wrote to Twiston-Davies, at his Tunbridge Wells address, in order to find out more about the obit area of his paper. It is a most extraordinary and disgraceful business. I shall harry Twiston-Davies till I find out more. I know Geoffrey Wheatcroft, not at all a bad fellow, despite being from New College. He wrote rather well about that strange man Gary Bennett (who once at a party in St Benet's asked <u>ME</u> if I could help him get the Chair vacated by Jack McManners!). At one time Jeremy Catto was to do MY obit in that paper, but it looks as if there has been a new deal all round, with my old pupil, Tim Heald, apparently driven away. I thought the AJPT obit quite good in itself, though I wish there had been a mention of leaving the BA over that disgraceful Blunt business. The wife of my old tutor, J.M. Thompson, a very difficult Welsh lady from the Bog of Tregarron, the daughter of a Church in Wales parson, had a deep hatred of Tompie's successor, 'a horrid little man from Manchester called Taylor'. Mrs T. died quite recently, just short of one hundred. AJPT had some odd prejudices. He despised Italians, but admired Serbs. I don't think he had much time for the French. He infuriated me with his review of Raymond Carr's great book in the <u>Sunday Times</u>. Carr, he said, had written about Spain from <u>inside</u>, had failed to put Spain in its international context. I wrote to Raymond at the time.

I have just been looking through my new University Diary. Several new Readers. Dixon is now a Professor. When I put in for the Wuggins Chair, in 1972, I was taken aside in Balliol SCR by Alastair Buchan:

'You haven't a chance in hell, old man, it has all been arranged, Dixon is to get it, he is supported by Lucy Sutherland.' But Dixon didn't get it! Though I was convinced at the time that he would.

Merton. Yes, Mertonians do seem to get elected. Harry Pitt and I were assessors for a History Fellowship. There was a short list of six, one a Mertonian. Halfway through proceedings, Harry and I got a note from the Senior Tutor to the effect that the College wanted to appoint someone under 30. There was only <u>one</u> candidate under 30. Then we got an unsolicited letter from the VC of Southampton University on the subject of that one candidate: yes, he had been rather difficult as an undergraduate, but, if elected, he would 'settle in' etc. etc. Of course he got the job. One of the candidates was even flown in from Naples. But there are one or two nice doctors. Medical Fellows are often rather nice. I had a bad bout in your old College after lunch there last week. William Thomas standing over my host, Martin Conway (who goes to Balliol at the end of the month) and myself, and holding forth on the subject of the Paris Sections.

What I DID see in Salamanca was VIVA FRANCO, in <u>huge</u> letters, high up on the walls of the Cathedral, along with the fasces of the Falange. In Toro I spotted a Calle Calvo Sotelo. One of the alumni of Salamanca was Belgrano. No mention of Titus [Oates].

Very brave of Xandra and you to have gone to Mexico. I imagine it is the <u>worst</u> food in the world, even worse than in Poland. And then is there not some <u>lethal</u> drink? Still, you have both survived.

I shall see Blair at dinner in SEH early next month, along, I imagine, with the Good Canon, the biographer of St Jerome. And I hope Blair will have news of Xandra and you. Poor Blair had a dreadful experience with the SNCF. I've always found them quite reliable.

Vitamin B seems to be keeping my left hand in working order.

I do get a bit fed up hearing what we all owe to the Few. True, I suppose, but in the course of my five obscure years in the Army, I cannot say that I warmed to RAF types. There was a perfectly HORRIBLE boy at my school called Hillary, and I cannot say I much liked the Cheshire brothers in Merton. Well, the fly-past is over now.

I'll let you know as soon as I hear from Twiston-Davies.

All good wishes to Xandra. I expect all of us will soon be getting a visit from the Pan-Liberal Viscount. Maurice Keen has laid him on a

195

permanent bed in Holywell Manor. It must be exciting to be a (young) historian in Russia just now. Perhaps we will soon know all about Kirov, etc. I was once denounced by a Pole, Tadeusz Lepkowski, in some Poznan review, as a 'bourgeois-reactionary historian'. That was in 1965. Lepkowski was then teaching in Cuba.

Let us meet then for lunch some time in Merton, the table there is LONG.

I am reading more and more about Spain.

A few days later (11 September) Cobb wrote to Worden again, still smouldering over the Telegraph's attack on his friend Trevor-Roper, which he thought 'quite gratuitous and vicious'. There was no mention of the wig but he said he was intending to arrive in St Edmund Hall 'wearing a skull-cap with a long silk silver tassel'. He was concerned that in his list of hated minorities 'I failed to include the CORNISH, possibly the most frightful of the lot.' He was also reading – with pleasure ...

... the eight pieces on the July Crisis (including my own, on France) which have now just come out in paperback. I am getting quite obsessed about July 1914, and, while still valid, I feel I MUST do the trip to Sarajevo, I just want to see that bridge over the narrow river, and Princip's footprints. Perhaps I should go back to Vienna, visit the Belvedere Palace and see the blood-stained uniform, the cocked hat, poor Sophie's dress, and the borrowed car. One of the children, a daughter, is still alive. I think my friend Vlado Dedijer went to see one of the boys when he was preparing his book. Now I must get hold of Asquith's letters to Venetia. I am also hooked on Modern Spain. The bloody RAF! Now we are going to be smothered with all the Battle of Britain stuff. The ONE thing I retain from my five (unwilling) years in khaki is a lasting dislike of RAF types.

The RAF also received a blistering PS to a letter he wrote to Michael Hodges on 11 September: 'WHAT a bore! All this fuss about the bloody RAF, the Battle of Britain etc. etc. this coming week-end. The Boys in Blue, red sports cars, bristling moustaches, all of them probably working in garages before the War. Bloody Biggles!

Bloody Bader! Bloody Cheshire! Bloody Hillary!' Earlier in the letter he commended the Bursar of Pembroke for his new book on Shrewsbury School which left out a lot even though it included Cobb, Judge Jeffreys and the man who was famously shot by Ruth Ellis. 'She hanged for it. Quite right, too, you cannot just go around shooting OSs (even in Hampstead).'

To Trevor-Roper, 21 October.

I had a phone call from Twiston-Davies this morning. He had been away. Apparently there have been considerable ructions in the obituary department, and now it is all Sealed Lips and so on. But he did tell me that there had been no penetration by the Peterhouse <u>mafia</u>. I conclude that it was an <u>inside</u> job, and that some people now have cold feet.

I went to the funeral of Dan Davin yesterday. It was a <u>grim</u> occasion because it was strictly non-religious. I think, in consideration to one's friends, one should be put away with all the proper drill, C of E, Church of Scotland or whatever. Still, the NZ High Commissioner made quite a good speech.

This morning I got a card to visit Your Place, the occasion being a book by one Cannadine published by Yale. I shall go.

Give warmest greetings to Xandra.

On 17 October, in a thank you letter to Blair Worden, he recalled a riotous evening in Wales long before.

I lived in a hotel (the Bellevue Royal) until I was expelled from it after entertaining the entire UCW rugger team in my room, with considerable damage to the plumbing in the Gents. Also some damage to three commercial travellers. The rugger team had been to Lampeter, on the way back they stopped off at Tregarron and ate all the tulips on the square by the War Memorial. I entertained them in my room till 3 am. I was asked to leave the hotel at 8 am and went to live in a pub. In Balliol one of my best pals was Jakobus de Wet, the grandson of the great General. But can it REALLY be true that I taught three of the five Moravian sergeants who later killed Heydrich English? It is of course possible.

In November he wrote to Worden after speaking at St Edward's, Oxford: 'I was very much impressed by the brand-new Blair Worden Auditorium in maroon and white (why, I wonder, did they adopt Merton colours?) and I gave my talk in the recently completed, fan-vaulted Blair Worden Amphitheatre. Unfortunately the Chapel was locked so she could not show me the Blair Worden West Window in stained glass.'

He wrote, on 21 May 1991, to Hugh Gough: 'I have difficulty in writing – <u>physical</u> not <u>mental</u>, my left hand trembles and typing seems impossible, & I have a lot I want to write, the answer seems to be a tape-recorder, if I can ever learn how to use one.' On a visit to his eighty-one-year-old sister ...

...her huge beige dog slobbered over me. I <u>hate</u> dogs and <u>love</u> cats & said, I thought convincingly, <u>Down Boy!</u> My brother-in-law laughed & said <u>she isn't a boy</u>. How would I have known? Anyhow for once Tories & Labour agree, <u>lots & lots</u> of Dogs are to be made illegal & Put Down (I hope painfully). I'd go anywhere on a clear anti-canine ticket.

On Waterloo Day 1991, 18 June, when his mother would have been 112, he wrote to Blair Worden feeling unwell:

I have been very <u>low</u>: some sort of pneumonia, coughing & coughing, naps in the afternoon, but now I am on antibiotics (fortified by Spanish red) so hope soon to be chirpy again. I caught a cold on the Sabrine Shore & felt so run down at breakfast in the Master's Common Room that I could not eat my scrambled eggs & could not properly <u>see</u> your school friend Simon Baxter, though he was sitting opposite me & reading a bizarre paper called the <u>Observer</u>.

On 26 June he suggested that Hugh Gough call in at Wolvercote on 1 August and the two of them could enjoy cold salmon and Hook Norton 'in a very nice pub in Steeple Aston. I am just coming out of a long tunnel of illness & feel tired & fragile: the effect of antibiotics I suppose.'

1992

On 19 February 1992 a letter from Cobb was published in the Telegraph. It was a defence of his determinedly conservative not to say prim birthplace on the Essex coast. Frinton-on-Sea was alleged to be entering the twentieth century by allowing such innovations as public houses selling alcohol. He wrote: 'It was very nice to see your report on Frinton. But as a Frintonian by birth, I can say that it is not only a good place to end up, but also a good place to start out. Chip shops, burger bars and candy floss may be undesirable, but true Frintonians should be more than a match for them.'

In May 1992 he celebrated his seventy-fifth birthday in Normandy and wrote to tell Blair Worden about it. 'I am now older than the Russian Revolutions and <u>utterly</u> idle, sitting under a plum tree & reading about a young man of 20 who may have been wrongly guillotined.'

'We are now installed here in Whitby,' he wrote later in a Christmas card to Blair Worden, 'mostly in the basement, which is warm and is being painted jade and primrose. Outside there is a constant gale, but my breathing is much better than it was in the Wolvercote Pontine Marshes. We seem to be nearer to Norway than to Oxford.'

1993

In January he wrote again to Worden: 'A good mark for Whitby! The Oxfam shop here has had to close.'

On 2 October he wrote to Michael Hodges agreeing to one of their lunches, 'but not in this tacky little hole (Whitby) which I must say I dislike intensely. Let us meet sometime in November, in London (you would say where) or in Oxford. We camp here in austere discomfort in an alien world where people speak what sounds like Norwegian. I am a recluse; but my health is a bit better.'

To Trevor-Roper, 10 December.

It was very good to have heard from you: a reminder of civilisation & light to one living in uncouth northern exile, in a place where people have rings in their ears, are immensely _fat_, have faces like those of Ensor's crowd scene: _l'entrée du Christ a Bruxelles_, eat standing up, eat _walking_, speak what sounds like Norwegian (or possibly Faroese) and part with the greeting _See you after_. (After _what_?) Even the children (referred to, unhelpfully, as _bairns_) are fat and coarsefaced. I have _never_ felt so alien. Even in Aberystwyth (where there was a leavening of sheer malice), even in Sofia in a January fog. So we are hoping to move back South, we are thinking of the Abingdon area, & we have put the house here on the market, & so perhaps 1994 (the _bicentenaire du 9 Thermidor_) will see us back in a civilised environment, far away from _see you after_. I can tell you little about _Boghole sous l'Abbaye_ (my name for Whitby) as I hardly ever go out, save to buy wine. But there are many chapels, though the trawlermen are Anglicans & no supporters of priestesses & refer to lavatories as _Heads_. There is an RAF enclave, the members of which attend the grim, black Catholic church. The Anglican vicar is an ex-naval type. I tried most of the pubs, but soon got tired of being looked at as if I were a Martian (because I do not look like Scargill or Alan Bullock or J.P. Beastly) but I do go to pubs in Cleveland, where people are quite _friendly_, though they, too, speak a sort of lilting Icelandic. _The Sea, The Sea_, as Iris would say. Well, though born in Frinton (Major Attlee's holiday retreat), I have had enough of _any_ of it: North (ex-German), Channel, Irish, Atlantic, Pacific, Indian &ca &ca. I know that Namier used to _walk_ on it (the Dead one) but I have no wish even to _see_ it. In short, the best view of Whitby is The Prospect of (though Whitby Ontario is no doubt a _vibrant_ centre of Canadian culture).

I am about to read at least a thousand pages on Franco. In Oxford I excused myself from the _Sin of Pride_. I have _no_ Pride; _my_ Sin is Sloth (& _Wine_ but never of the Italian kind).

Is my successor ever seen in Oxford? _What_ am I to make of the hypothetical Charles III? My love to Xandra.

This seems to have been the last letter he ever wrote to Trevor-Roper.

1994

On 28 October 1994 he wrote to Tim Heald asking for the Gloucestershire address of one General and the Christian name of another. He then turned to Oxford matters and remarked: 'So my inbred old College is to have <u>une Gardienne!</u>' This was Dame Jessica Rawson, an expert on Chinese Art and History at the British Museum. 'She sounds <u>very</u> learned, like a distant power figure in a Barbara Pym novel. And Merton <u>does</u> have (and has had) Oriental connections.' He then asked if he could have lunch at 'Talleyrand Bannister' (his name for the Travellers Club on account of a staircase down which the French statesman allegedly slid) on 6 January because he wanted to go to the British Association annual drinks party followed by a night in Cambridge. He still had to find a bed in London for the night of 5 January. As a postscript he added: 'What about a competition to nominate the most suitable candidate as first President of the English Republic. I'd back Leslie Rowse.'

Heald replied with an invitation to stay the night of 5 January, which Cobb accepted a few days later. ('I'd love to stay at Yokello Hall.') He added an irritated question arising from a mention in a new book by Jeremy Paxman.

He mentions me as wearing bicycle-clips while being interviewed for the Chair of Modern History! He doesn't seem to do his homework very well. <u>No one</u> is <u>interviewed</u> for Oxford Chairs; one applies for them to the Registrar; the appointment is made by a Statutory Committee (which includes the Vice-Chancellor, a nominee from Cambridge &ca, &ca) & 2 representatives from the College to which the Chair is attached. Paxman does not seem to be very reliable, but no doubt he is an agreeable drinking man! <u>No one</u> reads my books (most of them out of print, anyway); but if they <u>had</u> they would know that the Brie (roughly the Seine-et-Marne), the site of <u>Euro-Disney</u>, is one of the <u>coldest</u> parts of France. In my <u>Police & the People</u>, I have accounts of people being dug out of 20ft snowdrifts & of small schoolchildren being carried off by wolves in 1795, <u>l'Année</u>

<u>du Grand Froid</u>. The wolves came all the way from the Russia of mad Tsar Paul. They were still around in the Brie as late as 1850!

On the 19th of that month he wrote to Heald responding to an invitation to his fiftieth birthday party - a dinner in the Royal Tennis Club's rooms at Hampton Court. The letter was headed 'Boghole' so presumably came from Whitby. 'Dîner aux chandelles,' he exclaimed. But advising against setting the Palace alight again, he wanted to know, 'Is the birthday actually <u>on</u> the 28th? Will there be speeches? Will the Governor be there? Will there be Rich Presents?' It took him three and a half hours to get from King's Cross to Cambridge and he only arrived at Sidney Sussex College where he was staying as the Lodge was closing. The following month, he promised he and Margaret would be looking at seven or eight houses in Abingdon. The letter was signed, defiantly but sadly, 'The Exile'. It was time for him to come back south where at least the un-French half of him belonged.

By March he was telling Worden that they would be out of the 'Hellhole' by July or August. There was a problem involving a chain with the Abingdon house on which they had agreed, but 'We've got to get away from whippets, class war, uncouthness, rings-in-ears, being looked through (almost the <u>whole of Whitby have Enoch Powell eyes) and feeling alien</u>.'

That same month on the 30th he wrote to Bernard Wasserstein exhorting him not to even think of trying to stop off in Whitby on his way south from Newcastle. 'This is a dreadful dump and we are trying to leave it.'

The letter was handwritten by Margaret though Cobb managed to sign the single word 'Richard' in his distinctive though wobblier-than-ever handwriting.

1995

The following 23 September he wrote to Heald. 'It is <u>so</u> good to have escaped from the dreadful Whitby. One should <u>never</u> travel north of Banbury.'

He had been under the knife at the John Radcliffe Hospital. 'I have had a lot of my inside removed at the JRH & seem rather the better for the loss – lots of colon taken away, so a smaller stomach. I really thought the Reaper had come to get me. The JRH is a wonderful place.' He signed off 'love from Richard (minus yards of inside: they do seem to issue one with much too much at birth or whenever).'

He read about the death of Bernard Wasserstein's father in the Telegraph but did not write to Wasserstein until 4 October because of his operation in the Radcliffe. He asked Wasserstein to pass on a 'deep-felt sense of loss' to his mother, brother and sister.

What struck me most about him was his youthfulness and his love of the Classics, especially of Greek. I hope that he was fully appreciated in his teaching posts in Israel. He certainly deserved to have been. And how proud he must have been of you, Bernie, as a historian! There is so much more I could say but I won't now. Your father struck me as a man totally disinterested: a very rare breed these days.

His handwriting was distinctly wobbly now, even when he attempted it, which was by no means always the case. In a short letter to David Gilmour that October – the 11th – he reluctantly declined an invitation to attend a talk on Curzon because 'I am still on the mend from quite a big operation I had at the JRH late July & I am not doing any evening trips.' He wanted a copy of the book, though, and after finishing it wrote to the author on 5 November, which he called 'Guido's Day'. 'I have reached the (sad) end,' he wrote, 'and am sad too, for I could have read on and on, you write so well & your touch is so light.' He thought Gilmour's biography 'a masterpiece' and believed the judges simply had to award him the Whitbread. He was reminded of Baldwin, his favourite Prime Minister, 'Lazy & enjoying Aix-les-Bains; & he, too, like you wrote so well.' He was also reminded of his father. 'Did you know? I was a Kitchener Scholar (1936?) – son of an officer with war service – my father was an RE officer in the Boer war, then later in the Sudan Civil. Deputy Director of Public Works. He wore a fez.'

Ten days later he wrote what seems to have been a final letter to David Gilmour, who had failed, contrary to Cobb's expectation, to win the Whitbread Prize for his book on Curzon. 'Who are the bloody Whitbread judges anyway? I bet there was not a single historian. I am <u>outraged</u>. But your marvellous book will get its reward. Somewhere towards the end you mention Bagnolles. There are 3 Bagnoles & 5 Bagnols. I think you mean one of the latter.'

1996

He died on 15 January. John Walsh, his colleague from Jesus College, visited him in Abingdon when he was obviously terminally ill and found him lying downstairs on a camp bed subsisting on claret and camembert. It seemed oddly appropriate.

The funeral was in the parish church at Abingdon a few days afterwards. His friends Geoffrey Ellis and Richard Brain read his own 'End Paper' and verses from the 21st chapter of Revelation. The address was delivered by his friend and former Balliol colleague Maurice Keen. Later, in early May, there was a grander memorial service at the University Church in Oxford. Antony Kenny, the Master of Balliol, read from Cobb's 'End of the Line' and the address was given by Douglas Johnson, the Professor of French History at London, an old friend and the man who had once made an epic train journey from Paris to London during which Richard had consumed most of a bottle of Calvados while protesting about its poor quality. The hymns were traditional and familiar, the services orthodox. At the funeral his Légion d'honneur and Fellowship of the British Academy were listed before his CBE. At the memorial the order was reversed. It's difficult to say which Cobb, still divided even in death by his professed dual nationality, would have preferred.

Le Monde, in the obituary he would, surely, most have prized, drew attention to this national schizophrenia while remarking that with his passing the world had lost 'l'une des figures les plus excentrique du monde universitaire.'

He would have liked that, while not necessarily agreeing.

Cast of Characters, being a list of some of those who feature in the letters of Richard Cobb, at least as far as their details could be ascertained and seemed pertinent, interesting or entertaining.

Andrew, Christopher (1941–) was Fellow of Corpus Christi College, Cambridge, from 1967 and Professor of History in the University until retirement in 2008. An expert on Intelligence and widely supposed to be responsible for MI5's Cambridge recruitment, a belief which sometimes interfered with his reputation for historical impartiality.

Arblaster, Anthony (1937–) was for almost thirty years Reader in Politics at Sheffield University. An Exhibitioner of Balliol College, Oxford, where took a Second in Modern History.

Aylmer, Gerald (1926–2001) was the founding Professor of History at York University and Master of St Peter's College, Oxford, from 1978 to 1991. His book *The King's Servants* ran to well over 1,000 pages and was based on Aylmer's PhD thesis, itself so long that it caused the university to place an upper word limit on future theses.

Backhouse, Sir Edmund (1873–1944) was the subject of a book called *The Hermit of Peking*, in which the author, Hugh Trevor-Roper, substantiated his subject's reputation as a fraud, charlatan and congenital liar.

Ball, Edward (died 1987) A Shrewsbury schoolfriend and contemporary of Cobb whose celebrated matricide (he finally pushed her and her Morris Minor over an Irish cliff after she refused him funds for a foreign holiday) occasioned Cobb's characteristically unusual book *A Classical Education* (1985). Cobb was suspected of being an accomplice and was subjected to official questioning at his Oxford College, an interrogation only sanctioned by the presence of the senior college law tutor.

Bainbridge, Beryl (1933–2010) Quirky novelist, expelled from public school outside Liverpool aged fourteen and an uncomfortable presence ever since. Five-times nominated for the Booker Prize but seemingly condemned to a perpetual *proxime accessit* status. Sometime smoker, drinker and all-round bad hat. A scion of the publishers Duckworth and close friend of the proprietor's wife, the novelist Anna Haycraft.

Bayly, Christopher, Sir (1945–) Balliol College, Oxford, historian who became Vere Harmsworth Professor at Cambridge in 1992. He came from Tunbridge Wells, which gave him a further affinity with Cobb, but he was really a protégé of his predecessor in the professorship, Jack Gallagher (qv).

Beales, Derek (1931–) Professor of History from 1980 to 1997, a Fellow of Sidney Sussex College, Cambridge, and described in one Cobb letter as a 'nice man in SS'.

Belgium, Prince Charles of (1903–83) Younger son of King Albert, Count of Flanders, known during the war as General du Bec (for reasons of security); served as regent of his country from 1944, when the Germans left, until the accession of King Baudouin in 1950.

Beloff, Max (1913–99) was ennobled as Lord Beloff of Wolvercote, the village on the outskirts of Oxford in which Cobb lived for much of his life. Beloff was Gladstone Professor of Government and Public Administration from 1957 to 1974 and was then Principal of the privately funded University of Buckingham from 1974 to 1979.

Bennett, Gary (1929–87) was chaplain of New College, Oxford, and wrote an anonymous preface to *Crockford*, the Church of England annual, in which he attacked Archbishop of Canterbury Robert Runcie for liberal cronyism. He committed suicide after exposure became seemingly inevitable.

Bhutto, Zulfikar Ali (1928–79) President of Pakistan from 1971 to 1979, father of the assassinated Benazir, also President of Pakistan. A Christ Church educated lawyer, he was hanged in prison, a victim, it was widely believed, of his successor and the political system of his native country.

Blanning, Tim (1942–) Historian and long-serving Fellow of Sidney Sussex College, Cambridge.

Blunt, Anthony (1907–83) Establishment art historian who was Surveyor of the Queen's Pictures for more than a quarter of a century after 1945, when he was appointed by George VI, and head of the Courtauld Institute for a similar period after his appointment two years later. On his very public unmasking as the 'Fourth Man' and Russian spy, along with Burgess, Philby and Maclean, he was stripped of the knighthood he had held since 1956. It probably did not help that he was a keen homosexual, nor ultra-snobbish in a mannered manner.

Boyle, Andrew (1919–91) was a BBC broadcaster and the author of *The Climate of Treason*.

Bowle, John (1905–85) held a Brackenbury Scholarship at Balliol College before teaching at Westminster School and at Eton and finally becoming an academic at a variety of American universities.

Brain, Richard (1928–) attended Shrewsbury School and Queen's College, Oxford. He worked as a publisher at Hamish Hamilton from 1954 to 1961, and then as Managing Editor for African Universities Press in Lagos. On his return he worked for Oxford University Press, where he edited the *Oxford Dictionary of Quotations* before becoming an Assistant Editor at the *Times Literary Supplement* in 1981, working there until his retirement in 2008.

Briggs, Asa (1921–) was a historian who, as Professor at Leeds University from 1955 to 1961, was responsible for hiring Cobb as a lecturer. One of Cobb's pupils, Margaret, subsequently became his wife and mother of four children. Briggs was Professor at Sussex University and then Vice-Chancellor from 1967 to 1976. Elected to the position of Provost of Worcester College in 1976, he stayed until retiring at age seventy in 1991. His best known books are *The Age of Enlightenment* and the definitive five-volume history of British broadcasting.

Bromley, John Historian and Fellow of Keble College, where he taught John 'Napoleon' Roberts (qv) French Revolutionary history.

Brooke, Christopher (1927–) Mediaevalist with a particular interest in ecclesiastical history. Successively Professor at the Universities of Liverpool, London and, from 1977, Cambridge. Author of the Gonville and Caius College history.

Buchan, Alastair, Hon. (1918–76) Third son of the novelist and Governor-General of Canada. Educated at Eton and Christ Church, was Montague Burton Professor of International Relations, which carried a Balliol Fellowship, from 1972 until his death.

Bullock, Alan, Sir (1914–2004) Historian most famous for a seminal study of Adolf Hitler and a three-volume history of the British Foreign Secretary Ernest Bevin, whom he much admired and closely resembled, not least in his relatively obscure West Country antecedents. Bullock was an Oxford historian, the first full-time Vice-Chancellor of that university and, most significantly, the first Master and in many respects the creator of St Catherine's College.

Burgess, Charlie, aka Cathal Brugha (1874–1922) Irish republican, De Valera's predecessor as President of the Dail, sworn enemy of Michael Collins, died of wounds received while fighting the British in O'Connell Street, Dublin, during the uprising.

Cannadine, David Nicholas (1950–) Cambridge educated historian, notably of class in the United Kingdom, who became a Professor at London University and was knighted in 2009.

Carr, Raymond (1919–) Former Bullingdon Club member, fox-hunting man (and writer) best known as an expert on Spanish history and Warden of St Anthony's College, Oxford, from 1968 to 1987.

Catto, Robert Jeremy Adam Inch (1939–) Usually known as Jeremy, was a Balliol educated historian, authority on mediaeval chivalry and church, and a famously concerned Fellow of Oriel College, Oxford, from 1969 to 2008.

Cawkwell, George was an affable classical scholar, an authority on Philip of Macedon, sound on Alexander and a *Times* obituarist.

Chadwick, Owen (1916–) was knighted in 1982 but as an ordained clergyman never used the title. He was Master of Selwyn College, Cambridge, from 1956 to 1983 and Regius Professor of History at Cambridge from 1968 to 1982.

Chavasse, Christopher (1884–1962) was the twin brother of Noel, who was the only man to win a Victoria Cross and bar in the First World War. Their father was Bishop of Liverpool and founded St Peter's College, known at first as 'Pot Hall', of which Christopher became the first Master in 1929. He was consecrated Bishop of Rochester in 1940. His forerunner Walter de Merton (*c*.1205–77) founded the eponymous college in 1264, was at various different times Lord Chancellor of England and died in office as bishop after falling off his horse fording the River Medway on his way home from Oxford. He is buried in his cathedral in a magnificent tomb.

Cheetham, Antony (1943–) One of the triumvirate of Cobb's famously least-loved Balliol students (the others were Stuart Holland and Martin Walker qqv). A successful publisher in later life.

Chenevix-Trench, Anthony (1919–79) Old Salopian who became Headmaster of Eton College from 1964 to 1970 and of Fettes in Edinburgh, where he died after a decade in office. Notorious flogger who habitually offered his victims a choice between a trousered caning and a bare-buttocked beating with a belt. The former hurt much more than the latter, which Trench was said to prefer. He was also said to be keen on the bottle, albeit in a furtive rather than heroic manner.

Cheshire, Sir Leonard (1919–92) was a fast-living, Alfa-Romeo-driving Merton College undergraduate who became a bomber hero, decorated with a Victoria Cross for his exploits with the 'Dam Busters'. After the

war he became the philanthropist founder, with his wife, of the eponymous Cheshire Homes. Much disliked by Cobb, who felt the same for
most RAF people such as Richard Hillary (qv).

Chester, Norman (1907–86) ran Nuffield College, Oxford, as Warden
from 1954 to 1978 and advised the Football League after conducting a
commission of enquiry at the request of his old friend Harold Wilson.

Chesterfield, 4th Earl of (1694–1773) Politician best remembered for
the letters he wrote to his illegitimate son by a governess and to his
godson who succeeded him. 'Advice', he wrote 'is seldom welcome and
those who need it the most like it the least.' He included himself as an
example of someone who was averse to advice though much in need
of it.

Christiansen, Eric (1937–) Fellow of New College, Oxford, who once
described himself as 'Danish by descent, English by education'. An
expert on the Crusades.

Cobban, Alfred (1901–68) Revisionist historian of the French Revolution.
He used his inaugural lecture as Professor at University College London
to propound the ground-breaking theory that the French Revolution
did not change nearly as much as hitherto believed. Cobb, sticking to
the particular, tended to steer clear of debates such as this.

Conway, Martin (1960–) Historian of the Belgian Right and a Fellow of
Balliol College, Oxford, from 1990 onwards.

Cowen, Zelman, Sir (1919–) Australian lawyer who was Provost of Oriel
College, Oxford, from 1982 to 1990, after his term as Governor-General
of Australia (1977–82) in succession to Sir John Kerr, who was controversially dismissed by Prime Minister Gough Whitlam.

Cowling, Maurice (1926–2007) was a Fellow of Peterhouse 1963-93,
when he was perceived as a constant thorn in the flesh of Trevor-Roper
during his mastership. Cowling enjoyed a reputation for Machiavellian
scheming and an extremely right-wing disposition. Mentor of many distinguished luminaries, especially at the *Daily Telegraph*.

Cracraft, Caroline, née Pinder (1941–) Somerville College, Oxford, educated historian and pupil of Cobb who married an American Professor,
moving to Chicago, Illinois, where she became Deputy British Consul
under the aegis of Cobb's old schoolfriend John Heath (qv).

Crisp, Quentin (1908–99) Flamboyant homosexual who achieved wide-
spread notoriety after publication of his book *The Naked Civil Servant*
in 1968. Delighted in shocking the strait-laced.

Cronin, John Desmond (1916–86) Champagne socialist who sailed, played polo and was a friend of Roy Jenkins. A Stonyhurst educated surgeon who represented Loughborough in Parliament from 1955 to 1979, he was a fluent French-speaker and a chevalier of the Légion d'honneur.

Davin, Dan(iel) Marcus (1913–90) A New Zealand Rhodes Scholar who became a Fellow of his Oxford College, Balliol, wrote novels and short stories, enjoyed a long association with the University Press and became something of an Oxford legend.

Davis, Natalie Zemon (1928–) Detroit-born historian who decamped to Canada in 1960 after falling foul of Senator Joe McCarthy and his anti-communist purges. Best known for her work on the French film about Martin Guerre and her subsequent book of that name.

Denniston, Robin (1926–) was formerly Managing Director of Hodder and Stoughton, but took up the top job at Oxford University Press in 1984. He took Holy Orders in 1979 and served as unpaid vicar of the Oxfordshire parish of Great Tew from 1995 to 2002.

Douglas-Hamilton, James (1942–) Younger son of the Duke of Hamilton and Earl of Selkirk although he renounced the title and took a life peerage after serving as an MP for Edinburgh West from 1974 to 1997. At Oxford he was President of the Union and a Boxing Blue despite apparently being quite one of the gentlest of his generation.

Douglas-Home, Charles (1937–85) was Editor of *The Times* from 1982 until his early death from cancer.

Douglas-Home, William (1912–92) Old Etonian playwright best known for *The Reluctant Debutante*, who famously refused to take part, as an officer in the Buffs, in the attack on Le Havre and served a prison sentence as a result. In 1951 he married Rachel, the daughter of the 4th Viscount Hampden. In 1970 she became Baroness Dacre, a title which had been in abeyance but which was revived for her benefit. This led to her contesting Trevor-Roper's right to take a similar title on his elevation to the peerage.

Dover, Sir Kenneth (1920–2010) was a Greek scholar who was also Professor and Chancellor of St Andrew's University in Scotland. Educated at Balliol College, he was later President of Corpus Christi College. Awkwardly honest about ancient Greek homosexuality and his own sometimes murderous (though evidently unconsummated) instincts, his views helped him achieve notoriety outside academic circles

Dudley-Edwards, Ruth (1944–) Scion of a well-known Dublin academic family and first wife of well-known Dublin writer, speaker, smoker and drinker Patrick Cosgrave. Journalist, biographer, author of humorous crime novels and all-round controversialist.

Eagleton, Terry (1943–) was Wharton Professor of English at Oxford University from 1992 to 2001 but would have been a controversially left-wing English don at Wadham College when Cobb was in Oxford. Widely accepted by the Establishment in later life, he was a maverick in youth.

Ellmann, Richard (1918–87) American biographer of Irish writers, most notably James Joyce. He was Professor of English at Oxford University from 1970 to 1984 and a Fellow of New College from the same date until 1987.

Elton, G(eoffrey) R. (1921–94) Authority on Tudor England, author of many books, notably *Renaissance and Reformation*, and Regius Professor of Modern History at Cambridge University from 1983 to 1988. A long-standing Fellow of Clare College, he was born in Germany and only took British nationality in 1947.

Favier, Jean (1932–) Historian of mediaeval France, he was Director of the National Archives in France from 1975 to 1994 and of the Bibliothèque nationale for three years thereafter.

Feiling, Keith (1884–1977) was a historian of the Tory Party and England in the 18th and 19th centuries. He was a don at Christ Church, Oxford, from 1911 to 1946.

Flowers, Lord (1924–2010) Cambridge educated physicist who produced an eponymous report in 1976 expressing opposition to fast breeder reactors. Fellow of University College London and Vice-Chancellor of London University.

Foot, M.R.D. (1919–) His first name is Michael but he is always known by his initials. Distinguished historian, principally of the Special Operations Executive, with whom he served in the Second World War, being deco-rated with the Légion d'honneur for his work with the French Resistance. Educated at Winchester College and New College, Oxford, he was Professor of History at the University of Manchester.

Franks, Oliver, Lord (1905–92) Liberal Renaissance figure who was variously a banker, moral philosopher, British Ambassador to the United States from 1948 to 1952 and Provost of Worcester College, Oxford, from 1962 to 1976. Chair of a series of well-known and influential commissions, he was best known as an Ambassador for misguidedly saying that he would like some crystallised fruits for Christmas after his French counterpart had asked for peace and his Russian for freedom. Also known widely as 'No lolly Olly'.

211

Fraser, Peter (1918–2007) acted as Warden of All Souls College, Oxford, with unexpected success, given his aversion to all sorts of bureaucracy. A noted Hellenic scholar, he had first got to know and love Greece when dropped behind enemy lines by the SOE during the Second World War. He won a Military Cross for gallantry, was arrested and interrogated by the Gestapo, always boasted a dry, wry sense of humour and was an accomplished ping-pong player.

Fuller, Roy (1912–91) and his son John (1937–) were writers and academics. The father worked in a building society but was also Professor of Poetry at Oxford University, whereas his son became a tutor in English at Magdalen College while following in paternal poetic footsteps.

Gale, George (1927–90) Intemperate, bibulous right-wing columnist and broadcaster, educated at Peterhouse, Cambridge, and briefly Editor of the *Spectator*.

Gallagher, John (1919–80) More often known as 'Jack', Beit Professor of Commonwealth History, a post which also involved a Fellowship of Balliol College, Oxford, from 1963 to 1970. Gallagher and Cobb were boon companions and notorious mischief-makers. In 1970 Gallagher returned to Trinity, Cobb's favourite Cambridge College. A Falstaffian figure, Gallagher collaborated with his successor as Beit Professor, 'Robbie' Robinson, who was more austere and elongated. He published little but was a celebrated supervisor not to mention a heroic drinker, which was one of several characteristics that endeared him to Cobb. His Oxford career is celebrated at the beginning of Cobb's *People and Places*, published by Oxford University Press in 1985.

Gallant, Mavis (1922–) Montreal-born writer who emigrated to Paris and remained there writing short stories in English. These were mostly published in the *New Yorker* before being collected in volume form. Despite being honoured by Canada and working briefly as a writer-in-residence at the University of Toronto, she remains an acerbic, witty exile in her adopted France.

Garrod, Heathcote William (1878–1960) was a classicist, sometime Professor of Poetry and a Fellow of Merton College, Oxford, for more than sixty years.

Garrone, Alessandro Galante (1909–2003) was a historian and jurist, and became a great friend of another famous Turin lawyer and professor, Norberto Robbio, almost an exact contemporary. His daughter was born in 1946, in the same year and the same city, Turin, as Sonja Gandhi.

Gilmour, David, Sir (1952–) Elder son of Lord Gilmour, himself a distinguished Balliol man, Editor of the *Spectator* and cabinet minister. Gilmour Junior was a pupil of Cobb's at Balliol College, and later a distinguished author and biographer of Curzon, Kipling and Lampedusa, as well as a friend and correspondent of Cobb.

Goodman, Arnold (1913–95) Ennobled and acquired celebrity status as Harold Wilson's solicitor. Master of University College, Oxford, from 1976 to 1986. Not a pretty face, or sight, but possessed of a scintillating intellect and a gifted after-dinner speaker which belied his bulk.

Goodwin, Albert (1906–95) was Professor of Modern History at the University of Manchester 1953–69. In retirement he was briefly a Fellow of All Souls College, Oxford, where he had earlier spent some years teaching. His final years were spent in Sherborne, Dorset. His book, *The Friends of Liberty: The English Democratic Movement in the Age of the French Revolution*, was published in 1979.

Gough, Hugh (1946–) was a PhD student of Cobb, a friend and correspondent and subsequently Professor of Modern History at University Collge, Dublin. He is the author of many publications, some of book length, mainly about aspects of the French Revolution. Now retired and consequently Emeritus Professor.

Gowing, Margaret (1921–98) The first Professor of the History of Science at Oxford University. Her main interests were the Second World War and the Atomic Energy Authority, where she was once the archivist.

Gowon, Yakubu (1934–) President of Nigeria from 1966 to 1975, who left for a quiet, semi-anonymous life in the UK, where he has become an international authority on the Guinea worm.

Gracq, Julien (1910–2007) Determinedly anti-establishment French author who turned down the Prix Goncourt and is best known for his 1951 novel, *La Rivage des Syrtes*.

Griffiths, James Graham (1908–81) Physicist and a keen rowing man with a lively interest in wine, he was President of Magdalen College, Oxford, from 1968 to 1979.

Grafton, The Duchess of (1920–) Always known by her second name, Fortune, was created Mistress of the Robes to Her Majesty the Queen in 1967 and has been, for many years, a pillar of life at court.

Guilloux, Louis (1899–1980) was a Breton who was born in St Brieuc and lived there all his life.

Hampshire, Stuart (1914–2004) Balliol historian who became a world-famous philosopher, Fellow of All Souls, and, from 1970 to 1984, Warden of Wadham College, Oxford. His name became part of a famous word-play involving the magisterial history, *Tudor Cornwall*, by his irascible colleague, A.L. Rowse.

Heald, Tim (1944–) A pupil of Cobb's at Balliol College from 1965 to 1967. Author, journalist and editor of this book.

Heath, John (1922–2009) Educated, like Cobb, at Shrewsbury School and Merton College, Oxford, he was Her Britannic Majesty's Ambassador to Chile from 1980 to 1982. Before that he was from 1975 Consul-General in Chicago which, as his *Times* obituary pointed out, was a more important post than a number of minor embassies. In Chicago his Number Two was Caroline Cracraft (qv), a former pupil of Cobb's while at Oxford University.

Herzstein, Robert E. Professor of History at the University of South Carolina, who wrote about such twentieth-century figures as Adolf Hitler and Henry Luce.

Hexter, 'Jack' (1910–96) was an American historian who was a Professor at Yale University from 1964 to 1978, an authority on Tudor and seventeenth-century British history, and a well-known polemicist. His attack on Christopher Hill centred on Hill's Marxism and branded him as a 'lumper', which was a category of historian Hexter abhorred, as opposed to a 'splitter', of which he approved.

Highfield, (John) Roger Long-standing Fellow of Merton College, Oxford, and latterly its historian. A very old friend of Cobb's, who also knew Garrod (qv). It was Highfield who recalled that Garrod, a confirmed bachelor, liked to entertain his former undergraduates at his room in college. Very often his ex-pupils were married and had families. Garrod gave the wives chocolate and brought out clockwork toys to entertain the children. A particular favourite was one which raised a glass to its lips when wound up. After his death many of his former pupils asked for a clockwork toy as a memento and Garrod's collection was thus dispersed.

Hill, (J.E.) Christopher (1912–2003) Marxist historian of sixteenth-century England and particularly of the Civil War and Cromwell's rule. Master of Balliol College, Oxford, from 1965 to 1978. He had been an undergraduate there and apart from reading history had famously (and proudly) scored the winning try the last time the college had won 'Cuppers'. A keen college man of unswervingly left-wing disposition. He was largely responsible for getting Cobb to the college but subsequently relations between the two men became frostier for doctrinal as much as personal reasons.

Hillary, Richard (1919–43) was at school at Shrewsbury with Cobb and later suffered horrific burns which were repaired by the famous plastic surgeon Sir Archibald McIndoe. Hillary wrote a celebrated book, *The Last Enemy*, before dying when his plane crashed in Scotland. Cobb disliked him and had a particular contempt for the Royal Air Force and those who served in it. It is difficult to say which came first, and Cobb's feelings were much the same for another RAF ace, Sir Leonard Cheshire (qv).

Hills, Denis (1913–2004) After reading Politics, Philosophy and Economics at Lincoln College, Oxford, he taught in Poland, Romania and Uganda, where he fell foul of the dictatorial Idi Amin and was rescued in a high-level diplomatic mission launched by 10 Downing Street. He wrote a succession of more or less controversial books about his various places of exile and played himself in a film of his Ugandan exploits.

Hilton, J.R. Tim (1941–) Read English at Balliol College and later became a distinguished art historian and biographer of Ruskin. He once attempted to set fire to Anthony Cheetham (qv) at a party given by Cobb and Maurice Keen (qv). He is the son of a left-wing Balliol-educated Professor of History at Birmingham University.

Hinsley, Sir Harry (1918–98) Bletchley Park stalwart who became Master of St John's College, Cambridge, from 1979 to 1989 and was Vice-Chancellor of the University from 1981 to 1983.

Hinton, Michael (1923–2000) Fellow of Worcester College, Oxford, from 1960 onwards, best known for his 1973 book, *Experiences: An Inquiry into Serious Ambiguities*.

Hodges, Michael (1946–) Old Etonian pupil of Cobb's at Balliol College in the early 1970s; a friend, correspondent and banker.

Holland, Stuart (1940–) was Labour MP for Vauxhall from 1979 to 1989 and one of Cobb's three least favourite Balliol history pupils. Cobb habitually referred to him as 'Catlover', which should have been a term of endearment as Cobb was particularly fond of cats. It wasn't.

Hopewell, John Prince (1920–) was a consultant surgeon at the Royal Free from 1957 to 1986. His colleague Quist never apparently made it into *Who's Who*. The two doctors were the all-powerful men in charge when Cobb was admitted to the hospital after suffering a fall when the worse for drink.

Howard, Philip (1933–) has worked for *The Times* from 1964 onwards and was the paper's Literary Editor in the 1980s. An Eton and Trinity College, Oxford-trained classicist, he is an authority on words and manners who has latterly written on both subjects for his newspaper.

Howard-Johnston, James (1940–) was the son of Xandra (later married to Hugh Trevor-Roper) by her first husband, the admiral. James was a Fellow of Oriel College, Oxford, and married to the author Angela Huth.

Hunter, Michael (1949–) was a research fellow at Worcester College, Oxford, from 1972 to 1975 when he took his D/ Phil. An expert on the 19th century medical pioneer Robert Boyle, he went to Reading but only stayed a year before transferring to London University where, in 1992, he became Professor of History at Birkbeck College.

Ingrams, Richard (1937–) Salopian founding editor of *Private Eye* (1963–86) and of *The Oldie* (1992-). Friend and correspondent of Cobb.

Jerome, St (347–420) Illyrian father of the church, often anachronistically displayed in cardinal's gear and of ascetic disposition. Best known for friendship with a lion.

Keegan, John, Sir (1934–) Taught at the Royal Military Academy, Sandhurst, for over a quarter of a century before being snaffled by the Editor of the *Daily Telegraph*, Max Hastings, in 1986. As well as his prolific journalism as Defence Correspondent of that paper, he is the author of numerous books on warfare. His most notable is probably *The Face of Battle* but some critics thought him politically naïve. His sister Mary married Maurice Keen (qv).

Keen, Maurice (1933–) Mediaeval historian and Fellow of Balliol between 1961 and 2000. He won the Wolfson History Prize and is a leading expert on chivalry in the Middle Ages. A long-standing colleague and friend of Cobb's, he co-hosted with him a number of memorable parties. Wykehamist and Ulsterman. He gave the address at Cobb's funeral and married, in 1968, Mary, the red-haired sister of a Balliol military historian, (Sir) John Keegan (qv).

Kenny, Anthony, Sir (1931–) A philosopher of monkish disposition who was Master of Balliol College, Oxford, from 1978 to 1979. Briefly a priest, he was ordained in 1955 but returned to lay state in 1963 and married three years later. His wife, Nancy, ran the Oxford Society. After Balliol, Kenny spent a decade as Warden of Rhodes House. He famously conducted a series of seminars for dissident Czechs during the Dubček era.

Keyes, Roger, 2nd Baron (1919–2005) was a one-book author. His biography of Leopold III was called *Outrageous Fortune* and won the South East Arts Literary Prize.

Knowles, David Dom (1896–1974) was a Downside-educated monk who fell out with the Benedictines and lived outside their community for much of his adult life. He was an authority on monastic history and became a Fellow of Peterhouse in 1944. From 1954 to 1963 he was Regius Professor of Modern History at Cambridge University.

Krailsheimer, Alban (1921–2001) was a historian of France, and the pre-eminent authority on Rance, who spent most of his adult life as a don at Christ Church, Oxford.

Ladurie, Emmanuel Le Roy (1929–) is best known for his work on Ancien Régime Languedoc.

Lang, Cosmo Gordon (1864–1945) was the Archbishop of Canterbury and Visitor during Cobb's time as a Merton student in the 1930s. He became Archbishop of York in 1908 and transferred to Canterbury after two decades, remaining there till his retirement in 1942. The Visitor of Merton College, Oxford, has for hundreds of years been the Archbishop of Canterbury – a more potentially useful and influential figure than the Bishop of Rochester, which was the eponymous founder's title and who was the Visitor earlier in the college's history.

Laval, Pierre (1885–1945), whom Cobb once almost knocked over in his hurry to catch the last Tube home, was four times President of France but most controversially so at the time of the German occupation during the Second World War, as a result of which he was tried and executed by firing squad.

Lefebvre, Georges (1874–1959) Seminal twentieth-century historian of the French Revolution. He had to wait until 1924 when he was fifty years old before publishing his epic study of the part played in the Revolution by the 'Paysans du Nord'. He coined the phrase 'history from below' and was a major influence on other historians of the Revolution, including Cobb.

Le Quesne, Laurence was a Shrewsbury history master who was largely responsible for making Richard Ingrams, Willie Rushton and Paul Foot editors of the *Salopian* in the 1950s. He could therefore be held responsible for inventing *Private Eye* and possibly even the entire phenomenon of the satirical subversive 1960s. He retired in 1994 after a lifetime at the school, preceded by a degree in modern history from Oxford.

Levi, Peter (1931–2000) Professor of Poetry at Oxford University from 1984 to 1989. A long-serving Fellow of St Catherine's College and a former Jesuit priest married to the widow of Cyril Connolly.

Levin, Bernard (1928–2004) Witty, irreverent columnist latterly for *The Times*, for which he wrote regularly from 1971 to 1997, but first known for his mercurial though short-lived 'Taper' column for the *Spectator*. He hated judges and most lawyers, and famously renamed Sir Reginald Manningham Buller, Bullying Manner. He was also keen on opera, fine dining and himself, and was an acerbic TV personality who suffered a long, cruel death from Alzheimer's.

Lewis, Jeremy (1942–) Publisher with Oxford University Press and Chatto and Windus, self-deprecatory autobiographer and biographer of Cyril Connolly, Allan Lane, Tobias Smollett and others. Friend and correspondent of Cobb.

Liddell, Guy (1892–1958) was a successful and well-connected intelligence operative until denounced as a double-agent by Goronwy Rees.

Lloyd-Jones, Hugh, Sir (1922–2009) was Regius Professor of Greek at Oxford University 1960–89 and a towering figure in his chosen field throughout the second half of the twentieth century.

Long, David (1946–) was a Balliol pupil of Cobb's and subsequently a lawyer who became a partner in the London firm of Charles Russell. His elder brother was at the same college and became Ambassador to Switzerland, Egypt and Hungary – consecutively.

Longford, Frank, Earl (1905–2001) Labour cabinet minister, publisher and advocate of unpopular causes, including penal reform, he befriended murderers and in particular Myra Hindley, whose release he passionately and incessantly advocated. Myra Hindley (1942–2002) was Ian Brady's 'moll' in the infamous 'Moors Murders'. Hindley served a life sentence but was said to have repented and reformed.

Lovatt, Roger (1937–) is a distinguished mediaeval historian and Fellow of Peterhouse who read Modern History at Balliol College, Oxford, where he was a pupil of Maurice Keen. Keen says he specialises 'with insight on the spirituality of late mediaeval mystics' and adds, 'He is a nice, cheerful, modest man – not really sombre at all but from Richard's point of view quiet, uninformed about the French (or any other) Revolution, and usually sober, though in more far-off days he had a penchant for driving fast cars.'

Lucas, Colin Renshaw, Sir (1940–) Fellow of Balliol College, Oxford, and Tutor in Modern History from 1973 to 1990. Professor of Modern History, University of Chicago from 1990 to 1994. Master of Balliol from

1994 to 2001, Vice-Chancellor of Oxford University from 1997 to 2004. A postgraduate pupil of Cobb, friend and correspondent.

Lyons, Martyn (1946–) Postgraduate pupil of Cobb's, born in the UK but subsequently Professor at the University of New South Wales, which he joined in 1977. A friend, correspondent and leading academic in Australia.

MacCormick, Neil (1941–2009) A prodigious intellect but also a genial and gregarious figure given to deerstalkers and bagpipes, who came to Balliol College, Oxford, from Glasgow as a Snell Exhbitioner, became President of the Union, got a First in Law and became Regius Professor of Jurisprudence at Edinburgh University, a post he held from 1972 until 2008.

Malraux, André (1901–76) Almost impossibly Gallic French author, adventurer and politician habitually pictured with a cigarette drooping from the corner of his mouth. Gallantry possibly a touch Munchhausenish but indisputsbly a friend of Charles de Gaulle and Minister for Culture from 1959 to 1969.

Mansel, Philip (1951–) Eton and Balliol College educated historian who divides his time between Istanbul and London, a prolific biographer and historian, and Cobb's obituarist.

Marder, Arthur (1910–80) American historian of the Royal Navy from 1880 to 1945. He spent the last year of the 1960s as a Visiting Fellow at Balliol College, Oxford. Subject of an essay by Cobb in *People and Places*.

Markham, Felix (1908–92) A Balliol Scholar and then Fellow of Hertford College from 1931 to 1975. An authority on the Emperor Napoleon, he was a tutor and friend to the troublesome (to the British) Prime Minister of Malta, Dom Mintoff.

Mansergh, Nicholas, Sir (1910–91) Irish-born historian of Ireland and of the British Commonwealth. He was Master of St John's College, Cambridge, from 1969 to 1979.

Massie, Allan (1938–) Border-dwelling, Glenalmond and Trinity Cambridge educated author whose prolific interests include the ancient world, modern literature and Scottish rugby.

Massingberd, Hugh Montgomery (1946–2007) was born with just the first of his double barrels, adopted the second in adulthood and abandoned the first towards the end of his life, ending up as 'plain' Hugh Massingberd. The name, together with an apparently fogeyish interest in genealogy and country houses, lent itself to ridicule. *Private Eye* called him 'Massivesnob'. He was obituaries editor of the *Daily Telegraph* from 1986 to 1994 and widely credited with reinventing the genre as a waspish statement of truth rather than a genuflectory obfuscation of it. Privately, however, he was a genial presence and had nothing whatever to do with Heald's alienation from the *Telegraph* which stemmed from other causes and individuals.

Maudling, Reginald (1917–79) was a large, brilliant Tory politician who became Chancellor of the Exchequer and was sometimes considered as a future leader of his party. In fact he stood but was defeated by Edward Heath. He drank himself to death when he was only sixty-one. Cobb knew him at Merton College, Oxford, where they were contemporaries. Maudling got a First in Classics and drove a Buick.

Mayer, Arno (1926–) American Marxist historian of Luxemburg origins who was Professor at Wesleyan, Brandeis, Harvard and Princeton Universities sequentially but not simultaneously.

Mayr-Harting, Henry (1936–) Regius Professor of Ecclesiastical History 1997–2003 and, despite being a Roman Catholic, a minor canon of Oxford's Christ Church Cathedral.

Melliar-Smith, Matthew (1943–) was educated at Sherborne School whence he took a Brakenbury Scholarship in Modern History at Balliol College, Oxford, where he became a pupil of Cobb's.

Mesrine, Jacques (1937–79) Parisien bon viveur and gangster shot dead at the end of the Métro line at the age of forty-two. The subject of an essay in *People and Places*.

Meuvret, Jean (1901–71) Sometimes described as the 'historian's historian' because he was highly rated by his peers though little known to the public at large. Ancien regime expert, especially on the reign of King Louis XIV.

Mollet, Guy (1905–75) Very briefly Prime Minister of France from 1956 to 1957. Though leader of his country's socialist party from 1946 to 1969, he became the victim of his own unpopularly repressive Algerian policy.

Montefiore, Alan (1926–) was a Fellow of Balliol College, Oxford, from 1961 to 1994. He was a don in the Politics, Philosophy and Economics discipline, well known for a lecture on 'The Jewishness of the non-practising Jew'.

Morpeth, George (1942–) A student and friend of Cobb, who attended Balliol as a mere Viscount but later succeeded to the Earldom of

Carlisle. Carlisle moved to a Baltic state where he successfully eluded the attempts of the editor of this book to make contact. The editor recalls once helping Morpeth put Cobb to bed after dinner. A friend of Lord Michael Pratt and of Edward Mortimer (qv), two more of Cobb's Old Etonian pupils.

Mortimer, Edward (1943–) is the son of the bishop (qv) and a star pupil at Balliol, where he took a First in Modern History and an All Souls Fellowship, subsequently friend and correspondent of Cobb. He worked for *The Times* and *Financial Times* before going to the United Nations as chief speech-writer to Kofi Annan from 1998 and Director of Communications from 2001.

Mortimer, Robert (1902–76) Regius Professor of Theology at Oxford 1944-9 and then Bishop of Exeter until his retirement to Cumbria in 1973. Father of Edward, one of Cobb's favourite pupils at Balliol (see above).

Mousnier, Roland (1907–93) was a right-wing, Roman Catholic French historian.

Namier, Lewis, Sir (1888–1960) was a famous Polish-born British historian of the eighteenth century. His last wife, Julia (1893–1977), was a Russian émigré.

Norman, Frank (1930–80) Author of the autobiographical *Bang to Writes* and award-winning musical *Fings Ain't Wot They Used T'Be*. Artful Dodger sound-a-like and improbable brother-in-law of Wykehamist Maurice Keen (qv).

Obolensky, Dmitri, Sir (1918–2002) was for over a quarter of a century Professor of Russian and Balkan History at the University of Oxford.

Ogilvie, Robert (1932–81) A classics undergraduate and later Fellow of Balliol College from 1957 to 1970. He was Headmaster of Tonbridge School for five years and then Professor of Humanities at St Andrews University where he killed himself. Both his parents were heads of Oxford Colleges (father of Jesus, mother of St Anne's) and Ogilvie organised annual old-fashioned reading parties at his house, Errachd, by Fort William in the Scottish Highlands. He represented a conservative rump at a determinedly left-wing college in an equally left-wing period.

Osborne, D'Arcy, Sir, 12th Duke of Leeds (1884–1964) The consummate English aristo-diplomat, he played a pivotal but little-known role in Rome during the Second World War. Succeeded his cousin as the 12th and last Duke in 1963.

Pagden, Anthony (1945–) Oxford -educated historian whose main interests are European empires. After numerous and varied academic posts he became Professor of Political Science and History at the University of California, Los Angeles, in 2002.

Pares, Richard (1902–58) Historian of the eighteenth century, especially of the West Indies. Fellow of All Souls College and of his undergraduate college, Balliol.

Parfit, Derek (1942–) Old Etonian Balliol College historian of exceptional brilliance who took a First and won an All Souls Fellowship. He turned to philosophy and has produced such works as *Reasons and Persons* (1984), which those relatively few who were able to understand what he was writing said was a work of remarkable brilliance.

Parker, Alastair (1927–2001) was not his real name but the one by which he was always known. A historian of dashing appearance and considerable charm, he was a Fellow of Queen's College, Oxford, from 1957 to 1994. His speciality was appeasement and he was a dogged and slightly unexpected believer in the traditional values of the old Labour Party.

Patten, Christopher (1944–) MP for Bath from 1979, who famously lost his seat in the 1992 election and subsequently became Governor of Hong Kong until the handover in 1997. A former pupil of Cobb's, he was ennobled as Lord Patten of Barnes and has been Chancellor of Oxford University since 2003. Not to be confused with the other Tory Patten, Baron John (qv).

Patten, John (1945–) was Conservative MP for the City of Oxford and after a spell out of Parliament was MP for Oxford West and Abingdon until 1997, when he was ennobled as Baron Patten of Wincanton. From 1972 until 1994 he was a Fellow of Hertford College. Not to be confused with his near contemporary and namesake Chris (qv).

Paxman, Jeremy (1950–) Malvern and Cambridge educated journalist and author who lucratively fronts *Newsnight* and *University Challenge* with celebrated acidity.

Pearl, Valerie (1926–) Historian of the mid-seventeenth century and President of New Hall, Cambridge, from 1981 to 1995.

Pennington Don(ald) (1919–2007) Succeeded Christopher Hill as the Balliol College, Oxford, history tutor specialising in the seventeenth century. Fellow of the College 1965–82 and co-editor of a valedictory collection in honour of his predecessor.

Pitt, Harry (1923–2000) Fellow in Modern History at Worcester College, Oxford, from 1949 to 1980. Published little but popular and effective teacher.

Plumb, John, Sir, ('Jack') (1911–2011) was a Fellow of Christ's College, Cambridge, from his election in 1946 and remained a pillar of the college and the university until his death, serving as Master of the College, Professor of the University's History Department and most significantly one of its most dominating and visible presences throughout his adult life.

Pogge van Strandmann, Hartmut (1938–) was a colleague of Cobb's at Balliol College and again at Worcester College but finally fetched up at University College, Oxford, as a tutor in modern history and an Oxford history professor.

Powicke, Maurice, Sir (1879–1963) Oxford mediaeval historian who delivered the Ford Lectures himself in 1926–7 and was Regius Professor of History from 1928 to 1947.

Pratt, Michael, Lord (1946–2007) was the son of the 5th Marquess of Camden and also a Balliol pupil of Cobb's. It is said that when he saw his rooms in college he was appalled and decamped to the nearby Randolph Hotel while his mother, the Marchioness, returned the rooms to a suitable condition. When he died his obituary in the *Daily Telegraph* was described by a *Guardian* writer as 'the least hagiographic' in the paper's history. Nevertheless Lord Michael's funeral and memorial service attracted large crowds and many remembered him with real affection. He wrote three books, affected vividly coloured socks, co-respondent's shoes and three-piece suits and was not enamoured of anything as conventional and bourgeois as regular employment. Cobb liked him. A friend of George Morpeth.

Prest, John M. (1928–) History tutor and Fellow of Balliol College, Oxford, from 1954 to 1996. Expert on the nineteenth century.

Prestwich, John (1914–2003) was an Oxford mediaeval historian and for many years a Fellow of Queen's College where he wielded massive influence in conjunction with his wife, Menna (died 1990), who was a historian particularly of the seventeenth century and for many years a Fellow of St Hilda's College. Their son Michael, (1943–) is also a historian who was, for two separate periods, Professor of Modern History at the University of Durham.

Pryce-Jones, David (1936–) Old Etonian writer and right-wing polemicist of partly Jewish ancestry. Read history at Magdalen College, Oxford, where his tutor was A.J.P. Taylor, with whom he often disagreed, sometimes quite violently.

Pushkin, Alexander (1799–1837) Russian poet and not a particular Cobb favourite, but gave his name to an ocean liner built in East Germany in 1965. She had such old-fashioned features as cabins for six and separate taps for hot, cold and sea-water. Until 1979 she sailed during the summer between Leningrad and Montreal calling at intervening ports such as London and Helsinki. She was extensively rebuilt in the early 1990s and renamed as the *Marco Polo*, under which guise she spent many years as a successful cruise ship.

Quinton, Anthony, Lord (1925–2010) Stowe and Christ Church, Oxford, educated philosopher whose obituary described him exuding 'wit, energy, amiability and affection'. As such works as *From Wodehouse to Wittgenstein* suggest, his interests were catholic and his style gregarious. New College don who missed out on the top job there and went to be President of Trinity College from 1978 to 1987 instead. President of the British Library from 1985 to 1990 and responsible for its break with the British Museum and its move to controversial though custom-built new premises in the Euston Road.

Rae, John (1931–2006) Headmaster of Westminster School and an incorrigibly fashionable reactionary wolf in progressive clothing, a deceit which was only really discovered after the posthumous publication of his private correspondence.

Rees, Goronwy (1909–79) was Principal of the University College at Aberystwyth 1953–7. A friend of the spy Guy Burgess, he claimed to be a spy himself but was widely disbelieved.

Rhys, Jean (1890–1979) Dominican-born novelist best known for *The Wide Sargasso Sea*, a prequel to Charlotte Brontë's *Jane Eyre* first published in 1966, late in life, when Rhys (whose real name was Ella Williams) was in her mid-seventies.

Roberts, John (1928–2003) read Modern History at Keble College, Oxford, and subsequently became a Fellow of Merton College. After a spell at Magdalen College, he was Master of the Postmasters before decamping to Southampton University as Vice-Chancellor in 1979. Afterwards he returned to Merton as Warden in succession to Sir Rex Richards in 1984, serving in that post for a decade before retiring to his native Somerset. Cobb sometimes referred to him as 'Napoleon' on account of his hairstyle, interest in all things French and considerable ambition. Roberts also wrote a one-volume history of the world and presented a TV series on the same subject.

Robinson, 'Robbie' (1920–99) was Beit Professor of Commonwealth History and a Fellow of Balliol College, Oxford, from 1971 to 1989.

Rogister, John (1941–) Professor of History at the University of Durham, and authority on *parlements* of eighteenth-century France.

Rudé, Georges (1910–93) Marxist historian of Norwegian birth who was variously a professor at universities in Adelaide, Stirling and Montreal. He was best known as a historian of the French Revolution and especially of its ordinary architects whom he celebrated in his first, ground-breaking work on the crowd.

Runcie, The Rt Revd, Lord (1922–2000) was Archbishop of Canterbury from 1980 to 1991.

Santa Cruz, Lucia (1943–) Daughter of Chilean Ambassador, later mentor and reputedly girlfriend of Prince Charles. Beautiful member of the early Cobb set in Oxford in the early 1960s.

Schama, Simon (1945–) Brilliant, starred First pupil of Jack Plumb's at Cambridge; has written serious works, particularly of Dutch history, but is best known as the most successful TV historian of his time, most famous for his fifteen-part history of Britain. A pupil of Cobb's in a famous postgraduate seminar at Oxford.

Senior, J.R. Murray taught history at Shrewsbury from 1932 to 1951 and is remembered by an annual prize for the best historian in the Lower Sixth.

Skinner, Quentin (1940–) Distinguished Cambridge academic who became Regius Professor of History after a spell at Princeton and later becoming Barber Beaumont Professor of the Humanities at Queen Mary's, London. He won the Wolfson Prize in 1979 and, although more than twenty years younger than Cobb bore a passing physical resemblance to him.

Slack, Paul (1943–) is a Balliol-educated historian who became Principal of Linacre College, a postgraduate part of Oxford University, in 1996.

Soames, Christopher, Lord (1920–87) Portly Conservative politician who was last Governor of Southern Rhodesia but whose greatest achievement was arguably marrying Mary (1922–), youngest child of Sir Winston and Lady Churchill, and fathering several notable children including the Member of Parliament and friend of Prince Charles, Nicholas, the journalist Emma and the Countess Peel.

Soboul, Albert (1914–82) Friend and disciple of Georges Lefebvre (qv), a communist and keen exponent of 'history from below' who ended a distinguished academic career as Professor of the Revolution at the Sorbonne. Buried in the famous Père Lachaise cemetery in Paris, close to communist politicians and the famous wall of the communards where left-wing veterans of the Paris Commune were notoriously massacred.

Stone, Norman (1941–1) Glaswegian-born, Cambridge educated historian who succeeded Cobb as Professor of Modern History in 1984 and from which post he resigned in 1997, taking up a variety of senior academic positions in Turkey, which he much prefers on account of its relative political incorrectness. Famously cantankerous and right-wing as well as notoriously and heroically bibulous, he was a keen supporter of Mrs Thatcher and fluent in at least eight languages. Confessed to finding Britain 'boring', he likes to smoke and much enjoys tweaking establishment tails while operating in many ways from within the institution.

Southern, R.W. (1912–2001), widely known as 'Dick', was a mediaeval historian who was President of St John's College from 1969 to 1981.

Sparrow, John (1906–92) Warden of All Souls College, Oxford, from 1952 to 1977, well-known homosexual, garrulous gossip and almost as much an Oxford figure as his friend Maurice Bowra, Warden of Wadham College in the same university. Was elected to the job after a highly publicised election campaign against another well-known homosexual, the Cornish historian A.L. Rowse.

Spooner, William A. (1844–1930) Warden of New College but most famous for the eponymous 'Spoonerisms', some of the best of which are apocryphal but many of which, including 'Kinquering Congs their titles take', seem to have been real. Likewise sending an undergraduate down by 'the town drain' because he had 'tasted two worms'. He meant that the miscreant should leave Oxford by the down train because he had wasted two terms.

Starkie, Enid (1897–1970) was a flamboyant and eccentric Fellow of Somerville who wrote and lectured on French writers such as Baudelaire and Gide.

Stedman-Jones, Gareth (1942–) is a historian and political scientist who became a Fellow of King's College, Cambridge, in 1974.

Sutherland, Lucy (1903–80) Australian-born pillar of the Oxford establishment who, as a Somerville undergraduate, was the first woman to speak at the Oxford Union. After a war spent as a successful civil servant she returned as Principal of Lady Margaret Hall, a position she held from 1945 to 1971. She was an authority on the East India Company, particularly in the eighteenth-century, and also the Conservative thinker and politician Edmund Burke. She was a Dame.

Taylor, A.J.P. (1906–2000) succeeded Thompson (qv) at Magdalen College and was much disliked by Thompson's wife. Taylor was also a historian who wrote with brilliance and certainty about practically anything that took his fancy as well as selling his soul (according to his numerous enemies) to Lord Beaverbrook, for whose *Express* newspapers he was a flashy and frequent correspondent.

Thomas, Hugh, 1st Baron Swynnerton (1931–) is the author of *The Spanish Civil War* and was Professor of History at Reading University 1966–76.

Thomas, Keith, Sir (1933–) is a Balliol educated historian best known for his studies of witchcraft in the Middle Ages, and especially his book *Religion and the Decline of Magic*. Later President of Corpus Christi College, Oxford, from 1986 to 2000.

Thompson, James Matthew (1878–1956) was a Fellow of Magdalen College, Oxford, and the author of books on the French Revolution, Robespierre and Napoleon.

Tomalin, Claire (1932–) Widow of the journalist Nicholas, and subsequently wife of the playwright Michael Frayn, resigned as Literary Editor of the *Sunday Times* for reasons which, characteristically, Hugh Trevor-Roper was prepared to discuss and assess at length and with consummate authority. This he did in response to a letter from Cobb in a longish letter from Peterhouse dated 13 February 1986. He was so 'delighted' with the 'splendid' letter from Cobb that he read it aloud to Lady Dacre and they both 'enjoyed it immensely'. He personally deplored Tomalin's departure, which was due to her antipathy to Andrew Neil, the editor, whom Trevor-Roper considered 'a thug'. Trevor-Roper had written in protest at the paper's treatment of one of his reviews but did not expect it to do any good. Tomalin's successor, he had heard, 'was a fashion-writer on *The Times*'.

Trevor-Roper, Hugh (Lord Dacre) (1914–2003) Controversial historian who was widely felt never to have quite fulfilled his exceptional potential after a stunning early work on Archbishop Laud. Nevertheless he published widely and controversially and was Regius Professor at Oxford from 1957 to 1980 as well as Master of Peterhouse, the oldest of Cambridge University's colleges, for seven difficult years from 1980 onwards. He blotted his copybook by erroneously endorsing the Hitler diaries published by the *Sunday Times* but later found to be a spoof. He was under considerable pressure at the time and changed his mind before publication but it was, alas, too late. Best known as a letter writer for those to the *Spectator* written in cod seventeenth-century English under the name 'Mercurius Oxoniensis' but also a prolific writer to, among others, the art critic Bernard Berenson and, of course, Richard Cobb. Sometime British intelligence agent and married to Xandra, daughter of Earl Haig, the famous Field Marshal.

Trevor-Roper, Patrick (1916–2004) Brother of Hugh (qv) and a distinguished ophthalmologist as well as an outspoken pioneer of gay rights. He was one of a very few pratising homosexuals who gave evidence to the Wolfenden Committee, which advised legalising consenting acts of sex between adults. Naturally gregarious, he enjoyed a reputation as a keen and witty conversationalist.

Turpin, Kenneth (1915–2005) Classicist-turned-historian who was Attlee's secetary during the Second World War and subsequently became Provost of Oriel (his old college) from 1957 to 1980.

Tyacke, N.R.C. ('Nick') (1941–) Professional historian, educated at Balliol College, Oxford. Lifelong academic at London University and expert on England in the seventeenth century. An ebullient Wellingtonian.

Vaizey, John (1929–84) was an economist who was created a life peer in 1976. He was married to the art critic Marina Vaizey and their son Ed is a prominent Conservative MP.

Viot, Jacques (1921–) Career diplomat, writer, sometime Oxford don was French Ambassador to England from 1974 to 1976.

Vyvyan, C.G.C., Major-General (1945–) One letter, typed, to Blair Worden was 'signed by my Dijon Bicentenaire pen, a gift from Brigadier Vyvyan, the son of Electric Whiskers'. The nickname was coined by Jack Gallagher, who was a colleague of the senior Vyvyan at Trinity College, Cambridge. His son, a Balliol student of Cobb's, and by 2009 a retired general, tells a story of Gallagher leaving Trinity Hall and saying as he passed the Fellows 'haircut, haircut, haircut' just as if he were an Army drill sergeant. The Vyvyan son says that his father's whiskers were, by this time, less ferocious than heretofore.

Wade, William, Sir (1918–2004) was an academic lawyer and Professor at Oxford University from 1961 to 1976, when he returned to his alma mater and became Professor there as well as Master of his old college, Gonville and Caius, Cambridge. He frequently descended from his ivory tower to alter the course of practical law in court.

Walker, Martin (1947–) was, famously, one of Cobb's three least favourite pupils at Balliol College. He spent twenty-five successful years mainly as a foreign correspondent with the *Guardian* newspaper before joining United Press International and writing crime novels based in Perigord where he has a holiday home. Commonly known, though not to Cobb, as 'Sweetie'. His first wife, Anna Somers Cocks (not Cox as Cobb wrote) (1950–), was at the Victoria & Albert Museum before becoming Editor of *Apollo* and the *Art Newspaper*. She later moved to Turin with her third husband and became Group Editorial Director of Umberto Allemandi.

Wallace-Hadrill, Michael (1916–1985) was a mediaeval historian, a Fellow of Merton College, Oxford, for many years and Chichele Professor of Modern History from 1974 to 1983. His son was later the Head of Sidney Sussex College, Cambridge. Cromwell's head is alleged to be buried at an undisclosed spot in one of the quads.

Walston, Lord (1912–91) was an Etonian champagne socialist whose wife Catherine had a well-publicised affair with the novelist Graham Greene. He was a friend of Roy Jenkins and led an affluent life in an East Anglian country house which became a magnet for a certain sort of Labour Party supporter and the centre of a Fabian equivalent of the Cliveden set.

Wasserstein, Bernard (1948–) Balliol-educated Professor of History at the University of Glasgow (2000–3) and the University of Chicago (2003–). Prolific author and correspondent of Cobb's. Owner of a superior manual typewriter, 'borrowed' and much coveted by Cobb.

Wedgwood, Veronica, Dame (1910–97) was only the third woman to be awarded the Order of Merit. She was best known as an authority on the English Civil War and wrote an important work on the subject. She also wrote a biography of her ancestor, the potter Josiah and although never a career academic enjoyed a generally sound reputation in academic circles as well as having a more popular appeal.

Wernham, R.B. (1906–99) was an authority on the Spanish Armada and Professor of Modern History at the University of Oxford from 1951 to 1972. The post automatically conferred a Fellowship of Worcester College, just as it did when Cobb succeeded him.

Wheatcroft, Geoffrey (1945–) read Modern History at New College and was a publisher after going down but became an author and freelance journalist of generally right-wing persuasion.

Whiteman, Anne (1918–2000) was a History Tutor at Lady Margaret Hall from 1946 to 1985. On one occasion Cobb and his friend Jack Gallagher agreed that at an evening in Balliol they would attempt to get Anne Whiteman drunk. Miss Whiteman, who was substantially built, had a well-deserved reputation for being able to hold her liquor, and by the end of the evening it was Cobb, Gallagher and their male guests who were drunk and only Whiteman who remained sober. In the college lodge Whiteman mounted her bicycle carefully and correctly but as she rode off north she was seen to wobble. The drunken men let out a loud cheer at this apparent but slight sign of inebriation. Known to Cobb as 'Flight Sergeant'.

Willink, Lord, previously Sir Henry (1894–1973) was a Conservative MP who, at the time of the enquiry into Goronwy Rees's behaviour which bore his name, was the Master of Magdalene College, Cambridge.

Worden, Blair (1945–) Fellow of St Edmund Hall until becoming Professor first at the University of Sussex and then Royal Holloway College, London. An expert on the English Civil War, he is literary executor to Hugh Trevor-Roper.

Wormald, Patrick (1947–2004) Mediaeval historian of rare brilliance who won a seven-year All Souls Fellowship after an undergraduate career at Balliol College. He then taught at Glasgow University from 1974 to 1988 and ended as a don at Christ Church, Oxford. His best known publication is the first volume of *The Making of English Law*, published in 1999. He fought an ultimately losing battle against depression and alcohol. His father, Brian, also an historian, was a Fellow of Peterhouse, Cambridge, for sixty-six years.

Zaehner, Robert (1913–74) was an orientalist polymath, a student of Christ Church, Oxford, and a long-serving and influential MI6 officer who succeeded Radhakrishnan as Spalding Professor of Eastern Religions and Ethics in 1974, a post he held until his sudden and unexpected death in the street on the way to Evening Mass. He had converted to Roman Catholicism.

INDEX